BUSINESS OPPORTUNITIES IN MYANMAR

THIS INFORMATIVE BOOK on investment opportunities in Myanmar provides a most helpful background to understanding Myanmar's situation, its enormously resourceful people, deep culture and rich resources. The chapters provide information on different aspects of the economy and cultural setting which the reader will find most absorbing. An ancient civilisation strongly rooted in the Buddhist way of life, the country is set to play its part as a member of ASEAN by the end of this decade.

I congratulate the MBA participants of the business study mission in establishing a milestone in their selection of the information which is presented in this book and organising the chapters for easy reference.

REGGIE THEIN (VICE-CHAIRMAN, COOPERS & LYBRAND)

Titles in the Nanyang Business Report Series

Business Opportunities in Penang, Malaysia

Business Opportunities in Sichuan Province, China

Business Opportunities in India

Business Opportunities in the Philippines

Business Opportunities in Myanmar

Business Opportunities in the Yangtze River Delta, China

For further enquiries, information or feedback on the series, please write to the Editor at e-mail: prenhall@singnet.com.sg or Simon & Schuster (Asia) Pte Ltd, 317 Alexandra Road, #04-01 IKEA Building, Singapore 159965.

NANYANG BUSINESS REPORT SERIES

Business Opportunities in Myanmar

Edited by

Tan Teck Meng (Dean)
Low Aik Meng (Vice Dean and Director of MBA Programme)
John J. Williams (Chief Coordinator, Business Study Mission)
Ivan P. Polunin (Coordinator, Business Study Mission)

Nanyang Technological University
Singapore

Prentice Hall
Singapore New York London Toronto Sydney Tokyo

First published 1996 by
Prentice Hall
Simon & Schuster (Asia) Pte Ltd
317 Alexandra Road
#04-01 IKEA Building
Singapore 159965

Printed in Singapore

1 2 3 4 5 00 99 98 97 96

ISBN 0-13-713174-7
ISBN 0-13-713208-5 (pbk)

Prentice Hall International (UK) Limited, *London*
Prentice Hall of Australia Pty. Limited, *Sydney*
Prentice Hall Canada Inc., *Toronto*
Prentice Hall Hispanoamericana, *S.A., Mexico*
Prentice Hall of India Private Limited, *New Delhi*
Prentice Hall of Japan, Inc., *Tokyo*
Editora Prentice Hall do Brasil, Ltda., *Rio de Janeiro*
Prentice Hall, Inc., *Upper Saddle River, New Jersey*

CONTENTS

MACRO AND REGIONAL ISSUES

LAW, ACCOUNTING AND TAX

MANUFACTURING AND SERVICES

LABOUR AND HUMAN RESOURCES MANAGEMENT

TOURISM AND HOSPITALITY

ABOUT THE EDITORS

TAN TECK MENG is Professor and Dean at the Nanyang Business School. Since joining academia in the early 1970s, Professor Tan has combined his university responsibilities with extensive consultancy work, largely in the field of accountancy. He holds senior positions on a number of institutional boards and committees in Singapore including the Accounting and Auditing Services Working Group of the Economic Committee, the Public Accountants Board, the Board of Directors of Singapore Reinsurance Corporation Limited, the Institute of Certified Public Accountants of Singapore (ICPAS) Annual Report Award Competition Committee and the Income Tax Board of Review. Professor Tan is founding Director of the Entrepreneurship Development Centre (ENDEC) and in 1992 was elected to the Board of Governors of the MIT Sloan School of Management Society for Senior Executives. He is a council member of the ICPAS.

LOW AIK MENG is Associate Professor and Director of the MBA programme at the Nanyang Business School. He worked for five years as an accountant and an internal auditor before joining academia in 1975. He was Vice Dean of the Faculty of Accountancy and Business Administration at the National University of Singapore until he joined the Nanyang Technological University in 1987. He is currently Vice Dean at the Nanyang Business School and has been the Director of its very successful MBA Programme since its inception in 1991. Under his leadership, the MBA Programme has been building a network of contacts with businesses and government bodies in Singapore and overseas. He spearheads the thrice-yearly Business Study Missions which are an integral part of the MBA Programme. Associate Professor Low continues to be active in the accountancy profession and serves on several committees in the Institute of Certified Public Accountants of Singapore.

JOHN J. WILLIAMS is Associate Professor at the Nanyang Business School and Chief Coordinator of the MBA Business Study Mission programme. He has taught and carried out research projects in several countries including Canada, the U.S., Kenya and Singapore. Throughout the latter part of the 1980s, Dr. Williams served as Vice Chairman and Chairman of the Final Accreditation Exam Board for the Society of Management Accountants of Canada, which admitted him as a Fellow in the Society in 1992. Although active in consulting for government agencies in the U.S. and Canada during this period, he has published extensively in leading academic and professional journals and he continues to pursue the study of emerging regional economies in the Asean region.

IVAN P. POLUNIN spent 19 years with the British Tourist Authority, holding senior positions based in Tokyo, Singapore and Hongkong, during which time he was a consultant to numerous companies seeking entry into tourism markets in Asia. He is now sharing that experience at Nanyang Technological University in Singapore, where he heads the MBA programme in Hospitality and Tourism Management and is developing a new undergraduate tourism course. Mr. Polunin is a graduate of Oxford and Surrey Universities and is on the editorial board of *Tourism Management*.

PREFACE

The Master of Business Administration (MBA) programme of the Nanyang Business School at Nanyang Technological University requires participants to complete a Business Study Mission (BSM) before graduation. The purpose of these visits to other countries is to expose MBA participants to business opportunities and the realities of doing business in cultural environments different from Singapore.

This book presents the business reports emanating from the MBA Business Study Mission to Myanmar in June 1995. The BSM covered a period of ten days and included visits to the capital, Yangon, as well as to Mandalay and Bagan. Myanmar was chosen because it is one of the emerging economies in South-east Asia as a result of the government's new open door policy geared to a market-oriented economy. Through a series of economic reforms, Myanmar is shifting its internal direction from military objectives to social goals and economic upgrading. There is a concerted effort to attract foreign investment from around the globe. As testimony to the new stability, business interests from Singapore's public and private sectors have cultivated new economic relationships in Myanmar. In short, economic activity in Myanmar over the past several years has exceeded that of the last four decades. The investment potential is great and business optimism is plentiful.

In Yangon, the International Business Centre was the venue for the opening ceremony of the BSM, led by His Excellency, Lieutenant-General Khin Nyunt, Secretary 1 of the State Law and Order Restoration Council. Deputy Prime Minister, Vice-Admiral Maung Maung Khin, Dr. Cham Tao Soon, President of Nanyang Technological University and Professor Tan Teck Meng, Dean of the Nanyang Business School, delivered the opening addresses. Twenty-one other Ministers and Deputy Ministers accompanied the government delegation. This same venue was the forum for two full-day seminars led by some of

Myanmar's most eminent scholars and top level specialists from various government ministries.

After site visits to the Defence Services Museum, Shwedagon Pagoda, several companies and the Thanlyin Industrial Zone, the delegation flew to Mandalay accompanied by the eminent Dr. Khin Maung Nyunt, former Director-General of the Fine Arts Department and the Myanmar Historical Research Department of the Ministry of Culture. In order to imbibe the rich cultural heritage, the delegation visited the famous Mahamuni Pagoda, observed the traditional craft of gold leaf making, and toured the Shwe-In-Bin Monastery, Mandalay Palace, Kuthodaw Pagoda and Mandalay Hill. A full day was devoted to business site visits and a seminar featuring business opportunities and trade activities in the Mandalay region, led by leading authorities from the Institute of Economics, Ministry of Education and the Mandalay Chamber of Commerce.

A full day of travel from Mandalay by bus brought the delegation to Bagan, via the famous Mount Popa. In Bagan, a seminar combined with site visits, studied the cultural developments of Bagan and tourism potential in the region. The BSM concluded in Yangon, with further site visits and follow-up meetings and data-gathering.

These experiences instilled a profound sense of the importance of understanding the linkage between culture and doing business in Myanmar. This knowledge, in combination with the enthusiastic sharing and disclosure of information on new policy reforms, prompted us to request that the papers delivered by Myanmar authorities at the seminars be included in this book. Fortunately, the Myanmar response was affirmative and we are privileged to offer this compilation of information to readers of this book alongside the papers from the BSM participants.

In the economic world today, joint ventures with knowledgeable partners, whether in government or private sectors, or some combination of both, are the essence of successful economic development. The contents of this book are intended to facilitate an understanding of local conditions in Myanmar and to expose salient areas of business opportunities. Its appeal, therefore, is global as well as regional: to entrepreneurs and firms eager to provide capital, training, or technology; to government agencies contemplating trade and infrastructure development; to organisations servicing expatriates for subsidiary operations in Myanmar; to executives and managers of professional services; and to educational institutions for pedagogical and research purposes.

Editors:
TAN Teck Meng
LOW Aik Meng
John J. WILLIAMS
Ivan P. POLUNIN

ACKNOWLEDGEMENTS

The success of the Business Study Mission to Myanmar is attributable to considerable effort undertaken by many individuals and organisations. In Yangon, we extend thanks to His Excellency, Lieutenant-General Khin Nyunt, Secretary 1 of the State Law and Order Restoration Council and His Excellency Vice-Admiral Maung Maung Khin, Deputy Prime Minister and member of the State Law and Order Restoration Council, as guests-of-honour at the opening ceremony of the Business Study Mission. Thanks also to the many other Ministers, Deputy Ministers and guests for gracing this special occasion with their presence. The seminar series at the Yangon International Business Centre yielded knowledge and insight into Myanmar's economic reforms unattainable elsewhere. For the first session, thanks to master-of-ceremony, Daw Tin Hla Kyi; chairperson, Daw Yi Yi Myint; and panellists, U Myat Thein, Dr. Khin Maung Nyuat, Dr. Tin Soe, U San Khup, Dr. Khin Saw Nyein and U Waing. For the second session, thanks to master-of-ceremony, U Hla Myint; chairperson, U Maw Than; and panellists, U Maung Oo, U Tin Maung Win, Daw Yi Yi Myint, U Myat Kyaw, U Than Aung and Daw Nyunt Nyunt Swe. For the third session, thanks to master-of-ceremony, Dr. Nu Nu Yin; chairperson, Dr. Thet Lwin; and panellists, Dr. Naw Angelene, U Naing Bwa, U Hla Myint, U Htin Aung, U Khin Maung Lay, Dr. Tun Shin, U Maung Maung Yi and U Thin Maung. For the fourth session, thanks to master-of-ceremony, Daw Khin San Yee; chairperson, Daw Khin Thein Yi; and panellists, U Win Myint, Dr. Lwin Aung, and U Kan Zaw. Thanks also to Dr. Ng Kah Hwa, MBA Programme Director for Banking and Finance (NTU) and Mr. Ivan Paul Polunin, MBA Programme Director for Hospitality and Tourism Management (NTU) for presenting papers on Singapore's experience in developing capital markets and hospitality and tourism management, respectively.

For the seminar series in Mandalay, we thank Daw Khin San May, Associate Professor, Institute of Economics; Dr. Myo Myint, Associate

Professor, Ministry of Education; and U Tin Maung Win, Mandalay Chamber of Commerce. Thanks also to Dr. Khin Maung Nyunt for his stimulating seminar in Bagan.

For hosting our Business Study Mission at Karaweik Hall in Yangon and delivering the keynote address, thanks to Dr. Than Nyuant, Deputy Minister for Education. We are extremely grateful to Dr. Cham Tao Soon, President of Nanyang Technological University, for acknowledging our special guests at the opening ceremony and the opening banquet in Yangon.

Many institutions extended their gracious hospitality to our delegation and we thank those people at the Defence Services Museum, Shwedagon Pagoda, Myanmar-Singapore International Brewery and Thanlyin Industrial Zone in Yangon, as well as those people at the Mahamuni Pagoda, Shwe-In-Bin Monastery, Mandalay Palace and the Kuthodaw Pagoda in Mandalay. Our thanks also to our hosts in Bagan for the site visits they organised to infrastructure development projects and tourism projects in the region.

A very special thanks is extended to Dr. Khin Maung Nyunt for sharing his incredible archaeological and historical knowledge of Myanmar throughout our entire visit. Extremely personable, and with an unparalleled sense of humour, he brought to life with his eradition every temple, pagoda and mural inscription which elevated each MBA participant to the rank of historian.

We are grateful to the many pre-trip seminar speakers in Singapore in preparation for the BSM to Myanmar, including U Myint Soe, First Secretary, Myanmar Embassy, Singapore; Mr. Alan Tan, Senior Information Officer, Trade Development Board; Mr. Reggie Thein, Vice Chairman, Coopers and Lybrand; Dr. Myint Soe, Senior Law Partner, Murphy and Dunbar; Dr. Mya Than, Fellow, Institute of South-east Asian Studies; and Mr. Peter Low, Lawyer, Peter Low, Chong Tang and Partners.

Finally, thanks to all of our MBA participants for their diligent effort in gathering information, to the MBA office, to Grace Cheng and Adelene Ang for attending to all administrative details, to our Publisher Prentice Hall for their guidance, and to Alison Soo for her patience in bringing this book to fruition.

EDITOR'S NOTE

Myanmar's name referencing can be confusing. There is no separable family name and given name. The individual's name is always used in full. Adult men's names are formally prefixed by U (equivalent to uncle) and women, whether married or single, by Daw (aunt). Following conventional journalistic style, we have omitted these prefixes in the same way that Mr. and Mrs. are omitted when referencing scholars and authors. Within the text, the prefixes are retained where appropriate.

INTRODUCTION

Chapter 1

Myanmar: A Changing Context

BY
TAN Teck Meng
LOW Aik Meng
John J. WILLIAMS
Ivan P. POLUNIN

INTRODUCTION

Burma and Asian Growth

IN THE 1980s, four newly industrialised economies (NIEs) were dubbed "The Asian Tigers". For two decades, South Korea, Taiwan, Hong Kong and Singapore sustained the fastest economic growth rates in the world. None of them is well-endowed with natural resources and all cited hardworking and disciplined populations as their main assets. All had the common feature of being outward-looking and export-oriented. Burma, on the other hand, remained inward-looking, closed and struggled to be self-sufficient during these decades.

Twenty years earlier, if a visionary were asked to name potential Asian Tigers, then he might well have chosen Indonesia, the Philippines and Burma. These three countries were blessed in varying degrees with substantial, but not overwhelming, populations, natural resources (notably oil), extensive though damaged physical infrastructures left by former colonialists, international contacts and useful language skills. However, not one of these countries emerged as even remote contenders for tigerhood.

By the late 1980s, Burma had one of the lowest per capita incomes in the world and was recording negative economic growth. Under the leadership of General Ne Win, their 30-year experiment with a nationalised, centrally planned and closed economy was no longer sustainable.

Changes in Government

Public demonstrations against the old guard in 1988 led to the military backed State Law and Order Restoration Council (SLORC) assuming control of the government. Initial actions were taken to establish a market-oriented economy. The colonial name of the country and some major cities were changed back to traditional local forms. Thus, "Burma", an anglicised adaptation of the main Bamar ethnic group, reverted back to the ethnically neutral Myanmar and the capital, Rangoon, was re-named Yangon.

The world remained largely disinterested in Myanmar and only started checking the map when democracy-inspired demonstrations in 1988–89 led to riots and suppression. A long-delayed election followed in 1990. The SLORC expected Ne Win's National Union Party to win and were dismayed when the recently formed National League for Democracy, led by the imprisoned and charismatic Aung San Suu Kyi, daughter of Myanmar's former nationalist hero Aung San, won an overwhelming majority. Realising the serious miscalculation, SLORC arrested many of the NLD candidates and annulled the election results.

International disinterest turned into indignant concern when Aung San Suu Kyi was awarded the Nobel Prize for Peace. She was kept under house arrest and could not receive the award. Negative reports about human rights in Myanmar compounded the issue. SLORC's attempts to open up the economy met with a hostile or uncooperative response from potential investors in the west. However, some of Myanmar's South-east Asian neighbours saw things differently. An alternative political approach to the situation, termed "constructive engagement", was adopted most notably by Singapore, and tacitly supported by other ASEAN countries.

A Changing Context

The economic balance in east Asia was also changing at this time. The tiger economies were eclipsed by three new world leaders in economic growth: Thailand, China and Malaysia. These new stars are also Asian but they are closer to Myanmar geographically and in terms of trade links, primarily border trade.

The context in which Asian growth was happening changed significantly in terms of relationships and dependencies. Strong trade links with the U.S. were thought to be the engine of growth in the early 1980s. It was believed that Asian economies, therefore, would rise and fall with U.S. demand. In the late 1980s, the U.S. economy faltered but the Asian economies did not follow suit. Japan, which was experiencing a mini-boom and investing heavily in the region, was now seen as the vital growth ingredient. But Japan too slumped and the U.S., with its modest growth, has not taken back the baton. Meanwhile, the tigers and their chasers roared stronger than ever. Today, the dual forces of growth are anchored in China, which has witnessed strong growth in intra-regional trade, development and investment; and the region itself.

A New Group of Economies

The NIEs, emerging tigers, and even Japan, are turning their business gaze inward to the region itself. In the process, a "forgotten" and, as yet, undeveloped string of Asian countries, each going through political and economic change, and each linked by a single river, has captured world attention. The countries of Vietnam (population 70 million), Myanmar (43 million), Cambodia (25 million) and Laos (4 million), together with Yunnan Province in southern China, and north-east Thailand, comprise the emerging Mekong economies. Myanmar has the shortest share of the giant Mekong River, but the Ayeyarwaddy (formerly Irrawaddy), Myanmar's central riverine artery, is its close sister. Both rivers rise in the extreme eastern Himalayan foothills in Tibet.

Competition

The potential of Myanmar should not be viewed in isolation. Increasingly, sources of investment and development opportunities are to be found within a dynamic context that stretches from India in the west, to Japan in the north-east and Indonesia in the south. A Myanmar which fails to attract its Asian neighbours is faced with the prospect of continued stagnation.

But Myanmar is not the only suitor. Vietnam is another Mekong economy which has an equally low economic base and which is often compared with Myanmar for its investment potential. First, both are moving away from centrally managed, command economies towards market-oriented environments. Second, both need to modernise and rehabilitate their decayed infrastructures. Third, both offer a multitude of investment incentives and tax breaks. Fourth, both have identified oil extraction and tourism development as key sectors for foreign investment. Tourism is regarded as particularly attractive because it is a catalyst for multi-sector stimulation. It is labour-intensive but requires low skills. It is an export which earns foreign exchange without depleting local supplies. In addition, tourism gives each country international visibility and a much needed welcoming image.

So far, Vietnam, which opened its southern economy around Ho Chi Minh City before Myanmar, has attracted a lot more interest and investment. Vietnam became respectable for OECD investors when it renewed diplomatic ties with its former antagonist, the U.S. In 1995, it became the seventh member of ASEAN. Myanmar, on the other hand, still suffers pariah status because of its human rights image and political management. It is not yet a member of ASEAN.

While the similarities between these "competing" economies are striking, there are significant differences in their legal, financial and insurance structures, as well as religious, cultural, political and historical contrasts. The environment for investors in each country is both distinctive and unique.

Vietnam is not the only competing Mekong economy. The bravest investors in the region are also attracted to Cambodia which is striving for political consistency and transparency, factors vital to investors, so that it can commence its post-war recovery. Cambodia has a trump card in Angkor Wat although those who know the archaeological wonders of Myanmar would cite Bagan as an equal.

Singapore's Significance

Singapore is a key player in the changing investment environment. Its government has undertaken a significant paradigm shift in conceptualising a "second wing" initiative which aims to balance the long-practised policy of stimulating inward investment and the establishment of MNC bases in Singapore. The second wing is outward-oriented and strongly encourages, guides and even pushes Singapore companies and GLCs to form links with, and invest in, the surrounding region. The government and its agencies are often the lead investors. Prime Minister Goh Chok Tong, one of the most peripatetic Asian leaders in recent years, has headed mission after mission to initiate and develop such ties. As a result, Singapore is now a leading investor in the region. On the basis of overseas investment per capita, it is undoubtedly the leader in Asia. In Myanmar, it ranks first in number of foreign projects and still remains one of the few countries with direct air services to Yangon.

Singapore's characteristically pragmatic policy of "constructive engagement" today is regarded more with respect and less as self-interested opportunism. There is growing, although sometimes grudging, acknowledgement that SLORC might be making the right moves economically even if human rights activists are not happy. Singapore, one of the region's strongest advocates of Asian values, which favour community welfare over individual welfare and a hierarchical social structure infused with respect for age and status, does not share the west's discomfort when dealing with a non-democratic system. The complicated mix of Buddhist acceptance found in Myanmar, Confucian strictness underlying Chinese communities, and western individualism, inevitably colours judgements. However, the community approach shared by most Asian nations extends beyond national borders. Expanding alliances such as ASEAN, APEC and, most recently, ASEM, are evidence of this approach. Their contributions to regional growth should not be under-rated just because they appear to be "feel-good" rather than "do-good" gatherings.

Within this framework, one salient observation is that Myanmar has reached a threshold of stability. Moreover, it is genuinely striving to uplift the quality of life for each citizen in the country. On this foundation, it is inviting business and investment interests from around the globe to share in its future prosperity. But knowledge of local conditions in Myanmar is fundamental in this quest, and the contents of this book are intended to provide foundations amenable to this objective.

SYNOPSIS OF CHAPTER CONTENTS

Historical and Cultural

It is clear from the preceding section that Myanmar is experiencing monumental changes in moving to a market economy after decades of isolation. From a business perspective, these changes are permeating all facets of the social, cultural and economic fabric of Myanmar. The five chapters included in the first section of this book provide a frame of reference for understanding the context of doing business in Myanmar. The authors, all of whom are Myanmarese, offer an enlightening perspective of the current socio-economic status of Myanmar, its cultural heritage and the historical roots of its people, which make Myanmar the distinctive society that it is today.

The initial chapter by Myat Thein describes several economic indicators at the macro level in the manufacturing and trading sectors of the economy. He suggests that some of Myanmar's key social indicators compare favourably with other Asian countries while other aspects of Myanmar are woefully backward. Myat Thein concludes with a brief overview of the religious and traditional festivities which mark Myanmar culture.

Myo Myint, in Chapter 3, continues with the theme of Myanmar's history and culture. He contends that the physical characteristics of the country together with its geographical proximity to other countries in South-east Asia have played a significant role in the sharing and borrowing of cultural values and economic development. The author then gives a brief, but comprehensive, historical overview of the cultural, political, economic and religious influences that have poured into Myanmar from neighbouring countries.

In Chapter 4, Khin Mung Nyunt provides a lucid summary of the historical and cultural development of Mandalay, the ancient capital and the second city of present day Myanmar. After a description of the founding of Mandalay, the city is depicted historically in its religious, industrial, commercial, political and cultural contexts. Chapter 5 continues with Mandalay as the focus but attention is directed to ancient handicraft skills which generate considerable foreign exchange earnings. Daw Khin San May describes the manufacturing process of gold leaf, silk weaving, and gold and silver embroidery. Other cottage industries are mentioned, including bronze casting, stone carving and silverware.

In Chapter 6, Khin Mung Nyunt extends his prolific knowledge to an analysis of the historical and cultural development of Bagan. He portrays the political and religious rise of Bagan in vivid detail before articulating the factors attributable to its downfall. The chapter concludes with a discussion of Bagan architecture and the prominent remains of temples, pagodas and mural inscriptions which imbue Bagan with its distinctiveness and unique cultural heritage.

Macroeconomic and Regional Issues

This section consists of four chapters which cover important and emerging macroeconomic and regional issues. In Chapter 7, San Khup first considers several policies aimed at the structural transition to a market economy and the need to secure price stability while simultaneously controlling inflation. In particular, the formulation and implementation of the government's short-term plan (1992 to 1996) and the effects on the economy are explained. The author then examines the role of government policy related to infrastructure development and the nature of special projects devoted to roads, railways, air transportation, telecommunications and energy.

Trade development and various business structures in Myanmar are the focus of Chapter 8. Kin Maung Oo carefully outlines the objectives established by the Ministry of Trade and then evaluates Myanmar's major foreign trading partners in terms of exports and imports. In the latter part of the chapter, eight different forms for doing business in Myanmar are enumerated, together with a discussion on licensing laws, export-import licences, prohibited trade items, and various taxes and duties applicable to foreign trade.

In Chapter 9, Choo *et al.* begin with a description of eight areas of economic activity promoted by the government for business development. The authors then describe seven major geographical areas and their related commerce and industry. The chapter concludes with a functional analysis of the eight areas of economic activity within the context of their topographical settings.

Chapter 10 continues with the topic of regional development but with a focus on the Yangon region. Win Myint distils a number of programmes in five sectors which have top priority in the government's development plans.

Law, Accounting and Tax

This section comprises four chapters which deal with various legal, accounting and tax matters that are crucial to any form of business engagement in Myanmar. In Chapter 11, Tun Shin exposes the reader to the structure of Myanmar's corporate, economic and commercial laws. Seven major categories, ranging from state-owned economic enterprises and investment laws, to land, transport, dispute settlement and economy related laws, are presented.

Koh *et al.* continue the legal focus in Chapter 12 but with special emphasis on foreign investment. The authors first describe the forms of business incorporation procedures that are permissible, including those for registering companies. This is followed by a comparative analysis of investment incentives which are available across ten Asian countries. The authors conclude with several suggestions for amendments to the Myanmar Companies Act that may broaden potential business participation in the country.

Chapter 13 examines five major aspects within the accounting environment in Myanmar. Koh *et al.* discuss the regulatory framework, disclosure requirements for corporate reporting, audit practices, accounting firms and professional development. The authors conclude that substantial changes to accounting standards, audit practices and accounting education are required to meet the growing needs of a market-oriented economy.

In Chapter 14, Pathy *et al.* highlight major tax issues and important incentives that are offered under the Foreign Investment Law. A number of tax classifications and associated tax rates are discussed first, followed by a brief overview of profit, commercial and export-import taxes. The latter part of the chapter considers several important fiscal and non-fiscal incentives which are available to investors and others types of business interests.

Manufacturing and Services

This section consists of five chapters devoted to manufacturing and quasi-service sectors of the Myanmar economy. In Chapter 15, Goh *et al.* discuss the present status of manufacturing before turning their attention to the distribution of manufacturing operations among different forms of business enterprises. Next, the authors identify opportunities available in both export and domestic markets. In the latter part of the chapter, practical issues relating to the pre-production, production and distribution stages of manufacturing, and those impacting investment via government policy, cultural issues and foreign policy, are discussed.

Chapters 16 and 17 deal with Myanmar's banking and financial system. In the former, Myat Kyaw outlines the banking structure at the macro level and then summarises several recent reforms made to tax, interest rates and foreign exchange policies. In Chapter 17, Foo *et al.* place emphasis on the operational characteristics of the banking system and some of its weaknesses. They suggest a number of business opportunities which are viable under the existing framework while acknowledging that significant changes may be on the horizon.

The marketing function is the subject of Chapter 18 and Bin *et al.* offer a unique insight into the way it operates within the cultural environment of Myanmar. They employ a value creating and delivery sequence framework to assess three phases of marketing: choosing the value, providing the value and communicating the value. After developing this macro framework, which includes behavioural nuances specific to this culture, the authors describe the successful experiences of several prominent companies and warn of certain strategies that will not work.

In Chapter 19, Catlin *et al.* examine the modes of road, rail, water and air transportation. The current constraints on business caused by the under-development of each mode are enumerated. This is followed by an assessment of future needs and proposed development plans, together with specific suggestions for business opportunities in various geographic locations throughout the country.

Labour and Human Resources Management

This section of the book presents an array of information on one of the single most important resource advantages of doing business in Myanmar. In Chapter 20, Htin Aung outlines the roles and objectives of the Ministry of Labour. Also featured are the services provided by the Ministry and an overview of trade dispute processes.

In Chapter 21, Tan *et al.* analyse a number of general areas such as education, skills training, wage levels, and various labour laws and practices. Using these as anchors, they present some empirical findings related to specific companies in the manufacturing and hospitality sectors of the economy.

Tourism and Hospitality

This section of the book deals with the tourism and hospitality sector in Myanmar. In Chapter 22, Naw Angelene provides an overview of the government's new policies and plans for this industry. Not only is tourism one of the fastest growing industries in the world, it also is one of the fastest growing sectors in Myanmar. Besides tourism promotion, the author details some of the activities to be undertaken and sponsored by the government as part of a major promotional effort called "Visit Myanmar Year" scheduled to commence in October 1996.

In Chapter 23 Chong *et al.* extend the tourism focus to infrastructure issues such as accommodation, attractions, government promotional efforts and pricing of tour packages. Attention then is turned to various business and investment opportunities spanning service and infrastructure projects.

Cher *et al.* concentrate specifically on the management of human resources within the hotel industry in Chapter 24. They compare several hotels located in Yangon, Mandalay and Bagan on the basis of government versus private ownership. The factors examined include recruitment, selection, compensation and benefits, performance appraisal, training and development, career planning and industrial relations. The authors conclude with recommendations for government and suggestions that can be translated into business opportunities.

The final chapter in this section looks at a case study involving the construction and initial operations of a joint venture business hotel project in Yangon. In particular, Chapter 25 portrays some of the issues and difficulties associated with first mover advantage in a developing country like Myanmar.

Finally, there are considerable references throughout the book to various regions and cities in Myanmar. To facilitate an understanding of relative locations, a territorial map of Myanmar and its contiguous relationship to other countries is presented in Figure 1–1.

FIGURE 1–1
Map of Myanmar

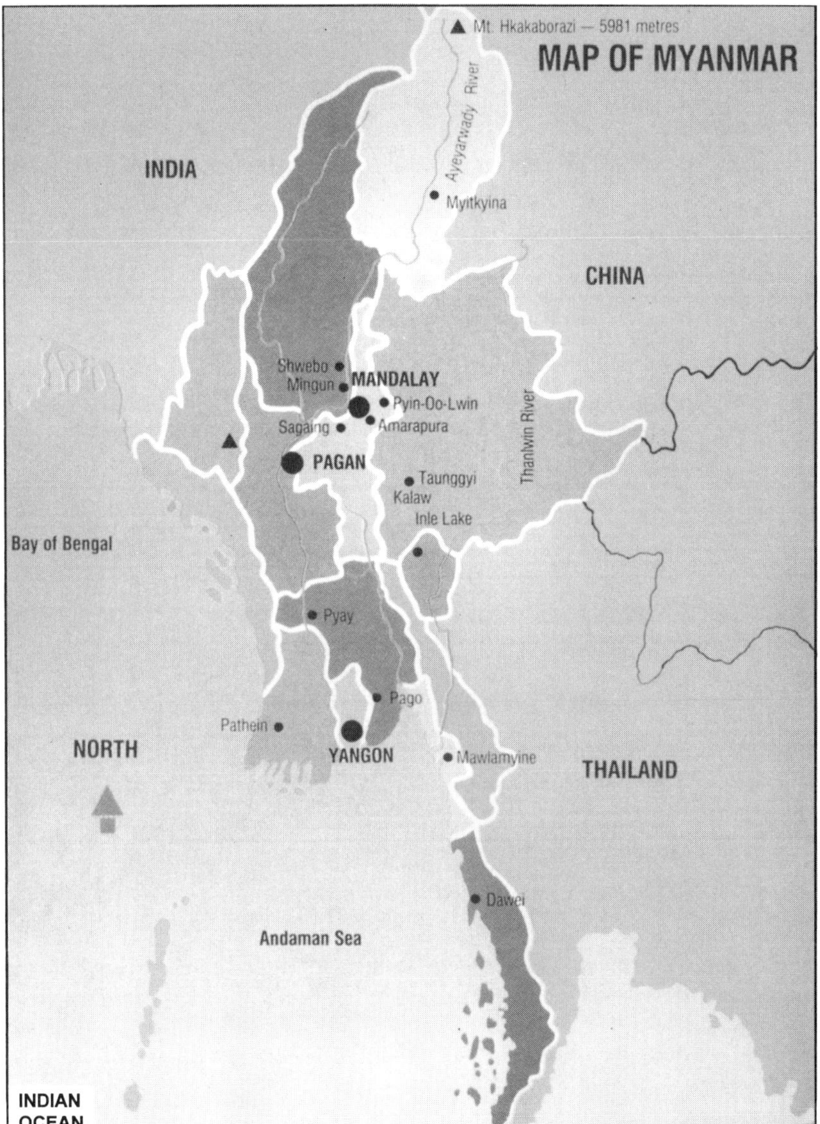

Source: *Myanmar – A Guide for Businessmen and Investors*, Coopers & Lybrand, 1994.

HISTORICAL AND CULTURAL

Chapter 2

Socio-economic and Cultural Background of Myanmar

BY
MYAT THEIN*

INTRODUCTION

THE MOST IMPORTANT task for Myanmar today is the promotion of economic and social development, while acknowledging the importance of the cultural heritage of the people. This chapter first outlines the socio-economic development of Myanmar and then describes the cultural background, with emphasis on aspects peculiar to Myanmar.

SOCIO-ECONOMIC DEVELOPMENT

When it took power in September 1988, the State Law and Order Restoration Council (SLORC) discarded the central planning type of economic management and adopted a market-oriented policy. The main objective of Myanmar's development policy then became one of developing overall economic growth in combination with preservation of the environment. Towards that end, a short-term plan was drawn up and is currently being implemented.

---

* Rector, Institute of Economics, University of Yangon, Yangon, Myanmar.

The key objectives are increased production, especially in agriculture, and increased export earnings from both goods and services.

Since adopting a market-oriented policy, Myanmar has recovered from the setbacks caused by the political disturbances of the late 1980s and gained momentum in its development efforts. GDP growth rates in 1992–93 and 1993–94 were 9.3 and 6.8% respectively (see Table 2–1).

Savings and investment rates in Myanmar are averaging 12% and 13% of GDP, respectively. These are not sufficient to sustain rapid economic growth. However, export promotion, market orientation and financial sector developments could stimulate greater domestic savings in the years ahead. Myanmar, as an export-oriented market economy in pre-war days, was able to save as much as 20% of GDP.

In the past, inappropriate macroeconomic policies and price controls adversely affected the agricultural sector. Since the decontrol of major agricultural products in September 1987, and the adoption of a market-oriented system, agricultural production has picked up momentum.

In the manufacturing sector, which accounts for 10% of GDP, output is divided evenly between the private and public sectors. Some privatisation has taken place, mainly in the form of leases, joint ventures and production on contract basis. The recently formed privatisation committees and subcommittees plan to transfer some of the state economics enterprises (SEEs) to the private sector according to contract methods. In the meantime, measures aimed at increasing the efficiency of existing SEEs still need to be pursued.

In the trading sector, liberalisation measures in line with market-oriented policies and decontrol of major agricultural products mentioned above, have boosted both domestic and external trade. However, Myanmar still remains heavily dependent on the export of primary commodities which include agricultural, forest and fishery products.

The liberalisation and market reforms have led to significant shifts at the sectoral level. There have been some successes, as illustrated by the growing role played by the private sector in the national economy.

Myanmar lacks a sound macroeconomic environment which is necessary for long term growth and development. Some tax reforms now exist such as the Commercial Tax Law of 1990. Budget proposals of ministries and departments are closely scrutinised. Nevertheless, there are still budgetary deficits. The money supply continues to expand fairly fast and inflation is between 20 and 30% per annum (see

TABLE 2–1
GDP Growth, GDP Changes in Composition and GDP Per Capita: 1985 to 1995

	1985–86	1986–87	1987–88	1988–89	1989–90	1990–91	1991–92	1992–93	1993–94 (P.A.)	1994–95 (P)
Constant Prices										
Gross Domestic Product (% change)	2.9	-1.1	-4.0	-11.4	3.7	2.8	-0.6	9.3	6.8	6.8
Agriculture (as % of GDP)	39.7	40.3	39.3	38.5	39.0	38.7	37.5	38.5	37.9	38.1
Industry (as % of GDP)	12.6	11.9	11.7	10.9	12.1	12.4	12.7	12.9	13.4	10.7
Infrastructure (as % of GDP)	4.4	4.5	5.0	4.8	5.1	5.2	5.5	5.7	6.1	5.9
Services (as % of GDP)	34.8	34.6	34.8	36.4	34.5	34.6	34.8	34.1	33.7	33.8
Per Capita GDP (% change)	0.9	-2.9	-5.9	-13.0	1.8	0.9	-2.4	7.2	4.0	4.8
Per Capita GDP (in kyats)	1,510.0	1,466.0	1,380.0	1,200.0	1,221.0	1,232.0	1,202.0	1,289.0	1,345.0	1,410.0
Current Prices										
Gross Domestic Saving (as % of GDP)	11.32	10.21	8.19	11.1	9.18	11.7	14.3	13.14	11.47	–
Gross Domestic Investment (as % of GDP)	15.45	14.6	12.67	9.6	9.49	14.64	14.8	12.52	10.52	–
Resource Gap	4.13	4.39	4.48	-1.5	0.31	3.21	0.5	-0.62	-0.95	–

Source: *Review of the Financial, Economic and Social Conditions for 1994–95* and earlier issues.
P.A. – Potential/actual
P. – Potential

Table 2–2). Price increases in the open market are generally followed by periodic price revisions for the remaining administered goods. These factors, combined with anticipation of further price increases, could precipitate chronic inflation.

TABLE 2–2
Budget Deficits, Money Supply and Inflation

Year	Budget Deficit (million kyats)	Currency in Circulation (million kyats)	Inflation Rate (change in CPI) (%)
1985–86	1,855.10	12,240	13.50
1986–87	1,243.20	17,035	14.75
1987–88	2,993.40	9,539	22.03
1988–89	5,594.50	16,890	22.50
1989–90	6,445.80	23,218	23.70
1990–91	10,350.00	35,140	21.91
1991–92	12,222.00	46,584	29.12
1992–93	11,160.20	63,871	22.30
1993–94	(17,463.00)	74,872	32.89

Sources: *Review of the Financial, Economic and Social Conditions* (various issues), Ministry of National Planning and Economic Development, and Selected Monthly Economic Indicators, CSO.

Prior to 1991–92, there was a deficit balance of payments. By 1993–94, Myanmar's external position was in an overall balance. Three developments are responsible for this turnaround: increased export earnings, services' earnings and inflows of foreign direct investment.

In social development, Myanmar is different from a number of developing countries in at least three respects. First, Myanmar does not have a population problem. The population grows at nearly 2% per annum and was estimated at 43.13 million in 1993–94. With a total land area of 676,577 square kilometres (261,228 square miles), the population density is 64 people per square kilometre which is fairly low by Asian standards.

Second, Myanmar's key social indicators are in line with those of more developed neighbouring countries. Of the countries shown in Table 2–3, only Bangladesh has a lower per capita income in U.S. dollars than Myanmar. Yet, many of Myanmar's social indicators compare favourably with those of her richer neighbours. For example, Myanmar's adult literacy and primary school enrolment rates are

TABLE 2–3
Comparative Social Indicators for Myanmar and Selected Asian Developing Countries

	Adult Literacy Rate (%)	Primary School Enrolment (%)	Daily per Capita Calorie Intake (% of requirement)	Population per Doctor	Infant Mortality Rate (per 1,000 births)	Life Expectancy at Birth (years)	Population with Access to: Health Services (%)	Population with Access to: Safe Water (%)	Population with Access to: Sanitation (%)
	1992	1990	1988–90	1990	1992	1992	1985–91	1988–91	1988–91
1. Myanmar	82	97	116	3,261	57				
ASEAN									
2. Indonesia	84	117	122	7,140	66	62	80	51	44
3. Malaysia	80	93	124	2,700	14	70	90	72	94
4. Philippines	90	112	108	8,330	40	65	75	82	69
5. Thailand	94	99	100	5,000	26	69	70	76	74
South Asia									
6. Bangladesh	37	77	94	6,670	109	52	60	–	32
7. Sri Lanka	89	107	99	7,140	24	71	90	71	60

Sources: 1. *World Development Report,* 1989, World Bank.
2. *Human Development Report*, 1991, 1994, UNDP.
3. *Review for the Financial, Economic and Social Conditions for 1994–95*, Ministry of National Planning and Economic Development.

higher than those of Malaysia. Myanmar's daily per capita calorie intake is higher than those of the Philippines and Thailand. Myanmar's population per doctor is less (i.e., better) than all the countries shown in Table 2–3, with the exception of Malaysia. However, Myanmar fares poorly if the population with access to health services, safe water supply and sanitation facilities, is compared to other countries.

Third, gender-bias against women in Myanmar is neither apparent nor acute. Some 50 years ago, an English clergymen, Reverend Appleton, who knew a lot about Myanmar (Burma), had this to say about the women of Burma: "The women of Burma are the freest of all the women in the East, and although tacitly paying lip service to the superiority of men, they are very much the equal companion of men. In Buddhist Law, if husband and wife separate each takes the dowry brought by him or her to the marriage, together with half the increase that has been added during the years they have lived together. The Burmese women are intelligent and capable; many friendly observers regard them as having more backbone and character than the men. They take an active share in the management of the home, much of the petty trade of the country is in their capable hands, while in the villages they share with their menfolk the work of planting and harvesting."[1] This observation clearly shows that the equality of women is an important cultural tradition of Myanmar.

CULTURAL BACKGROUND[2]

Myanmar's cultural foundation stretches back many centuries, at least to the reign of the Pyu Kings in the fifth century A.D. The greatest period of cultural activity began with King Anawratha, the Burmese King of Bagan. In 1057, he occupied Thaton of Suvannabhumi, the land of gold, and brought back from the Mons Theravada Buddhism as well as their culture. In fact, from that time onwards, it was possible to speak of a distinctive Myanmar language, Myanmar art and Myanmar culture.

The Myanmar language is quite distinct from those of neighbouring countries. It was through the introduction of Theravada Buddhism in the 11th century that it gained its place as a literary language. Myanmar

---

1 Quoted in Kyin, "An Ambassador Speaks", Mimeograph, 1994, p. 23.

2 This section is largely based on the speeches of His Excellency Thadoe Maha Thray Sithu U Kyin, Ambassador of the Union of Myanmar, 1951–1960.

literature also has been greatly enriched by translations from Pali and Sanskrit.

Seeing Bagan today, with its magnificent pagodas and monasteries in various stages of decay, one can easily imagine what a great city it must have been almost one thousand years ago. From this location, in the arid plains of Myingyan, grew Myanmar art, culture and history. The best decorative art-frescoes, relief-work, sculptures and carvings are found in temples, monasteries and pagodas, like the Ananda pagoda in Bagan and the Shwedagon pagoda in Yangon. In 1586, Ralph Fitch, the first-known Englishman to visit Myanmar, described Yangon as “the fairest place in the world”.[3]

Buddhist religion plays a large part in the life of the people of the “golden land”. National and local religious festivals keep them busy throughout the year. The Myanmar New Year, or *Thingyan*, which is around mid-April, is celebrated merrily and noisily. Elderly and devout Buddhists, who do not care to join the celebrations, keep sabbath. That is, they live on one meal a day, observe the eight or ten precepts of Buddhism and cease anything done for worldly profit.

After *Thingyan,* there is a religious or traditional festival every month of the year. Not all of these are merrymaking celebrations, nor are they all celebrated nationwide. For example, the watering festival of the Bodhi tree on the full-moon day of *Kason* in May, is a very religious occasion. It was on the full-moon day of *Kason* that Buddha was born, became enlightened and then passed away. Bodhi means omniscience, and it was under the Bodhi or Bo tree that Buddha gained enlightenment. Buddhist lent, which is around June, July and August in the rainy season, is a period of religious retreat and a time when marriages do not usually take place.

At *Thadingyut,* the lighting festival which marks the end of lent, it is customary for young people to dress up smartly and to pay their respects to their elders, and beg forgiveness from them for any sins that they might have knowingly or unknowingly committed. The elders, in return, ask the young to quash any sins that they, the elders, might have committed against them.

Another festival, held just before *Thadingyut*, is the boat racing festival. It is being revived by the present government with all the

---

3 Quoted in Kyin (see footnote 1).

attendant pomp and ceremony of the Myanmar courts of olden days because it is a traditional equestrian festival.

The last festival during the month of *Tabaung* (March) is called *Thareponzedi*. It is strictly a local or regional festival and is held in the vicinity of nearby pagodas. This festival, more than any others, provides an opportunity for people to sell and buy local handicrafts and assorted products.

Many festivals are accompanied by folk songs, stage dancing and marionette shows. Open-air theatrical plays and marionette shows often last through the whole night. Folk dancing is still very popular in Myanmar. The peculiar feature of this event is people dressed up as a mustachioed uncle-figure called U Shwe Yoe. Folk songs often reveal, in a jovial manner, some of the hardships and problems of daily life.

In contrast to folk dancing, stage dancing is a court dance both in conception and execution. It grew out of the need for princes to be skilled in dancing and music which were regarded as royal accomplishments. There were 18 arts which Myanmar princes had to learn before they could become kings. Myanmar court dancing or stage dancing assimilates elements of Thai dancing from the 18th century.

Finally, mention must be made of the traditional warm hospitality of the Myanmar people. Perhaps this has its roots in the Buddhist philosophy of impermanency and selflessness, of not leaving anything of their own in this world as they prepare for the next existence. Whatever the reason, natural warm hospitality is ingrained in Myanmar character and is clearly visible, not only in their smiles, but especially in their love for entertaining people as guests with food, songs and dances, and in their readiness to share their food with a visitor if they happen to drop by at meal time. Myanmar people take great pride in their hospitality.

Chapter 3

Myanmar: A Historical and Cultural Perspective

BY
MYO MYINT*

INTRODUCTION

THE SUBJECT OF this chapter is the same as the name Nanyang, or the Southern Seas. Although the term "South-east Asia" was first used by the British under Admiral Mountbatten in World War II to refer to a theatre of military operations in the war against the Japanese, and later earned wide currency in academic circles, the Chinese have understood South-east Asia as a geographical unit and a distinct entity since the early Christian centuries. The name also reflects the relative homogeneity of basic South-east Asian culture.

The theme of this chapter is how Myanmar became actively engaged in culture, borrowing and sharing with other countries in South-east Asia, and how Myanmar culture, based on Buddhist values and ideas, has played an important role in Myanmar history. In other words, it shows that Myanmar has never been isolated historically and culturally in the region.

Before addressing the issue, some points of caution are in order. First, history is not the

* Associate Professor, Department of History, Mandalay University, Mandalay, Myanmar.

business of historians alone, but, rather, the business of everyone. Most political and economic problems are historically rooted in the past. In order to understand economic problems, one must examine non-economic factors such as religion and cultures. Scholarship on Indochina, including Myanmar, is thin compared to islands of South-east Asia. Research on Myanmar history and culture in the South-east Asian context is scarce and still awaits the expert minds of native and foreign scholars.

Second, the present boundaries of the nations of South-east Asia, including Myanmar, are of recent origin. They were drawn by colonial powers at a time when early South-east Asian nations had different concepts of frontiers. Therefore, when we talk about the Myanmar state in historical times, it may not be demarcated by present boundaries. Sometimes it may refer to cultural or ethnic boundaries.

Finally, although Myanmar shares many similarities with other South-east Asian nations, it should not obscure the fact that South-east Asia is also a region of ethnic and cultural diversity, and that Myanmar is different from other South-east Asian countries in many aspects.

PHYSICAL LANDSCAPE

South-east Asia may be defined as the area south of China and east of India. It includes the present political units of the Union of Myanmar, the Kingdom of Thailand, Laos, Cambodia, the Democratic Republic of Vietnam, the Federation of Malaysia, Brunei, the Republic of Indonesia, the Republic of Singapore and the Republic of the Philippines. About 400 million people are living in a total land area of 1.5 million square miles.

South-east Asia is a tropical land lying across the equator, influenced by the Asian and Australian monsoons. A geographical crossroad, it controls passages between the Indian and Pacific Oceans. It constitutes both a barrier and a highway. The land, with jungles and mountains, divides; the water, with rivers and seas, unites. Rising in the central plateaus of Asia, high mainland mountain ranges unfold, running mostly in a north-south direction. These land barriers are difficult to cross. Four mighty rivers, also flowing north-south, help to ease travel. The Red River flows through northern Vietnam; the Mekong flows through, or borders on, Laos, Myanmar, Thailand, Cambodia and

Vietnam; the Chao Phraya flows through Thailand; and the Ayeyarwaddy flows through central Myanmar. All of them broaden out as they approach the sea, thus creating vast fertile deltas.

Situated in the north-east corner of South-east Asia, Myanmar shares borders with two South-east Asian countries and three non-South-east Asian countries. With an area of 261,267 square miles, it extends over 1,200 miles from north to south. Its borders total 3,170 miles in length. Myanmar shares 1,118 miles of border with Thailand, 148 miles with Laos, 1,358 miles with the People's Republic of China, 45 miles with Bangladesh and 501 miles with India. The coast line of Myanmar stretches 1,650 miles, from Bangladesh to southern Thailand, and borders the Indian Ocean.

Put Myanmar within the geographical context of South-east Asia and one cannot fail to appreciate its historical importance in the region. Geographical proximity creates special relationships and Myanmar has long cultural, economic and political relationships with all of her neighbours. Despite physical barriers, contact or trade with her neighbours and other South-east Asian countries were never completely blocked. The following points of historical importance should be noted. First, Myanmar is next to India and is like a cultural door through which Indian religious influence spread to other mainland South-east Asian countries. Through the passes of Rakhine (Arakan), Yomas and by way of the Bay of Bengal, Myanmar received Indian cultural influences like other South-east Asian countries. These include ideas of kingship and state, cosmology, architecture, law, literature and art.

Second, flourishing traditional caravan trade routes between Yunnan and Assam passed through Bhamo in Myanmar. Even in Roman times, emissaries went from Rome to the Han Dynasty through Myanmar in A.D. 92 and A.D. 121. In the 19th century, Britain made repeated attempts to use the same trans-Myanmar trade route to Yunnan via Bhamo.

Third, Myanmar's thriving seaports, such as Sittwe (Akyab), Pathein (Bassein), Yangon (Rangoon), Bago (Pegu), Thanlhlyin (Syriam), Motama (Martaan), Mawlamyaning (Moulmein), Dawe (Tavoy) and Myait (Mergui) participated in Indian Ocean trade. Although the Myanmar kingdom was based on agricultural resources, Myanmar kings never underestimated the importance of trade as they obtained handsome revenues from the seaports. They appointed foreign officials to supervise the seaborne trade. In the 17th century, Myanmar exported rice, slaves and earthen jars to Malacca.

Finally, neighbouring Thailand dominated Myanmar foreign relations until the 19th century. The Myanmar-Thai love-hate relationship resulted from nearly three centuries of warfare, which culminated in the destruction of Ayuthia in Thailand in 1777. Both countries tried to control parts of the Taninthayi (Tenasserim) region for Indian Ocean trade, and to dominate the adjacent Shan States. A neglected chapter in Myanmar-Thai relations is the cultural influence of each upon one another. Thai influence on Myanmar music, drama and art is considerable while Myanmar cultural influence in northern Thailand, including Chiangmai, is still apparent (and in parts of Laos). Many religious missions were exchanged between the two countries over the centuries and up to the present time. As a backdoor to China, Myanmar's strategic importance cannot be ignored.

CULTURAL LANDSCAPE: SHARING AND BORROWING

Myanmar shares many cultural features with South-east Asian countries. First, even in prehistoric times, Myanmar shared its culture with other South-east Asian countries. Recent finds of fragments of mandibles, teeth and skulls of Pithecanthropus-Sinanthropus (Java man-Peking man) in various parts of south China and north Vietnam provide a link in the chain between Java and northern China. They suggest that this human type was once widespread throughout south-east and eastern Asia, and was in fact the earliest form of "aborigine". Roughly fashioned stone tools, mainly made from river pebbles and which are thought to have been used by this type of primitive man, have been found in Europe, north Africa and northern China, as well as throughout South-east Asia and northern India.

Second, the most characteristic South-east Asian Neolithic civilisation is thought to have developed about the third and second millennia B.C. This is the quadrangular adze civilisation that used a finely polished stone axe with a quadrangular cross-section and which is found throughout South-east Asia. One eminent scholar suggests that it is possible that the combined quadrangular and shoulder adze civilisation founded a South-east Asia-wide common culture base which was later acted upon by Indian and Chinese influences.

Third, another South-east Asian cultural complex, the Megaliphic practices, included the erection of huge stones to enhance the social prestige of a person, living or dead, who was thereby commemorated. These practices are still widespread among the mountain peoples of South-east Asia. This custom was bound up with the belief that the living acquired wisdom from their ancestors who, in turn, promoted fertility in the soil and livestock.

Fourthly, the Dongson civilisation traditionally is regarded as the first metal-using culture in South-east Asia. It is named after a region in north Vietnam where the first significant bronze objects were excavated before World War II. Among the finds were large bronze drums of a kind found throughout the Indochinese peninsula and Indonesia. Rice is the main staple food throughout the area and its cultivation is accompanied by rituals and beliefs everywhere.

Fifth, throughout most of the region, maternal relationships were as important as paternal ones. Inheritance patterns indicate the bilaterality and high position of women. The strongest values of South-east Asian societies are apparent in their languages which contain elaborate sets of pronouns used to express social distance and relationships between superiors and inferiors, intimates and strangers. The maintenance of hierarchical relationships is important to South-east Asians. The nuclear or individual family structure is important in much of South-east Asia, as opposed to the importance placed on the extended family in India. Caste, one of the essential features of Hinduism, was never adopted in South-east Asia.

Sixth, linguistic unity is recognised across the colonial boundaries of South-east Asia. Modern Vietnamese and Khmer have common linguistic ancestors. The Thai language is not only spoken in Thailand, but in parts of south China, in Vietnam, in the Shan States of Myanmar, in western and north-eastern Cambodia, and in the extreme north of peninsula Malaysia. Variants of Indonesian/Malay languages are spoken throughout Brunei, Indonesia and Malaysia, and in the southern Philippines, the south coastal region of Thailand, Cambodia and Vietnam. The Tibeto-Burman languages constitute one such group spoken by Myanmar (Burmese), Naga, Chin, Lolo, Akha and other people in north-western parts of South-east Asia. It is vaguely related to the language of the Karens of eastern Myanmar and western Thailand, and to that of the Mao and Yeo people of northern Thailand, northern Laos, northern Vietnam and southern China.

Seventh, the countries of South-east Asia were neither "little India" nor "little China". Although the impact of these two great countries cannot be dismissed, South-east Asian countries have to be considered as culturally independent units. Strength and importance of indigenous cultural traditions have to be recognised. Myanmar and Cambodians were good at adapting Indian or Chinese art, religion, or political theory to suit their own needs and values. Historians call this process the localisation of culture. While Indian artistic and architectural concepts played an important part in the development of South-east Asian art, the glories of Bagan (Pagan), Angkor and the temple complexes of Java stem from their own individual character.

Finally, there are important common themes in the historical experiences of South-east Asian countries. In the modern period, the problems faced by its people in seeking independence, and those of governments in seeking to operate within independent states, often possess great similarities.

MYANMAR HISTORY AND CULTURAL DEVELOPMENT

With the demise of the Pyu, a Tibeto-Burman race who established their kingdoms along the Ayeyarwaddy from the fifth to eighth centuries, the Myanmar people entered the Kyaukse area where they learned the techniques of irrigation from the Mons. Then they entered the valley of Ayeyarwaddy and established their first kingdom at Bagan in the ninth century. Elements of Mahayana Buddhism, Brahmanism, and spirit worship prevailed in the early part of Bagan history.

The turning point in Bagan history came when King Anawrahta ascended the throne in A.D. 1044. This great king, who first unified the Myanmar kingdom, attacked Thaton, the Mon capital in lower Myanmar, and brought back the sacred Tripitaka Buddhist texts which, in turn, led to the introduction of Theravada Buddhism at Bagan. Lower Myanmar at that time formed the cultural entrance to South-east Asia from India and the west. From India, there were introduced such cultural techniques as alphabets, religion and rites, ideology, the concept of sovereign right, arms and strategies, elementary irrigation and the technique of rice farming. Receiving inspiration and support from Ceylon, Theravada Buddhism was developed under the patronage of the Myanmar kings. Merits, as the path to salvation, led to the donation of land, slaves and labour to the order of monks, Sangha, and the building of temples by the king, officials and the people.

Today, there are 2,217 historic monuments and temples under the care of the Archaeological Department. They are masterpieces of Myanmar art and architecture and form the richest archaeological sites in South-east Asia, rivalling the splendour of Ankor and Borobudur. The period from the 11th to the 13th century was the heyday of Theravada Buddhism in Bagan. From the religious point of view, Theravada Buddhism with its spiritual value system, took root and spread to other countries of South-east Asia such as Thailand, Cambodia and Laos. Unlike previous creed Buddhism, it was not simply a court religion but it spread to the common people.

The monk organisation Sangha, came to play an important part in Myanmar society. Monks performed Buddhist rituals, taught the doctrine and perpetuated the religion. Monasteries became the centre of learning. Treatises on Buddhist ethics and morals were compiled by monks. The order of Buddhist monks thus became one of the pillars of Myanmar society together with the monarchy. They represent the continuity of Myanmar society up until today. One scholar has advanced a theory that donations to the Buddhist orders, by both the people and the king, weakened the tax base of the kingdom and led to the downfall of Bagan. Bagan fell to the Mongols in 1289. Although it was no longer the political centre, Bagan religious and cultural traditions became the model for later Myanmar dynasties.

The fall of Bagan was followed by Shan domination of Myanmar. They founded the city of Inwa (Ava) in 1364, legitimising themselves by adopting Bagan culture and traditions. Shan domination in upper Myanmar forced many people to migrate to Tougoo, a Myanmar stronghold in the Sittaung valley. While competing with Shans in the north and Mons in the south, the Myanmar people established the Toungoo dynasty in 1486. One of its great kings, Bayinnaung (1551–81), not only unified Myanmar for the second time but he also established the largest empire in the Indochinese peninsula.

British historian, G.E. Harvey, described the Bayinnaung Empire as "the greatest explosion of human energy in Indochina". Bayinnaung conquered Chiangmai twice, in 1564 and 1569, and captured Ayuthia. He also extended his rule to Laos. Manpower mismanagement and administrative inefficiency by his successors led to the decline of the Bayinnaung Empire. The country fell into chaos following attacks by the

Rakhine and Portuguese on Bago. The dynasty was later restored by King Anaukpetlun (1605–28). Centrifugal forces were at work again for some time and the Mons conquered Inwa in 1752.

In the midst of anarchy, a new centre of Myanmar power emerged from Shwebo, a town north of Mandalay. A Myanmar leader named Alaungpaya founded a new dynasty called Konbaung in 1752. Konbaung kings moved their capitals around the confluence of the Chindwin and Ayeyarwaddy rivers. The capitals were Shwebo (1752–65), Inwa (1765–83 and 1823–37), Amarapura (1783–1857) and Mandalay (1857–85). The Konbaung dynasty experienced an expansion of its empire east and west, foreign wars with the British and, finally, the end of the dynasty.

From a cultural viewpoint, two Konbaung kings were significant. One was King Hsinbyushin (1763–76) who conquered all of Myanmar and then subdued Manipur, Assam, parts of East Bengal, Laos and Thailand. His conquest of Thailand resulted in the removal of the Thai population from its capital to Myanmar. Among those taken to Myanmar were Thai dancers, musicians and artisans whose services at the court enriched Myanmar culture. A Thai version of the Ramayana became popular in the court and its theme was used in Myanmar drama.

Another king deserving of attention was King Mindon (1853–78) who founded Mandalay and was regarded as the most pious and diplomatic king of the dynasty. On losing more than one-half of his kingdom and facing British expansion, he tried to strengthen Myanmar identity and values by giving strong support to the monks and Buddhism. Building pagodas, donating to monasteries and monks, convening the Sixth Buddhist Council, blessing the foundation of the Shwegyin sect and recording the Tripitaka texts on 729 stone tablets were all directed towards the attainment of this goal. He was believed to have been quite willing to compromise with the British on territorial questions but he refused to budge on cultural points. On one occasion, the British Resident insisted on wearing shoes in the presence of the king, a custom which is contrary to Myanmar custom and an insult to the king. Thereafter, King Mindon no longer permitted the Resident to meet him. The so-called "shoe question", which contributed to the loss of Myanmar independence, ironically became a nationalist issue during the colonial period for regaining independence.

During the colonial period, with cultural crisis in Myanmar because of political and economic changes, the peasants made a traditionalist response based on Buddhist millennialism against their rulers. The Saya San Peasant Rebellion (1930–31) was a reaction to alien rule using traditional ways and ideas. So were the "political" monks who cooperated with the nationalist politicians in the struggle for national independence. The early awakening of Myanmar nationalism and formation of political parties in the colonial period were also inspired by Buddhism. Only in the later stages was the nationalist torch taken over by secular elites in the late 1930s.

Chapter 4

Historical and Cultural Development of Mandalay

BY
KHIN MAUNG NYUNT*

GEOGRAPHICAL SETTING

MANDALAY, THE LAST capital of old Myanmar and the second capital of modern Myanmar, lies in the very centre of the country. Strategically situated for trade, communication and administration, it is accessible by land, water and air. On the west flows the Ayeyarwaddy River, the country's principal natural waterway, with the pagoda-dotted Sagaing and Mingun hill ranges on its western bank. On the east run the thickly wooded, blue Shan mountains. To the north stretches a vast terrain, punctuated here and there by offshoots of the Mogok mountain range. Two ancient capitals, Inwa and Amarapura, lie to the south just ten miles away.

* Professorial Chair of History, Mandalay University; Director-General, Department of Archaeology, Mandalay University; Chairman, Committee on Myanmar History; Member, Myanmar Historical Commission; Member, Council of University of Culture; and Member, Central Executive Committee of Writers and Journalists Association of Myanmar.

NATURAL ENVIRONMENT

There is a Myanmar folk song which epitomises the natural environs of Mandalay. Rendered in English it runs as follows:

He who wishes to live long
Should seek the shelter of Mandalay Hill
Which is kissed by the green waters
Of the Emerald Nanda Luke.

The description in this song befits the Mandalay of over 100 years ago when the natural environment of Mandalay was sylvan and idyllic, and unspoiled by the vandalism of so-called modern development. Wooded hills, groves and vales, lakes, ponds, streams and falls, nurtured by waters from the Shan mountains, formed one of nature's choicest landscapes, traces of which may still be discerned from an aerial view.

THE LEGEND

Like other ancient capitals of the world, Mandalay abounds in legends. One particular story is connected with Mandalay Hill which overlooks the Palace City. In fact, the real name of Mandalay City was not Mandalay. It was officially named Ratanapon by its founder King Mindon (A.D. 1853–78), meaning literally "a heap of precious treasures". Mandalay is the name of the Hill. But because King Mindon was legendarily associated with Mandalay Hill and the City was created at the foot of the Hill, the city became more well-known as Mandalay.

Legend has it that when the Lord Buddha with his disciples made a sojourn on the summit of Mandalay Hill, he met an ogress named Sanda Mukhi who was dwelling there. After the ogress had listened to the preaching of the Lord Buddha, she was happy and so grateful to him that she felt that she should offer him something. As she could find nothing, she cut off her two breasts and offered them to Buddha. Whereupon Buddha gave her a divine prophesy saying that the ogress would be reborn a prince who, on becoming king, would found a new city at the foot of Mandalay Hill. This king would promote Buddhism and there would be peace, prosperity and progress in his kingdom. The Myanmar people believed that this divine prophesy came true when King Mindon founded the new city of Ratanapon in 1856–57 on the very site Buddha had pointed at when he made his prophesy, and when the Fifth Buddhist Synod was convened by King Mindon in A.D. 1871.

HISTORY

Legend apart, the practical reasons which prompted King Mindon to move his capital from Amarapura to Mandalay were municipal, commercial and progressive. Amarapura was getting congested with the growing population. There was limited space for expansion. The marshy lands around it were unhealthy. After the deposition of his elder brother King Pagan (A.D. 1846–53), who lost the second Anglo-Myanmar war of A.D. 1852, King Mindon adopted a policy of peace although he never signed peace with the British.

Soon, agriculture and trade prospered. Merchants, both native and foreign, thronged to the capital to set up their quarters, offices and shops. Foreign envoys also arrived, mostly from western countries, to establish their residential missions in the capital. King Mindon was the most enlightened monarch of the late Kingbolt dynasty. He was farsighted and diplomatic. He knew that his country was backward and weak. To be able to withstand the imperialism of western industrial nations, his country had to be modernised. Territories lost to the British in the two wars could not be recovered by fighting with primitive weapons. But they might be regained by diplomacy or, if not, taken back by force when his country became strong. So the king decided to introduce reforms and launch a programme of modernisation.

Amarapura was inadequate for such new ideas and requirements. The terrain around Mandalay Hill was vast and healthy, befitting the site of a modern city. So the wise king made up his mind to build a new capital there, regardless of the protest against the move by both clergy and laymen.

Some scholars of Myanmar history, like Mr. Taw Sein Kho and Charles Duroiselle, suggested that as the ethnic origin of Myanmar people was Mongoloid, the nomadic instinct inherent in Myanmar kings was the motivating factor behind the frequent shifting of the capital throughout history. This suggestion is far-fetched because capital shifting is not peculiar to Myanmar. It has happened, and is happening, in other countries as well. We have the cases of Chang-an, Nanjing and

Beijing in China, and Kyodo and Tokyo in Japan. In India, there were many capitals before New Delhi. Bonn and Berlin in Germany are modern examples.

THE FOUNDING OF MANDALAY

The foundations of Mandalay were laid in the years 1856–57. Rituals and ceremonies were performed during its building, according to traditional practice and custom. But there was no human or animal sacrifice in those rituals, as erroneously recorded by some European historians. Archaeological excavations at the ancient capitals of Myanmar have revealed no evidence of such practices. Myanmar kings, including Mindon, being devout Buddhists would not have allowed a ritual that involved the taking of life.

The Palace City is a square area surrounded on all four sides by a high, thick wall of brick and mortar, and a wide moat. A flat and spacious area serves as a promenade between the walls and moat. The latter is fed by a canal which brings fresh water from the Shan mountains in the distant east. The moat is crossed by four bridges, one on each side of the city which is entered by four gates. The Palace City was built according to traditional Myanmar architectural design. Inside, laid out in square and oblong blocks, were the dwellings of soldiers and people ranking from minister to gate keeper.

In the centre on a raised platform stands the palace, officially named Mya Nàn San Kyaw, and commonly called Shwe Nan Taw (Royal Golden Palace). It is a complex of elaborately carved, gilded and mosaic-decorated wooden buildings. The original palace was bombed by the British towards the end of World War II. The present palace was reconstructed by the present government.

At the time of the kings, no commoner was allowed to live inside the Palace City. It was a city exclusively for royalty and the aristocracy. Only the King, Crown Prince and Queen, and lesser queens and the royal children, resided in the Palace itself. The Privy Council, government offices and law courts were also inside the Palace City, near the Palace.

King Mindon moved into the new palace in 1859. The whole court and population of Amarapura followed the king. Ratanapon, the capital, lay outside the Palace City. It was a carefully planned city built with advice from European town-planners and engineers, notably from Italy and France. With the Palace City as the Mandala (the hub), buildings were spread out in square or oblong plots from its four sides. On the north-east, east, and south-east sides were army quarters and barracks, each named after their respective regiments. On the west and south-west sides were houses and bazaars. The streets were named after the commodities sold, such as bamboo sellers' street, lacquerware sellers' street, vegetable sellers' street, fishmongers' street, and so on. The streets along which craftsmen and artisans lived were also called by the names of their trade, such as stone sculptors' street, glass makers' street, bronze smiths' street, carpenters' street, cartmen's street, and so forth. There were separate wards for ethnic groups and alien residents, such as China street, Indian street, Manipuri village, Siamese quarters, Laotian ward, Yunnanese quarters, Roman Catholic quarters and so on. The streets were laid out in a grid pattern. Buildings were of brick, teak, bamboo and thatch, in rows of square or oblong blocks, with shady trees in the front and spacious backyards for growing vegetables for home consumption.

MANDALAY THE HOLY CITY

Being a pious king and a devout Buddhist, King Mindon modelled his new city on Rajagaha, the city in India where Lord Buddha resided for a long time. Thus, he built many religious monuments (pagodas, temples, shrines, monasteries, rest houses, and meditation centres) in, and around, Mandalay. Assuming the role of royal promoter and inheritor of Buddha Sasana, King Mindon convened the Fifth Buddhist Synod in 1871 at which learned monks gathered for many months to revise and edit the Tipitakas, or the three sets of Buddhist Scriptures namely, the three Treatises of Discourse, the five Treatises of Priestly Disciplines and the seven Treatises of Buddhist Philosophy. The edited treatises were inscribed on alabaster stone slabs, numbering 729 in all. They were set up in serial order in the precinct of the Maha Loka Marazein Pagoda which the king built in 1857. This was the second time that the Tipitakas had been recorded since the demise of the Buddha over 2,500 years ago. The collection of these inscribed tablets is unique in the Buddhist world. Being an authorised version of the Buddhist Bible highly prized by all oriental scholars, this collection is often referred to as the "world's biggest book".

Another religious monument of world fame, which is credited to Mindon, is the Kyauk Taw Gyi Pagoda that lies right at the foot of Mandalay Hill. It is a temple housing an immense alabaster Buddha Image in sitting posture, sculpted from a single piece of stone brought from the Sagyin hills about 50 miles north of Mandalay. Tens of thousands of devotees contributed their labour, working in teams, to transport the big rough stone. A canal was dug to ferry it on a bamboo raft to the construction site. After completion in 1865, King Mindon performed the dedication ceremony of the Sacred Image. This great event was recorded in colourful pictures by court artists on folding papers. Enlarged reproductions of these historic pictures are displayed at the Pagoda. They depict the royal pageant, with the Myanmar armed forces of Mindon's time in traditional dress.

There are many monuments of religious merit around Mandalay which were built not only by the king but, also, by his queens, princes, princesses, ministers and men of substance. A walk on Mandalay Hill, around the recently installed corridors of the Pagoda on the summit, affords a panorama of the city and the many chapters of its history.

MANDALAY THE INDUSTRIAL CITY

Modernisation was one of the motivating factors behind the move to Mandalay. While King Mindon devoted himself to the construction of the holy city, the programme of industrialisation was entrusted to his beloved younger brother Crown Price Kanaung. The Crown Prince and his Minister U P.O. Hlaing were scientifically minded and well-informed about the progress and prosperity achieved by European nations in their application of science and industrialisation. Eager to catch up, they engaged Italian, French and German experts to help their industrialisation programme. Young Myanmar students were sent abroad to learn applied sciences, mechanics, industry, navigation, ship-building, weapon-making and so forth. Machines and equipment were bought and set up in the neighbourhood of the capital. Nine years after the founding of Mandalay, there were already over 40 new industries established, including iron foundries, rice and sawmills, metal smelting factories, weaving factories, a gun and artillery making factory, a soap factory, shipyards, indigo factories and, to Myanmar, indigo so fine that it was exported to Yunnan. The north-west, west and south-west outskirts of the city were demarcated industrial zones because of their proximity to the Ayeyarwaddy River and surrounding lakes.

A tragic turn of events in 1866 interrupted the industrialisation programme. A palace rebellion broke out in which the Crown Prince and two other senior Princes lost their lives. This did not stop the industrialisation programme but slowed it down and sent King Mindon into a sad mood from which he never fully recovered. He was now beset with the succession problem. With over 40 royal sons and daughters, who was to be the next Crown Prince? Prince Kanaung's death was not only a great blow to King Mindon but an even greater blow to the nation. King Mindon was a contemporary of Emperor Meiji of Japan. The two sovereigns began modernisation of their respective countries at almost the same time. But while modernisation in Myanmar came to an abrupt end with the loss of independence in 1885, followed by stagnation, Japan's modernisation proceeded uninterrupted by political events, as the country became one of the leading industrial nations of the world.

After annexing upper Myanmar, the British dismantled all factories and machines and sold them off as scrap. It was British imperial policy to keep the colonies as suppliers of cheap raw materials and consumers of finished products. The remains of some of the old factories can still be seen in, and around, Mandalay. One was converted into a brewery in the early days of British rule. Today, it produces the famous Mandalay beer.

MANDALAY THE COMMERCIAL CITY

With royal patronage and encouragement, foreign and local trade prospered in Mandalay. King Mindon promoted agriculture and exported its produce to neighbouring countries: beans, wheat and corn to British Burma and India; cotton, indigo and jade to China; teak and forest products to British India, France and England. Land, oil, teak, and precious metals and stones were royal monopolies. But anyone or any company could trade freely in the kingdom, provided custom duties were paid and trade regulations were observed. Commercial treaties were signed with England, France and British India for the extraction of natural resources such as logs, minerals and rubies, and for the opening of banks and construction of trans-border railways connecting Myanmar and Yunnan. Three steamships were purchased from the British and, with two cargo sampans attached to each, they made regular runs on the Ayeyarwaddy River, transporting passengers and cargo between Mandalay and Bamaw, an outpost and thriving trading town on the Myanmar-China border.

It was via Bamaw that most Chinese from Yunnan entered Myanmar. Many set up businesses in Mandalay and grew rich. Some gained access to the court and received royal favours. One striking case was that of a Yunanese Chinaman named U Set Shwin who came to Myanmar as a penniless boy. Through thrift, perseverance and industriousness, he became a trader. When he moved to Mandalay, his honesty and amiable nature won the affection of a nobleman who introduced him to King Mindon. In no time, he had become the king's favourite. He was given a royal permit to work the jade mines at Mogaung. This was a very special favour and luck smiled on him. Many jade stones of high quality were discovered in his mines. He rose to become the king's merchant and married the daughter of a nobleman from Yamethin town. He built a gilt wooden monastery in typical Myanmar architectural style, the Shwe Inpin Monastery, which today is one of Mandalay's tourist attractions. Inscriptions on his tombstone, and that of his wife, near the monastery graphically tell his success story. There are other similar success stories of Chinese, not only in Mindon's time but, also, during the early part of the British colonial rule. Mr. Au Bon Pa was one outstanding case. He started in Daik-U in Pegu Division where he began his business career selling "tiger balm". His descendants now live in Singapore.

Mandalay in Mindon's time was quite a business centre. Chinese, Indians, Arabs, Armenians, Italians, Frenchmen, Germans, Englishmen and Scotsmen resided in Mandalay either to trade, to be employed in the king's service or to gather information for their agencies. Thanks to the tradition of religious tolerance and freedom, faiths other than Buddhism had arrived in Myanmar since the early times. In Mandalay, Chinese joss houses, churches of different denominations, Hindu temples, mosques, and other prayer houses can be found. King Mindon made friends with the leaders of these faiths and made contributions to their welfare.

MANDALAY THE CENTRE OF DIPLOMATIC ACTIVITY

Myanmar played an important role in foreign relations in the late 19th century. It was King Mindon's policy to cultivate friendship and maintain good relations with all countries, and to learn from them whatever was beneficial to his own country. Having lost a major portion of his kingdom to the British, Mindon wanted to retain intact what was still left – upper Myanmar. So he used diplomatic means to have the world recognise his country as an independent nation. He sent out senior envoys on goodwill missions to the then leading nations of the world including England, France, Italy and British India, and received foreign envoys in return, as well as from neighbouring China, Siam and Vietnam. He even tried to open diplomatic relations with the United States of America and Tzarist Russia by sending his representatives there with credentials and gifts. European and English envoys who visited Mandalay and were received at the Court, wrote graphic accounts of what they saw and experienced.

MANDALAY THE CULTURAL CITY

From the deposition of the last king Thibaw in 1885, Mandalay ceased to be the capital. The seat of government was moved to Yangon, a booming seaport town in the delta which, because of its good location and the presence of the world renowned Shwedagon Pagoda, gained preference over Mawlamyine, another seaport on the south-east coast. But as the centre of Myanmar culture, Mandalay still has no rival. All elements of culture, fine arts, performing arts, architecture, sculpture and literature continued to thrive in the old capital of Mandalay even after the monarchy ended.

Throughout the British colonial regime, Mandalay withstood the impact of western education, administration and cultural infiltration. Mandalay gained material development and modern amenities introduced by the British. But thanks to the predominance of Buddhism, the monastic education given by the Buddhist monks and the devotion of artists, Myanmar cultural heritage thrived and is well-preserved today in Mandalay.

Foreign tourists who want to have some knowledge of typical Myanmar culture must visit Mandalay to observe daily life and visit old monuments, pagodas and historic sites. Even in the heyday of British colonial rule, the significance of Mandalay as the metropolis of Myanmar culture was recognised by no less a person than the British Viceroy of the Indian Empire, Lord Curzon. When he visited Mandalay in early

1901, he saw the palace occupied by British troops. Being a lover of oriental antiquity and desirous of preserving the cultural glory of the last seat of the Myanmar monarchy, he immediately gave orders for the troops to be moved out and for the whole palace complex to be preserved as a national museum.

Over time many foreigners have written accounts about this last Myanmar capital, extolling its past glory and present cultural wealth. Examples include two fully-illustrated volumes entitled *Silken East* by Scott O' Connor (1904); *Mandalay and Other Cities of the Past in Burma* (1907) by the same author; *A Narrative of the Mission sent by the Governor-General of India to the Court of Ava in 1955* (1958) by Sir Henry Yule; *The Mandalay Palace* by Charles Duroiselle; and *Mandalay*, with colourful photographs (1994) by Paul Strachan. There is much literature on Mandalay.

The government is endeavouring to preserve Myanmar's cultural heritage by maintaining ancient movements and cities, excavating archaeological sites, reviving fine arts and performing arts, holding traditional national festivals and encouraging and patronising Myanmar language, literature and history. The Ministry of Tourism was formed not merely to boost tourism as a foreign exchange earner, but to make Myanmar cultural identity more well-known to the world. The year 1996 has been designated "Visit Myanmar Year". For those who are serious about Myanmar culture, "Visit Mandalay" should be a top priority on their tour programme.

CONCLUSION

To conclude, the following is the first stanza from the famous poem, *On the Road to Mandalay* by the English poet Rudyard Kipling:

> By the old Moulmein Pagoda, lookin' lazy at the sea,
> There's a Burmese girl-a-settin; and I know she thinks o' me;
> For the wind is in palm-trees, and the temple bells they say:
> Come you back, you British soldier; come you back to Mandalay!
> Come you back to Mandalay.
> Where the old Flotilla lay:
> Can't you 'ear their paddles Chukin' from Rangoon to Mandalay?
> On the road to Mandalay

Where the flyin'-fishes play.
An' the dawn comes up like thunder outer China 'crost the Bay!

Chapter 5

Mandalay: The Handicraft Centre of Myanmar

BY
DAW KHIN SAN MAY*

INTRODUCTION

MANDALAY, WITH A population of about 700,000, is the second largest city in Myanmar. It is located on the east bank of the Ayeyarwaddy and is about 640 kilometres from Yangon. Since it lies in central Myanmar, it is connected to all major cities by air, road, river and rail.

It is a great trading centre with its famous market, the Zegyo Bazaar, and is one of the main distribution centres of agricultural products in upper Myanmar. All crops, including rice, but mostly dry zone crops, such as chillies, onions, oilseeds, pulses and beans, flow through various channels to Mandalay where they are marketed and distributed all over Myanmar. Mandalay and the surrounding region are noted for sesamum seeds, groundnuts, tobacco, wheat, cotton, pulses and beans, betel nuts and tangerines which are all exported to neighbouring countries.

With the advent of the market economy, many private industries have sprung up in Mandalay. And with the designation of 1996 as

* Associate Professor, Institute of Economics, Mandalay University, Mandalay, Myanmar.

"Visit Myanmar Year", many hotels, private as well as government-owned, have been built which creates an impression of modernity.

The history of Mandalay is a tale of two cities. It became the capital of the Myanmar kings from 1857 when King Mindon moved his capital to Mandalay from nearby Amarapura. King Mindon and his son King Thibaw, the last king of the last Myanmar dynasty, left a great cultural heritage in Mandalay. Today, it is well-known for its classic handicrafts. There are six notable cottage industries in, and around, Mandalay.

GOLD LEAF

One very important ancient craft is the manufacturing of gold leaf (*Shwe Saing*). This is concentrated in Myatpa Yat Quarter, in the south-eastern part of the city and is a hereditary occupation found nowhere else in Myanmar.

About 35 to 40 cottage industries work together to produce gold leaf. The initial part of the work is done by five to seven households, each employing three or four skilled workers. The remaining work is done by about 30 households using 20 to 30 specialised workers.

The production process is rather complicated. First, gold blocks are melted down and purified. The liquid is poured into a conical-shaped vessel to produce finger-shaped gold bullions. Then, these are flattened by rollers of two different sizes. Next, they are beaten out by skilled craftsmen who make thin sheets of gold, called *shwe-let*, which means golden finger. In olden days, the beating was done mainly by manual labour and it took several days. Now, the craftsmen of Myatpa Yat can produce one *shwe-let* in four to five hours. A roll of *shwe-let* looks like a gold ribbon, about four feet long and one inch in width. One tical of gold can produce four *shwe-let*s.

These *shwe-let*s then are sent to another household where they are made into gold leaves. Small pieces of gold, about one inch in width and one-quarter inch in length, are cut off from the *shwe-let* and placed between sheets of bamboo paper called *shwekhat setku* (gold leaf making paper). Layers of *shwekhat setku*, holding small pieces of *shwe-let*, are wrapped with deer skin and then beaten by skilled craftsmen to get the required film-like thinness of the leaf. The films of gold are then joined to get two-by-two inch gold leaves. These are placed between *shwehlaung setku* (gold holding paper).

Shwehlaung setku is made of straw and it is manufactured in Amarapura.

Gold leaf is sold in packets known as *shwe-let*. Four rolls of *shwe-let* amount to 25 to 28 packets of *shwe saing* which contain 100 gold leaves each. Different households produce their own brands. The market price for one packet containing 100 gold leaves is about K1,200. It is a profitable business because Myatpa Yat has a monopoly of the gold leaf making business.

Devotees buy gold leaf to gild pagodas and images of Buddha. Mandalay gold leaf meets national demand and the cottage industry flourishes along-side Buddhism. The gilded pagodas of Myanmar get covered with an estimated 10 to 20 ticals of gold a day.

SILK WEAVING

Mandalay is also well-known for its *luntaya gyeiks* (woven silk material). Silk material has been used since the days of the Myanmar kings. Gold silk was woven exclusively for the royal household. Today, *luntaya gyeiks* are popular with Myanmar ladies and the demand is increasing. Silk weaving enterprises are found in Nan Shay, east of the palace, and in the nearby towns of Amarapura and Sagaing.

Luntaya gyeik is woven on a handloom using 100 or more shuttles to produce intricate wavy designs. It is believed that the intricate weaving technique was introduced by Assamese and Manipurian weavers who were brought to Myanmar during the reign of King Bagyidaw (1819–37). However, some scholars have noted that the intricate wavy designs existed in the Bagan era. A wall painting of a guardian angel wearing a sarong with a wavy design can be seen at the Apeiyadana Pagoda Cave in Bagan.

Production begins with the spinning of silk into silk thread. This is then boiled in colourful dyes in earthen pots to get the desired colours. It takes 15 to 30 days to weave two metres of wavy design cloth. The more intricate the design, the more shuttles are used and the longer it takes. One cottage industry has 20 to 30 looms. It is estimated that Nan Shay, together with Amarapura and Sagaing, produce 500 to 800 *luntaya gyeiks* per month, which is more than sufficient for home demand.

There are about 50 *luntaya gyeik* designs. The most famous are Hteik Kaung Tin and Sapenwe. Local silk supplies are insufficient, so most of the silk used in Mandalay is imported from China. Prices range from K6,000 to K14,000 depending on quality and design. The profit is from K1,000 to K3,000 per two metres.

GOLD AND SILVER EMBROIDERY

Another Myanmar handicraft which is becoming popular, especially among tourists, is gold and silver embroidery. It is an ancient craft and the materials used reflect the influence of the Moghul courts of India. Production is concentrated in Nan Shay and Myatpa Yat. Since the Bagan era, the colourful dresses of royalty were embroidered with gold and silver thread, glass beads, pearls and shining sequins stitched on silk material. The gold and silver thread is called nagada thread.

Embroidered tapestries vary in size from one-foot square to 20 feet by 10 feet. They are earning an international reputation and are popular tourist souvenirs. Renowned artist, U Sein Myint, presented a Myanmar tapestry to the United Nations in 1990. He now owns one of the largest tapestry industry workshops in Mandalay. Another overseas example is in the Blue Elephant Restaurant in London. This tapestry portrays the ten stories of Buddha's previous existence, with each story explained in Myanmar characters.

A tapestry is known as a *Kalaga* in Myanmar. The use of a *Kalaga* as a screen or curtain was a tradition in Myanmar courts. The most ancient, and historic, *Kalaga* design is Buddha's footprint with 108 auspicious marks. Other historic designs depict Lawkanat, a guardian angel of the Universe; dancers; Kanarie and Kanaya mythical birds from Myanmar culture; and peacocks. The whole Myatpa Yat Quarter specialises in gold and silver embroidery, with the exception of those engaged in gold leaf making.

The process of producing a tapestry is usually led by a painter and artist. Three or four stitching craftswomen work together, for a week or two, to produce a two foot by four foot tapestry. Great skill is required to create the various pieces that make up the design. First, an artist draws the design on a piece of cotton cloth. The required materials then are stitched on to the drawing. The pieces that make up the design are cut off from the drawing cloth and stitched on to the velvet or cotton cloth to become a tapestry.

The value of a tapestry depends on its size and design. The one presented to the United Nations is valued at K120,000. Nowadays, tapestries are fashioned into pretty souvenir items, such as wall plaques, jackets, caps and handbags to attract the tourists. The growth of this cottage industry depends on the development of tourism. Promotion of this kind of industry promotes Myanmar culture and earns foreign exchange.

The other ancient crafts of bronze casting, stone carving and silverware are less popular than the above mentioned crafts. They are briefly described below.

BRONZE CASTING

Bronze casting works can be found in Tanpawadi or the Kyi Thun Yat Quarter (the Bronze Village) in Amarapura, which indicates that this craft may have existed from the days of King Bodawpaya (1782–1819). Bronze casting was mainly used to mould images of Buddha and large bells that were hung in the compounds of most pagodas. One outstanding example is the famous Mingun Bell, the world's largest ringing bell, which weighs 55,555 viss, or over 90 tonnes. It was cast by the craftsmen of Bodawpaya.

STONE CARVING

Stone carving, a hereditary occupation, is done in the Kyauk Sit Tan Yat Quarter, near the great Mahamuni Pagoda. There, the craftsmen make statues and images of Buddha out of Sakyin stone, which is quarried at Sakyin village near Madaya town, not far from Mandalay. This industry is very much associated with Buddhism.

SILVERWARE

Most silverware is produced in Ywataung, a few miles from Sagaing. Because silver is scarce, it is difficult to find genuine and authentic silverware. Ywataung silver smiths also produce bronze and copper ware. It is feared that this cottage industry might disappear due to lack of skilled labour and the scarcity of raw materials.

While these crafts are of limited economic importance, they contribute to the importance of Mandalay and its surrounding region, as a place of rich culture and tradition combined with growing trade and industry.

Chapter 6

Historical and Cultural Development of Bagan

BY
KHIN MAUNG NYUNT*

GEOGRAPHICAL SETTING

MYANMAR IS A tropical country which typically experiences heavy rainfall during the monsoon season. However, in the very centre of Myanmar, there is a rain-shadowed area called the Dry Zone, a semi-desert sandy land, sparsely covered with thorny bushes, shrubs and cactus, fossil woods, isolated clusters of palms, hardy trees and ravines of the zone. It is a parched land, or "Tatta-desa" as Mon inscriptions call it. Annual rainfall is less than 40 inches. Bagan occupies an area of 25 square miles in the heart of the Dry Zone.

Approximately 30 miles to the south-east of Bagan rises Mt. Popa, a 5,000-foot extinct or dormant volcanic outcrop of the nearby mountain range. Eight miles south-east runs a range of low hills called Tuyin which average 1,000 feet in height. The Ayeyarwaddy River flows on the western bank of Bagan, along an

* Professorial Chair of History, Mandalay University; Director-General, Department of Archaeology, Mandalay University; Chairman, Committee on Myanmar History; Member, Myanmar Historical Commission; Member, Council of University of Culture; and Member, Central Executive Committee of Writers and Journalists Association of Myanmar.

ever-changing course between eroded banks. On the river's west bank, facing Bagan, is another range of hills named Tant Kyi Taung Tan, behind which the sun sets every evening.

HISTORICAL BACKGROUND

The place described above is an unlikely site for a civilisation. There is no fertile alluvial soil in which to grow paddy, no thick teak forest from which to extract timber and no rich minerals to mine. Yet, Bagan grew there and stood as the capital of the first Myanmar empire for nearly three centuries. Over 2,000 surviving monuments and thousands of stone inscriptions found within 16 square miles of Bagan testify to the existence of a well-developed ancient civilisation on this dry land. How and why Bagan was founded at such an inhospitable site are questions still not answered satisfactorily.

On the strength of archaeological and epigraphic evidence, scholars of Bagan history have generally agreed that there were two key economic reasons for Bagan's existence. Both relate to areas some distance from Bagan. One was the Kyauk-Se area, 200 miles north-east, in the present-day Mandalay Division. The other was the Minbu area down-river, on the west bank of the Ayeyarwaddy River in Magwe Division. Lithic inscriptions at, and around, Bagan mention 11 economic centres in the Kyauk-se area and six in the Minbu area. These were called "Kharium", meaning the hub or the centre. Those in Kyauk-se, referred to as the "Eleven Myittha Khariums", were Pnile, Myitmana, Myit-tha, Myin gon daing, Ya-mon, Panan, Mekkhaya, Tapyet tha, Thin daung, Tamokso and Khan-lu. Those six in the Minbu area were Saku, Salin, Lei kaing, Mapinsaya, Paung lin and Kya bin.

While Khariums or economic centres lay in the Dry Zone, they were very fertile, being covered by an irrigation network, a technology brought by Proto-Myanmars from central Asia in times immemorial. The Shan mountains, the Minbu hill range and the five rivers, Ayeyarwaddy, Sa-mon, Duhtawaddy, Zawgyi and Panlaung, were the main sources of fresh water feeding the irrigation system. The Khariums were the granaries of Bagan, producing no less than 76 varieties of crops, fruit and vegetables. Scholars agree that the irrigation works of the Bagan period were among the oldest and best in South-east Asia.

FOUNDING OF BAGAN

Not far from the Tuyin hill range, on the sandy plain of Yon Hlut Kyun, are 19 villages which are believed to have been the first settlements of Bagan. The name Bagan, philologists opine, is derived from Pyu-gama meaning "village of the Pyus". A contemporary Khmer inscription referred to Bagan as Pu-gam. After the Nan-Chos sacked the Pyu city states the Pyus, who were Proto-Myanmars, moved to the Dry Zone and founded their first settlements there.

Myanmar chronicles claim that Bagan was founded in A.D. 108 and that a long dynasty of 55 kings ruled over the Bagan kingdom for 12 centuries, from A.D. 108 to 1287. As strong archaeological evidence has not yet been found, the A.D. 108 date is regarded as legendary. The brick city walls and the Sarabha Gateway, still standing today, were built by King Pyinbya in A.D. 849, in the fourth year of his reign. He was the 34th king in the dynasty. There are, however, many undatable monuments of different sizes and designs in various stages of decay which might have been built by earlier kings. But lithic inscriptions so far found have no date earlier than the tenth century, though they cross-refer to kings prior to Pyinbya. We may safely regard the tenth century as the beginning of the authentic history of Bagan.

According to Myanmar chronicles, Bagan changed its capital four times. The first was Pauk-kan, built by King Thamudarit, who founded the Bagan dynasty in A.D. 108. The second was Thiripyitsaya, built by Thiligyaung, the seventh king; the third was Tampawadi (now Pwasaw) built by Thaiktaing the 12th king; and the fourth was Arimaddana pura, a Pali name meaning "the city which crushes its enemies", built by King Pyin bya in A.D. 874. Today it is called Bagan.

CAPITAL OF THE FIRST MYANMAR EMPIRE

Bagan only became an empire in the time of Anawrahta (1044–77), the 42nd king. He was followed by a line of 14 kings, who ruled Bagan for over two centuries during which Bagan rose to the height of its glory and greatness, and then met its final downfall.

It is interesting to note three stages of progress in Bagan's political organisation. Like the economic centres, its political or administrative centres were called Kharium. Many settlements, called Taiks, spread out from each Kharium. When Taiks expanded, through conquest or colonisation, they were collectively called Naing-gan. Naing-gan means state or empire. All Taiks united under King Anawrahta to form his Naing-gan. Anawrahta's Naing-gan or empire extended up to Kantu and the Yunnan border in the north and east, down to Dawei and Thandok in the south-east to Taninthayee in the south, and right down the Kra Isthmus to Takun Pa, and over to Salankre (Junk Ceylon), Na Kuiw (Nagara) and Bengal in the west. Anawrahta's seals, which were votive tablets and epigraphics bearing the names of these places, were found in each of these locations.

BAGAN THE ROYAL CITY

Under Anawrahta, Bagan grew to be a peaceful and prosperous city. With a strong army, headed by his faithful paladins, and a chain of 43 outposts established along the borders, he was able to defend his far-flung empire and maintain law and order within it. An administrative hierarchy, spread as a network over his kingdom, enabled him to efficiently manage the irrigation system and to develop agriculture, the principal source of revenue. He built four weirs and canals, called Kinda, Ngalaingzin, Pyaung bya and Kume on the Panlaung river, and three weirs and canals on the Zawgyi river. He populated these irrigated areas with villages and appointed officers to supervise the maintenance of the system. These areas became known, in Myanmar history, as Lei-Dwin, meaning "rice country".

Anawrahta's Bagan was a cosmopolis which attracted people from neighbouring Cambodia, Laos (Linzin), Theingo (Sri Lanka), Bengal, China and Zimme, who came to serve under Anawrahta. Stone inscriptions from this time mention Myanmar ethnic groups like Mons, Palaung, Shan and Chins, as well as Chinese, Cambodians, Laotians, Indian, Bengalis, and Ceylonese.

BAGAN THE HOLY CITY

In 1056, a learned Buddhist monk named Shin Arahan came to Bagan. He was a missionary monk from Thaton, the capital of the Mon kingdom in lower Myanmar. It was he who introduced Theravada Buddhism to

Bagan. He became Anawrahta's "Raja guru" (teacher-adviser to the king). With his advice and assistance, Anawrahta carried out religious reforms, breaking down the power of corrupt priests known as "Aris" and stamping out animistic worship and primitive customs. Monasteries were built where learned monks of the Theravada School of Southern Buddhism were patronised. They were encouraged to teach the pure form of Buddha Dhamma. At the behest of Shin Arahan, Anawrahta sent his envoys to Manuha, the king of Thaton, to get from him copies of the Tipitakas (30 sets of Buddhist scriptures). When Manuha refused, Anawrahta besieged and took Thaton in 1057. He returned home in triumph bringing with him the sacred scriptures, relics and learned monks. King Manuha, his court, and several artists and craftsmen from Thaton, were also taken as captives to Bagan.

The conquest of Thaton brought immediate results and contributed to the development of Bagan, the holy city. Firstly, many learned monks from Thaton joined Shin Arahan in his missionary work and in preaching of Dhamma, guided by the Tipitakas. Secondly, Theravada Buddhism superceded Mahayana Buddhism and, in religious education, Pali superceded Sanskrit. Thirdly, the Mon alphabet was adopted. For the first time, the Myanmar language was written down. The earliest inscription in Myanmar is dated 1058, a year after the conquest of Thaton.

BAGAN THE SEAT OF LEARNING

As Theravada Buddhism flourished and spread, many monasteries were built at Bagan. Here, novices were trained for monkhood and the laity was taught the three Rs and moral instruction. There were also types of monasteries where secular subjects such as astrology, medicine, carpentry, masonry, gymnastics, occult science, and various arts and crafts were taught to laymen. These monasteries were called Pwe-Kyaung. The word Kyaung means both monastery and school and, indeed, monasteries were schools. In its heyday, Bagan was the seat of learning for the sacred Pali language. Buddhist monks came from abroad to Bagan for higher learning. Its monasteries were considered equal to the old universities of Taxila and Nalanda in India.

ANAWRAHTA AND FOREIGN RELATIONS

Anawrahta's fame as the great royal patron of Theravada Buddhism spread to Buddhist centres throughout South-east Asia. He made alliances with the Buddhist kingdoms of Haripunjaya in Northern Thailand, Patikkra in East Bengal and Nagara Sri Dhamaraja in Malaya. In about 1060, Anawrahta sent military assistance to King Vajaya Bahu I of Ceylon on the latter's request, to repel a Chola invasion. In 1071, he despatched a religious mission, composed of Myanmar learned monks, with cannonic texts to Ceylon to help the Ceylonese king revive Buddhism. Myanmar chronicles record the exchange of religious and diplomatic missions between Anawrahta and the Chinese Emperor, and the visit of the former to the latter's court to ask for the Sacred Tooth Relic of the Buddha. He received a jade image instead. When Anawrahta died, Bagan was one of the strongest Buddhist kingdoms in South-east Asia.

BAGAN UNDER ANAWRAHTA'S SUCCESSORS

A line of 14 kings succeeded Anawrahta, ruling Bagan over a period of 292 years. The longest reign was that of Alaung Sithu which lasted 50 years. The two shortest were those of Narathu and Naratheinkha, both of whom ruled for three years. The average reign was 20 years per king. Of the 14 kings, only two matched Anawrahta in terms of leadership, accomplishments and greatness – Kyanzittha and Alaung Sithu. Kyanzittha was a great soldier and a wise statesman. He led all military campaigns during Anawrahta's reign and his own. He united the kingdoms of Mon and Myanmar, and adopted Mon culture for Bagan. He completed the Shwezigon Pagoda, an immense solid structure left unfinished by his predecessor Anawrahta, in 1090. A year later he himself built the graceful and artistic Ananda Temple.

Alaung Sithu was Kyanzittha's grandson, known in Myanmar history as the "traveller king" because he toured extensively. Aboard his royal barge and attended by a large flotilla, he journeyed to Bengal, the Coromandel Coast of India, Ceylon, Malaya and the Cape of Negrais, establishing contacts with royalty and rajas in these countries, and returning with maritime knowledge and experience and gifts. During his long reign, he devoted time to works of religious merit and public welfare. Thatbyinnu, the tallest temple in Bagan, Shwegugyi and many other religious monuments were built by him. He repaired old irrigation networks, constructed new ones and reclaimed new land for agriculture. He also systematised the weights and measures of his kingdom. New villages and towns were built where war captives were accommodated. New monasteries were built for teaching his people. Alaung Sithu was indeed a benevolent monarch.

Most of the other kings were mediocre or weak in comparison. But they tried to be good Buddhist kings by doing religious work. Even a tyrant like Narathu built the massive castle-like temple of Dammayangyi. Another bad ruler Narathihapate, who was defeated by Kublai Khan's hordes, built the Mingalazedi Pagoda.

THE DOWNFALL OF BAGAN

There is an old Myanmar saying: "if you speak of Bagan history you must keep a stick on your shoulder." Bagan history is so long and complicated that heated arguments about it are inevitable. One may be challenged to fight in the process, so it is wise to have a stick to defend yourself.

For generations, Myanmar and neighbouring China maintained friendly relations through diplomatic exchanges and two-way border trade. But when the foreign ruler Kublai Khan came to power in China, things changed. Assuming himself to be the only universal monarch, Kublai Khan spared no other kingdom from subjugation. King Narathihapate of Bagan sent envoys to Khan on an equal footing, refusing to pay tribute by way of submission. This led to the outbreak of war. In the fierce battle fought at Nga Saung Chan near Bamaw, on 3 December 1283, the Tartar hordes defeated the Bagan army. Marco Polo gave a graphic account of this in his Travelogue. Narathihapate had to retreat to the Delta. For some months, the Tartar soldiers occupied Bagan. In 1285, a peace mission headed by the king's guru monk Shin Ditha Pamaukkha, was despatched to Kublai Khan in Beijing. The monk won over the Emperor and the Tartar troops were withdrawn. Although three kings ruled in unbroken succession after Narathihapate's death, none could restore the greatness of Bagan, and it slowly faded into obscurity.

THE CULTURE OF BAGAN

An exhaustive study of the cultural development of Bagan could exceed a life time. The late G.H. Luce, Professor of Oriental Studies at Yangon University, who devoted his life to the study of Bagan and produced his three-volume illustrated magnum opus entitled *Old Burma: Early Bagan*, is said to have made as his last wish that, if he were reborn a man in his next existence, he would return to Bagan to continue his study.

BAGAN ARCHITECTURE

It is said that "in the palmiest days of Bagan the pagodas and monuments could be counted by the myriads". Many totals are found in legends and chronicles but the inventory of structures, made by the Archaeology Department two decades ago, totals 2,217. A new inventory is now being made with the assistance of the UNDP. Since many new ruins have been discovered after clearing the jungle, the latest inventory will be greater. The latest inventory appears in Mr. Pierre Pichard's three volumes entitled, *Inventory of Monuments at Bagan* (Paris, 1992).

Pagodas, which form the majority of Bagan's monuments, are of two types. The first is the stupa or Zedi, a bell-shaped brick, or stone brick structure built in a series of receding terraces, topped by a finial. These solid pagodas contain relics of Buddha or a Buddhist saint; or, they mark a sacred spot. The solid pagoda has a sealed chamber, often in its base, in which votive objects and jewellery from the donor are enshrined together with sacred relics. The second type of pagoda is a hollow, vaulted temple for housing a Buddha image. It is square in plan and sometimes has projecting porches. Above the temple rise a series of receding roofs. A bell-shaped stupa or curvilinear finial crowns the structure.

In 1955, the late U Lu Pe Win, Director of Archaeological Survey, classified Bagan's monuments into nine categories:

(i) Stupa, whose dome is modelled on a reliquary; e.g., Bu paya.
(ii) Stupa, whose dome is modelled on a tumulus; e.g., Lawkananda, Shwezigon, Shwesandaw, Mingalazedi.

(iii) Stupa of Sinhalese type; e.g., Sapada, Pebingyaung.
(iv) Temple based on north Indian model; e.g., Ananda.
(v) Temple of central Indian type; e.g., Mahabodhi.
(vi) Temple based on south Indian model; e.g., Gawdawpalin, Sulamani.
(vii) Cave temples based on Indian models; e.g., Kyauk Ku Umin, Kyanzittha Umin.
(viii) Ordination hall; e.g., Upali Thein.
(ix) Library; e.g., Pita Kattaik.

This classification does not include Bagan monasteries and non-Buddhist monuments such as Hindu temples.

He further differentiated the temples into Mon style and Myanmar style. Mon style temples have dark corridors, dimly lit by perforated windows and bright frescoes of variegated colour with Mon writing. Examples of Mon style temples are the Pato Thamya, Nagayon, Abeyadana, Kubyaukgyi of Myinpagan and Nanpaya. Myanmar style temples are tall and imposing, and airy and bright inside. Examples include the Shwegugyi, Thatbyinnu, Sulamani, Htilominlo and Gawdawpalin. The Ananda and Dhammayangyi temples are intermediate forms.

Regarding Bagan architecture there is an old Myanmar saying: "Massiveness that is Dhammayangyi, loftiness that is Thatbyinnu, gracefulness that is Ananda." These three famous temples, and Shwezigon, represent the range of Bagan architecture.

Dhammayangyi is a hollow, vaulted temple built by King Narathu during his short reign of three years. Its name symbolises the Light of Buddha's Dhamma. It is one of Bagan's architectural marvels. It has withstood the ravages of time, natural disasters and vandalism throughout its long life. A massive and strong structure, it has been hardly affected by earthquakes; not even by the serious quake of 1975. The finest of brick work can be seen in this Temple and its enclosing wall. In plan it is similar to Ananda, but only the outer corridor is accessible. All the entrances to the inner corridor are blocked by brick work, for some unknown reason. The upper storeys are reached by a flight of steps built into the wall.

Thatbyinnu, at 201 feet, is the tallest monument in Bagan. It was built in the mid-12th century by King Alaungysithu. Thatbyinnu signifies "Omniscience", one of the attributes of Lord Buddha. Its general plan is not dissimilar from Ananda but it does not, like Ananda, form a symmetrical cross. Only the eastern porch projects from the wall. The central stairway, flanked by two standing Guardians, faces the eastern hall and entrance. The steps lead to a circumambulatory corridor around the central mass. Climbing one of two stairways built into the thick walls, one reaches the top of the vestibule, from where an external flight of stairs leads to the upper storey. The high cubicles, the corner stupas on the terraces, the flamboyant arch pediments and the plain pilasters combine to give a soaring effect to the monument. The two tiers of windows in each storey make the interior bright and airy.

The structure has five storeys. The first and second were used for Monks' residences, images of Buddha were kept on the third, the fourth was used as a library, and a pagoda containing holy relics was built on the fifth storey.

Ananda Temple

The most artistic and graceful temple in Bagan is Ananda, built by King Kyansittha in 1091. The name symbolises the "endless wisdom" (Ananta Panna) of Lord Buddha while Thatbyinnu symbolises his "Omniscience". It is square in layout with each side measuring nearly 200 feet. Large gabled vestibules project from each side, converting the plan into a perfect Greek cross. Two tiers of windows in the walls of the main structure provide good lighting and ventilation. Inside are four deep niches, each containing an imposing standing Buddha measuring 31 feet in height and facing the four cardinal directions. These represent the four Buddhas that have already been revealed. The whole edifice is ornamented with plaster mouldings, stone sculpture, wood carving, glazed plaques and terracotta tiles, all of which depict the birth and stories of Buddha.

Because of its religious and historical significance, its graceful architecture and artistic accomplishment, Ananda Temple is the object of fame and admiration both at home and abroad. Myanmar classical literature describes this temple as an exact replica of Nandamu Cave in the Himalayas, which was miraculously revealed to King Kyanzittha by Holy Saints. But historians hold that the great skill and high artistic imagination of the builder-donor, its architects and artists, could alone inspire such a description by classical writers.

Shwezigon Pagoda

Shwezigon is a solid cylindrical structure resting on three square terraces. It is a prototype of Myanmar stupas. It has a bold waistband around the bell-shaped dome, above which rise a series of concentric mouldings, ending in a finial crowned by a *hti* (umbrella). Around the terraces of the pagoda, set in panels, are enamelled plaques illustrating scenes from the previous lives of Buddha. On each of the four sides of the pagoda there is a small hall, housing a 13-foot standing Buddha from the Gupta school of art. These four statues, made of bronze, are covered with gold leaf. They face the four cardinal directions and represent the four Buddhas who have already attained Nivarna. Kokusandha Buddha faces north, Konagamana Buddha faces east, Kassapa Buddha faces south and Gotama Buddha faces west. Anawrahta built this Pagoda in 1059, but left it unfinished. King Kyanzittha completed it in 1090.

History tells us that King Anawrahta brought a sacred relic of Buddha's frontal bone to Bagan. The relic was unearthed at a ruined stupa in Thayekhittaya, an ancient Pyu capital. It was carried on the back of a white elephant to Bagan. The elephant knelt down at a sandy site which the king believed to be an auspicious place for enshrining the relic. He named the place "Zeya Bumi" (land of victory) and began building the Shwezigon Pagoda. It was built of stone blocks brought by hand from quarries in the Tuyin hills about seven miles away. Pious devotees lined up along this distance forming a human chain and stone blocks were passed from hand to hand to the site. Enshrined in the pagoda are the frontal bone of Buddha and a replica of Buddha's Sacred Tooth, presented to Anawrahta by the king of Sri Lanka.

Shwezigon Pagoda is held in great veneration by Buddhists in Myanmar and around the world. Myanmar kings used to visit the pagoda to worship and to renovate it after they had ascended the throne.

Epigraphy

Bagan epigraphy may be classified into stone inscriptions, ink writings, glazed plaques and terracotta inscriptions and Pei and Parabailk writings. Stone inscriptions form the major corpus of Bagan epigraphy. They are records of religious dedication inscribed on sandstone slabs set beside the dedicated object, be it a pagoda, temple, monastery, rest house, meditation cave, water tank dam, reservoir or canal. They usually mention the name, address, rank and occupation of the donor; the aims of the dedication; and a description of the dedicated object, the expenditure incurred, a prayer for merit, curses on those who vandalise the dedicated object and the donor's sharing of religious merit to all sentient beings. From these inscriptions can be gleaned economic, political and social data of the time because of references made to contemporary events and conditions. The following provide three examples.

The Myazedi stone inscription dated 1112, records the dedication made by Prince Yazakuma, son of King Kyanzittha, of a gold Buddha statue and several villages of slaves to gain religious merit for his dying father and as a token of filial gratitude. This dedication is in four languages – Mon, Myanmar, Pali and Pyu – on each of the four sides of a stone pillar. Like the Rosetta Stone in Egypt, the Myazedi inscription provides the key to deciphering old Pyu Script and verification of the accession dates of some Bagan kings.

The Kyanzittha Palace Mon inscription records in detail the ritual and ceremonies observed and performed during the founding and building of the new palace between 1101 and 1102. From this inscription, we learn about court life in Bagan, the persistent influence of Brahmanism and Naga worship, which still continued in the face of long established Theravada Buddhism. The inscription also describes the ground plan of the palace and technical engineering terms, some of which still puzzle scholars.

The third example is the inscription of Shin. This records the dedication to religion, by the head monk Shin Dithapamaulkha, of land, slaves and paddy received from King Narathihapate as a reward for successfully leading a peace mission to Kublai Khan in 1285. The inscription is the monk's story, starting with the despatch of the mission, the long and difficult journey to China, peace talks with Kublai Khan at the Beijing Court, the return journey, the withdrawal of the Tartars, the reward received and ending with the dedication of the reward to religion. This inscription is a primary source for the history of Bagan's foreign relations.

There are hundreds, perhaps thousands, of stone inscriptions in, around and beyond the Bagan area, belonging to different periods of Bagan history. Many have been collected, catalogued and preserved in museums. Many remain hidden under the earth, vegetation or debris. Many have been destroyed or used in the construction of roads and housing.

Ink letters, found on the walls of monuments, contain descriptions of events, facts about the donor, horoscopes, medicinal formulae, proverbs and graffiti. They also provide source material for Bagan's social history. Glazed plaques and terracotta inscriptions inscribed or embossed on baked earthen tablets and glazed plaques, usually depict scenes from Jatakas or stories of Buddha's birth. They carry captions or short explanations of the scene depicted.

Pei and Parabaik inscriptions are found in pagodas, on images, or deposited in earthern pots buried in the precincts. Pei are palm leaves for writing on. Parabaiks are folding sheets, made of metal (including silver and gold), wood or thick rice paper. They are usually found in monasteries. They contain written scriptures, prayers, jatakas or writings on secular subjects, such as astrology, medicine, occult science and sometimes details of daily accounts, revenue and expenditure. They are useful in the study of economic conditions of the time.

Mural Paintings

Among the variety of decorative and votive arts that adorn Bagan monuments, frescoes or mural paintings deserve special study by art experts. Many have decayed, some have been vandalised, and some have been concealed under whitewash by pious devotees. Those that still survive are in varying states of preservation. Under the UNDP programme, art restoration experts were hired from abroad to restore the decaying frescoes and to train local teams in the art restoration. Temples noted for their bright coloured frescoes with Mon writings, are the Patothamya, Nagayon, Abeyadana, Kubyaukkyi of Myinpagan and Nanpaya temples.

The traditional technique of mural painting started with the smoothening of the surface of the wall to be painted by applying a mixture of lime, and animal and vegetable matter. When the surface was dry, the master painter drew an outline with ink, chalk or lead. Then he or his apprentices filled in the colours, which were made from local animal, vegetable and mineral materials, including ochre, lime, charcoal, chalk, vermillion, cinnabar, neem resin, vegetable lacquer, lac, saffron, realgar orpiment, copper sulphate, iron oxide or rust, egg shell, animal fat and soot.

Myanmar traditional painting has no perspective. Simple lines are drawn to make the picture lively. Short, long, curved and zigzag lines are cleverly applied, and bright and luminous pigments are used. No space is left empty. Geometric, floral or fantastic designs fill in the gaps. A whole story is depicted in one picture, with scenes separated by floral boundaries. Space is left for writing a caption or explanation of the picture. Mostly Jatakas were depicted, but artists also portrayed scenes from daily life in Bagan.

Ten Traditional Arts and Crafts

Arts and crafts which developed and flourished in the Bagan period, and which signify an aesthetically beautiful object, are classified under ten names, each with the prefix "pan" or flower. In addition, "pan" signifies craft, occupation or trade. The ten arts and crafts are:

(i) Pan Pe, the art of ironware.
(ii) Pan Tein, the art of gold and silverware.
(iii) Pan Tin, the art of bronzeware.
(iv) Pan Tau, the art of plaster moulding.
(v) Pan Yan, the art of masonry.
(vi) Pan Pu, the art of wood and ivory carving.
(vii) Pan Ta Mau, the art of stone sculpting.
(viii) Pan Put, the art of a tunner.
(ix) Pan Chi, the art of painting, drawing and colouring.
(x) Pan Yun, the art of lacquerware making.

These ten are referred to in Myanmar literature in the following couplet:

Flowers of ten different kinds
Not meant for offering at shrines

For easy memorisation the head monk of Zetawun Monastery at Monywe composed a rhyme enumerating the ten:

Pe, Tein, Tin, Tau, Yan, Pu, Mau, Know ye!
Put,
Chi, Yun

MACRO AND REGIONAL ISSUES

Chapter 7

Macroeconomic Policies with Special Emphasis on Infrastructural Development

BY
SAN KHUP*

INTRODUCTION

THE STATE LAW and Order Restoration Council, on assuming power in late 1988, charted an entirely different political and social system. It initiated a period of transition which, as experience has shown, entailed economic and social hardship. This was complicated in Myanmar's case by three years of severe economic recession from 1986–87 to 1988–89. Therefore, in initiating a market-oriented system, utmost care has been taken to avoid further exacerbation of the economic and social conditions of the people. Circumstances called for economic recovery quickly and, at the same time, a transformation that minimised adverse affects.

* Director-General, Planning Department, Ministry of National Planning and Economic Development, Yangon, Myanmar.

ECONOMIC DECLINE: 1986–1989

Before 1988, the economy registered negative growth for three consecutive years (1986–87 to 1988–89), precipitated by declining trade. Consequently, GNP declined in real terms by 15.2% in 1988–89. Per capita income registered an even sharper decline of 20.5% during the same period causing social and economic hardship. Leading macroeconomic indicators, such as exports, investments and imports, also registered considerable decline with an inevitable effect on the development of the economy. Inflation, which had never been an important factor in the past, became a serious problem, rising from 9.2% in 1986 to 23.9% in 1987, and to 16.8% in 1988. Thus, the structural transition which caused hardship was compounded further by the bad shape of the economy.

ECONOMIC RECOVERY WITH PRICE STABILITY

While undertaking the formidable task of structural transformation, the government took great care to ensure that it was systematic and orderly, and enhanced the output of goods and services. The government was greatly constrained by a severe shortage of foreign exchange needed for spare parts, and raw materials needed to enhance industrial and agricultural production. This situation was aggravated further by a great decline in loans and grants which declined by a hefty 57.7% during the six years of the present government as compared to the six preceding years. The government's ability to manage foreign exchange was also eroded by a fall in the share of government receipts to less than 50% of total export value due to opening up of the private sector to foreign trade.

On the positive side, liberalisation measures (i.e., decontrol and deregulation of a wide spectrum of economic activities through revised and new laws, rules and regulations) have enabled the private sector to participate extensively in almost all economic activity. This led to an increase in output of both goods and services. Liberalisation measures that have had a significant positive impact on production include the promulgation of the Foreign Investment Law in 1988 and the State-owned Enterprises Law of 1989. These laws allow the private sector to engage in all types of economic activity, except those few reserved exclusively for the state sector. In addition, the private sector had access to large financial credits, technical assistance and training courses. Of particular importance was the removal of controls and regulations relating to the cultivation, marketing, transportation, milling, and storage of agricultural products which, in turn, gave strong incentives to the agricultural sector, the mainstay of the economy. Another major and effective reform is opening up foreign trade to the private sector, hitherto monopolised exclusively by the state. Credit also goes to the government for instituting reform measures in an orderly, gradual and consistent manner, and for exercising care in not upsetting and disrupting existing output.

Against this background of stabilisation and structural reform, annual plans were formulated for 1989–90 to 1991–92. The objectives were to restore economic recovery and to stabilise prices as quickly as possible. The declining trend of the economy was reversed. During the first two years, the economy achieved modest growth of 3.7% in 1989–90 and 2.8% in 1990–91. However, the recovery process suffered a setback in 1991–92 because of extremely inclement weather and shortages which both adversely affected agricultural output and related industries. As a result, the economy recorded negative growth of 0.6%. Other key macroeconomic indicators, such as investment, exports and imports, registered significant upward trends in real terms, indicating that the economy was definitely on the path of growth and recovery. Inflationary pressure, which had been a problem before the reforms, was more or less contained. There are indications that the inflation rate is slowing down steadily.

Having achieved a measure of political and economic stability, the government then turned attention to accelerating the pace of economic development by formulating the Short-term Plan (1992–93 to 1995–96) whose main objectives are to achieve an average annual growth rate of 5.1% and to pursue a determined export drive. Special emphasis was given to agricultural production, especially paddy, and to more effective utilisation of natural resources. To give impetus to the implementation of the Short-term Plan, the first and second years were designated "Economic Years". Efforts were made to increase public saving, to channel these savings into productive investments, and to promote exports and foreign exchange earnings. A budget austerity drive also was enforced and allocations were made strictly on the basis of priority. The results so far are very encouraging. Actual growth rates of 9.7% in

1992–93 and 5.9% in 1993–94 were much higher than projected. All sectors, except forestry, performed well. The forestry sector registered negative growth because emphasis was shifted from extraction to value added wood-based products. Border extraction also was phased out.

The third year of the Plan (1994–95), is designated "All Round Development Year". A sustained effort has been made to maintain and enhance the momentum of growth achieved in the previous years by giving special emphasis to the harmonious progress of productive sectors such as agriculture, livestock, fisheries and mining. The service sector has supported the production sectors. Commitment, close supervision and coordination rendered by leadership at various levels, and an equally enthusiastic response by the people at large, has resulted in a very satisfactory growth rate of 6.8% in 1994–95 as compared to the projected rate of 6.4%. Growth during the past three years has averaged 7.5% as compared to the planned 5.1% for the whole period. This success is largely attributable to the substantial growth in agricultural production, particularly paddy. There have been equally satisfactory developments in mutually related macro factors such as investment and foreign exchange earnings, particularly from exports. This success, in the face of numerous constraints and difficulties, has created much more favourable economic conditions for future development. GDP performance is shown in Table 7–1 while the performance of investment, exports and imports is shown in Table 7–2.

TABLE 7–1
Gross Domestic Product
(At 1985–86 Constant Producers' Prices)

Year	Value (kyat in Million)	Annual Growth Rate (%)
1985–86	55,989.3	2.9
1986–87	55,396.8	-1.1
1987–88	53,177.8	-4.0
1988–89	47,141.1	-11.4
1989–90	48,883.1	3.7
1990–91	50,259.5	2.8
1991–92	49,933.3	-0.6
1992–93	54,756.6	9.7
1993–94*	58,001.0	5.9
1994–95**	61,949.8	6.8

* Provisional actual ** Provisional

INVESTMENTS

Investments at current prices have increased by 5.3 times from 1983–84 to 1993–94. The state sector share of total investment declined from an annual average of 72.7% during the period 1983–84 to 1988–89, to 46.7% during the period 1989–90 to 1994–95. Correspondingly, the private sector share increased from 24.2% to 52.3%, reflecting the significantly enlarged role played by the private sector in the market-oriented economy. Gross investment in real terms during the six years ending 1994–95 exceeded the six preceding years by 17.5%.

TABLE 7–2
Total Investment, Exports and Imports (At Current Prices)
(Million kyat)

Year	Total Investment	Annual Growth Rate (%)	Export Value	Annual Growth Rate (%)	Imports Value	Annual Growth Rate (%)
1985–86	8,649.5	2.0	2,566.1	-18.1	4,802.0	-4.7
1986–87	8,617.6	-0.4	2,418.5	-5.8	3,936.1	-18.0
1987–88	8,682.7	0.8	1,655.2	-31.6	4,065.7	3.3
1988–89	7,295.5	-16.0	2,168.9	31.0	3,443.0	-15.3
1989–90	11,826.6	62.1	2,834.1	30.7	3,395.0	-1.4
1990–91	22,318.4	88.7	2,952.6	4.2	5,522.8	62.7
1991–92	27,571.0	23.5	2,952.9	-0.9	5,336.7	-3.4
1992–93	31,184.4	13.1	3,590.0	22.7	5,365.3	0.5
1993–94	37,258.2	19.5	4,227.8	17.8	7,923.3	47.7
1994–95*	48,377.5	29.8	4,772.6	12.9	9,117.0	15.1

* Provisional

INVESTMENT BY THE STATE SECTOR

The structure of investment by the state reveals significant changes between the two periods. In the period 1983–84 to 1988–89, investment in production sectors constituted 41.2% of the total, and processing and manufacturing claimed by far the largest portion or 28.1% of the total. This is expected because the state operated and managed economic enterprises as the main source of income during the period of the socialist economic system. In the latter period, 1989–90 to 1994–95, the production sectors declined to 9.4%, and processing and manufacturing to a mere 3.9%. The fall in the production sectors is even more pronounced if expenditure on irrigation is taken out of this sector and re–classified under infrastructure. It should be noted that investment in infrastructure was about 40% during the two periods.

The share of investment in construction increased significantly from 7.3% to 14.1% while power declined perceptibly from 9.8% to 5.1%. The latter was probably due to the need to conserve foreign exchange. The share of investment in transport and communications remained unchanged for the same reason. The share of investment in oil and gas declined during the latter period. This was probably due to the great increase in private sector investment in this area, assisted by foreign direct investment. Overall investment and the structure of state investment are shown in Tables 7–3 and 7–4, respectively.

TABLE 7–3
Overall Investment by Ownership
(Million kyat)

Year	State Sector		Co-operative Sector		Private Sector		Total
	Value	%	Value	%	Value	%	
1983–84	7,132	78.8	120	1.3	1,805	19.9	9,057
1984–85	6,474	76.4	108	1.3	1,895	22.3	8,477
1985–86	6,424	74.8	177	1.5	2,049	23.7	8,650
1986–87	6,409	74.4	158	1.8	2,051	23.8	8,618
1987–88	6,226	71.7	156	1.8	2,301	26.5	8,683
1988–89	4,384	60.1	82	1.1	2,829	38.8	7,295
1989–90	6,584	55.7	90	0.7	5,153	43.6	11,827
1990–91	10,289	46.1	125	0.6	11,904	53.3	22,318
1991–92	12,455	46.1	91	0.3	14,490	53.6	27,036
1992–93	13,455	43.1	150	0.5	17,579	56.4	31,184
1993–94	15,678	42.1	1,030	2.8	20,550	55.1	37,258
1994–95	22,885	47.3	272	0.6	25,221	52.1	48,378

INFRASTRUCTURAL DEVELOPMENT

The government's determination to promote the development of infrastructure is clear from the fact that it set four major tasks, one of which was "to provide secure and smooth transportation". Accordingly, the government made an all out effort to promote infrastructural development. This has been constrained by shortages of foreign exchange for infrastructure projects in which this component is high. The development of electric power, transportation and communication depends significantly on the availability of foreign exchange. Thus, effort has concentrated on the accelerated development of roads, railways, buildings and airport runways which require lower import content. At the same time, various methods have been derived for the import substitution of many items.

TABLE 7–4
State Sector Investment by Structure (Million kyat)

Sector	1983–84 to 1988–89		1989–90 to 1994–95	
	Value	%	Value	%
Productive Sector	**15,293**	**37.5**	**7,655**	**8.6**
Agriculture	1,598	3.9	1,746	1.9
Livestock and Fishery	877	2.2	629	0.7
Forestry	1,031	2.5	1,114	1.3
Mining	1,344	3.3	967	1.1
Processing and Manufacturing	10,443	25.6	3,199	3.6
Infrastructure	**18,408**	**45.2**	**40,338**	**45.4**
Power	3,655	9.1	4,185	4.7
Construction	2,691	6.6	11,494	12.9
Transport Communications	4,714	11.6	9,743	11.0
Others:	3,674	9.1	7,458	8.4
(a) Irrigation	2,390	5.9	4,749	5.3
(b) Oil and Gas	1,149	2.8	544	0.6
(c) Hotel and Tourism	135	0.1	1,320	1.5
(d) Border Area Development			845	1.0
Services	**7,071**	**17.3**	**40,812**	**46.0**
Trade	1,163	2.9	2,533	2.9
Social	3,196	7.9	13,959	15.7
Financial	116	0.1	1,323	1.5
Other Administrative Organisations	2,596	6.4	22,997	25.9
Total	40,772	100.0	88,805	100.0

Special Projects

Major projects requiring substantial investment and that are politically, economically and strategically important to the country, are designated as "special projects". They are given priority in budget allocations and coordinated by the highest authority to ensure fast completion. Most special projects are infrastructural in nature. They directly and indirectly help the output of goods and services, and comprise irrigation networks, electric power plants, roads, railways, bridges and so forth. Another priority is border area development. A high-powered central committee, a work committee and sub-committees, the first two of which are chaired by the Chairman and Secretary (1) and a ministry, have been formed to oversee the implementation of border area development. As at the end of 1994–95, K2.1 billion has been invested in border area development, of which infrastructural investment on electric power, roads, bridges, transport and communications, amounted to K895 million or 41.9% of the total development expenditure. Another area of substantial investment is social infrastructure where K270.9 million has been spent on education and health.

Soon after assuming power, the government placed special emphasis on the upgrading and renovation of existing infrastructural facilities and networks, and adopted the slogan "to renovate, upgrade and maintain a city, town, village, school, hospital, etc. is to have essential characteristics befitting as such". Budgets were allocated and public cooperation and participation activated. People's participation was systematically mobilised to undertake community related infrastructural development works of both a physical and social nature. In line with the slogan, "to renovate and upgrade the cities and towns to possess characteristics of cities and towns", the Yangon and Mandalay City Development Committees and Township Development Committees (municipalities) all over the country carried out enormous infrastructural works with their own funds and supplemented by grants from the state. They literally reshaped, renovated and recreated new towns and wards.

After restructuring and renovating of the existing infrastructure, constructing the new infrastructure and upgrading the existing infrastructure as special projects were implemented as phase 2. One area receiving special emphasis, and which is making rapid headway, is the development of tourism facilities and the construction of hotels and lodging houses. By the end of 1994–95, there were 257 hotels and lodging houses with a total of 4,339 rooms, of which 214 with 4,040 rooms; 83.3 and 93.1%, respectively, are in private hands. The private sector has helped considerably with credit facilities and technical assistance.

ROADS

Much has been achieved in road construction, with the building of new roads and the upgrading of existing ones. The State Public Works Department, which is responsible for construction and maintenance of roads and bridges, has built 2,165 miles of new roads and upgraded 2,128 miles of existing roads during the past six years. In addition, the two city development committees and township development committees all over the country treat road construction, maintenance and upgrading as a priority. The community at large, with guidance and supervision from their regional leadership, is undertaking extensive infrastructural development works, particularly community road construction on a self-help basis. The Public Works Department also built 64 bridges, spanning 28,962 feet. An additional 41 bridges, spanning 23,916 feet, are also under construction. These include six major bridges across big rivers to aid transportation and accelerate development. The progress of union highways and main roads, by type, is shown in Table 7–5. Construction and upgrading of roads by the Public Works is shown in Table 7–6.

TABLE 7–5
The Progress of Union Highways and Main Roads by Type (Miles)

Year	Bitumin Road	Metal Road	Gravel Road	Earth Road	Total
1985–86	5,484	1,479	3,498	3,955	14,416
1986–87	5,502	1,497	3,532	3,946	14,477
1987–88	5,533	1,544	3,561	3,896	14,534
1988–89	5,492	1,570	3,660	3,880	14,602
1989–90	5,582	1,630	3,647	4,042	14,901
1990–91	5,616	1,714	3,619	4,020	14,969
1991–92	5,679	1,706	3,681	3,994	15,060
1992–93	5,700	1,699	3,737	3,982	15,118
1993–94*	5,730	1,762	3,780	5,249	16,521
1994–95**	5,760	1,911	4,020	5,079	16,770

* Provisional actual
** Provisional

TABLE 7–6
Construction and Renovation of Various Types of Roads from 1988–89 to 1994–95 (Miles)

Particulars	Funds Allotted (K Million) 1988–89 to 1994–95	Bituminous Road 4–6 Lanes	2 Lanes	1 Lane	Others	Gravel Road	Earth Road	Total
Completed:								
Construction of roads	367.83	3	43	18	71	5	28	168
Upgrading of roads	1,369.32	8	228	179	54	126		595
Incomplete:								
Construction of roads	1,528.37		44	93	281	393	1,190	2,001
Upgrading of roads	3,498.18	41	110	378	438	414	152	1,533

RAILWAYS

While some rolling stock has been procured and constructed, the main thrust for the railways is the construction of new tracks in strategic areas to facilitate mass and bulky transportation. There are 438 miles of new track which have been constructed during the past six years. Important tracks completed include the 102-mile Aungban-Pinlaung-Loikaw stretch linking Loikaw, the capital of Kayah State, with Shan State; the 25-mile Myotha-Nahtogyi track; the 37-mile Shwenyaung-Yatsauk track; the 121-mile Pakokku-Gangaw-Kalay track; the Namsan-Shwenyaung track of 28 miles; the Ye-Dawai track of 10.7 miles and the Chaungoo-Pakokku track of 45 miles. A number of overhead bridges and engineering works also have been constructed.

TELECOMMUNICATIONS

Myanmar Post and Telecommunications carried out a number of projects to upgrade and modernise telecommunication facilities, both on its own and in cooperation with foreign firms. Auto telephone systems have been installed in some townships with contributions from the community.

AIR TRANSPORTATION

Myanmar Airways is concentrating on domestic routes while international operations are cooperating with a foreign airline. A foreign airline also has been given permission to operate on certain domestic routes, especially for the convenience of tourists. Yangon Airport has been extensively upgraded and renovated, permitting increased air traffic. Two international airports are being built. A number of runways have been upgraded and extended in strategic locations in order to accommodate large aircraft.

ENERGY

Emphasis is being placed on financing and developing electric power to promote economic and social development. Renovation of existing power capacity and development of hydro projects have been implemented in many parts of the country. In addition, two 18-megawatt capacity hydropower stations are under construction. Two 93-megawatt capacity gas generated power stations have been installed as a short term measure to augment power capacity using the natural gas reserves recently found onshore. When offshore gas resources come on stream in two years' time, present power constraints, along with the foreign exchange situation, will be considerably improved. This, in turn, will go a long way towards solving the present infrastructural bottlenecks. Feasibility studies into hydroelectric power show that the country has much potential in this area, amounting to about 33,000 megawatt capacity.

Chapter 8

Trade Development and Doing Business in Myanmar

BY
KIN MAUNG OO*

INTRODUCTION

AFTER MORE THAN two decades of centralised planning, the State Law and Order Restoration Council assumed power in September 1988 and repudiated the socialist economic system and moved towards a more open, market-oriented economy. Since then, steps have been taken to decontrol the agriculture sector, encourage foreign investment, legalise border trade, encourage private sector participation in foreign trade, and allow the setting up of companies, joint ventures and chambers of commerce.

Due to these measures, the net value of the trade sector in constant 1985–86 prices increased over the three years from 1992–93 to 1994–95 by 8.9%, 5% and 7.4%, respectively. Trade was K13,638 million in 1994–95 and constituted 22% of GDP.

* Managing Director, Inspection and Agency Services, Ministry of Trade, Yangon, Myanmar.

TRADE POLICY

Policy pronouncements on foreign trade are in line with the independent foreign policy of the country. They reflect a belief in trade liberalisation and a wish for free and fair trade in the world. Myanmar is a founding member of the General Agreement on Tariffs and Trade (GATT) and, accordingly, its external trade practices are governed by GATT's leading principles. Myanmar is also a member of the World Trade Organisation. It can trade with any country in the world except those embargoed by United Nations' resolutions and a few countries with which it has cut diplomatic relations.

Three basic principles of trade have been laid down regarding the administration and carrying out of trade activities, in line with the market-oriented economy:

(i) Trade activities should be in the interests of the state and the people.
(ii) Trade activities should not be a burden on the people.
(iii) Trade activities should aim at structuring a long-term viable trading system rather than a short-term profit perspective.

The Ministry of Trade recognises that in the context of a market-oriented economic system, the private sector is the prime mover of the market mechanism. The private sector is receiving a lot of attention from the Ministry and effort is being made to encourage and support active participation in foreign trade. The following objectives overarch this position:

(i) To support internal and external trade activities aiding the economic development of the country.
(ii) To upgrade the commercial efficiency of public and private trading houses.
(iii) To increase foreign exchange earnings through the promotion of exports.
(iv) To encourage the trading activities of co-operatives and private entrepreneurs.

Trade Agreements

Myanmar has bilateral trade agreements with the Republic of Korea, the People's Republic of China, Thailand, Bangladesh, India, Pakistan, Vietnam and Laos in the Asian region, and with seven countries in Eastern Europe. These agreements are general in character and they aim to develop and strengthen trade relations based on the principle of equality of rights and mutual benefit. Articles in the agreements generally are based on the most-favoured nation (MFN) principle of GATT.

Volume of Trade and Balance of Trade

Since moving towards a market-oriented economy, the volume of external trade has increased in absolute terms and it reached a peak of K14,289 million (US$2,381 million) in 1994–95. However, like many other developing countries, Myanmar has experienced persistent trade deficits over the past ten years. The volume of trade and balance of trade are shown below (see Table 8–1).

TABLE 8–1
Volume of Trade and Balance of Trade (Million kyat)

Year	Exports	Imports	Total Volume	Deficit
1983–84	3,420	5,197	8,617	1,777
1984–85	3,195	5,041	8,236	1,846
1985–86	2,654	4,802	7,456	2,148
1986–87	2,514	3,936	6,450	1,422
1987–88	1,679	4,066	5,745	2,387
1988–89	2,193	3,443	5,636	1,250
1989–90	2,847	3,395	6,242	548
1990–91	2,962	5,523	8,485	2,561
1991–92	2,932	5,337	8,265	2,405
1992–93	3,655	5,365	9,020	1,710
1993–94	4,228	7,923	12,151	3,693
1994–95*	5,172	9,117	14,289	3,945

* Provisional

Direction of Trade

Myanmar foreign trade is mainly with other Asian countries. China, Singapore, Japan, Thailand, India and Malaysia are the main trading partners. Regionally, the European Economic Community ranks second in importance. With changes in the pattern of trade, the direction of trade also may change. The structure of Myanmar foreign trade with major trading partners is shown below (see Table 8–2).

TABLE 8–2
Myanmar Trade with Main Trading Partners: 1993–94
(Million kyat)

Country	Value		Percent	
	Exports	Imports	Exports	Imports
South-east Asian Countries:	**1,728.6**	**2,594.4**	**40.88**	**32.74**
Singapore	819.8	820.2	19.39	10.35
Malaysia	98.7	567.3	2.33	7.16
Thailand	736.8	865.4	17.43	10.92
Others	73.3	341.5	1.73	4.31
Other Asian Countries:	**1,797.5**	**4,275.1**	**42.50**	**53.96**
People's Republic of China	209.8	1,261.4	4.95	15.92
Sri Lanka	45.0	0.1	1.06	0.01
India	634.8	281.4	15.01	3.55
Japan	187.6	2,020.1	4.43	25.50
Pakistan	113.8	30.0	2.69	0.38
Bangladesh	94.0	183.4	2.22	2.31
Hong Kong	453.0	134.9	10.71	1.70
Republic of Korea	35.0	292.5	0.83	3.69
Others	24.5	71.3	0.58	0.90
European Economic Community	**123.7**	**455.9**	**2.93**	**5.75**
Others	**578.0**	**597.9**	**13.67**	**7.55**
Total	4,227.8	7,923.3	100.00	100.00

Myanmar-Singapore Trade

Rice and rice products, pulses and beans, sesame seeds, teak and hardwoods in the form of logs and sawn timber, fresh and dried prawns, fish and fish products, base metal and ores, are exported to Singapore. Petroleum and petroleum products, iron and steel, machinery, electrical appliances, transport equipment, plastic materials, chemical materials and products and miscellaneous food preparations, are imported from Singapore.

While the volume of two-way trade has increased annually, the balance of trade has fluctuated. This trend is shown in Table 8–3 for the period 1989–94. Mr. Tan Thim Fook, Managing Director, Fulbrim (S) Pte. Ltd., Singapore, was appointed promoter for foreign investment for Singapore in January 1993. There is no formal bilateral trade agreement between Myanmar and Singapore at present.

TABLE 8–3
Balance of Trade (Million kyat)

Period	Exports	Imports	Balance
1989–90	258.89	316.69	(57.80)
1990–91	845.80	532.43	313.37
1991–92	683.03	663.53	19.50
1992–93	601.63	575.83	25.85
1993–94	819.78	820.26	(0.48)

A high-level Trade and Investment Committee for the development of trade and investment between Myanmar and Singapore, led by Lt. General Khin Nyunt, Secretary 1 of SLORC, has been formed. Brig. General Abel, Minister for National Planning and Economic Development, is the secretary.

Border Trade

Government policy aims to develop and strengthen bilateral trade relations with neighbouring countries including the People's Republic of China, LAO People's Democratic Republic, Thailand, India and the People's Republic of Bangladesh. Border trade is the mechanism for this trade expansion. In July 1988, a border trade agreement between the Myanmar Export Import Services (MEIS) under the Ministry of Trade, and Yunan Province Import Export Corporation of the People's Republic of China was signed. A border trade agreement with India was signed on 1 January 1994 and implemented on 12 April 1995.

Discussions and exchanges of notes on border trade agreements are progressing with the remaining three neighbours. Public and private enterprises are now actively engaged in border trade which was estimated to worth K1,066 million, or nearly 8.8% of total trade volume, in 1993–94.

Composition of Exports

Increasing and diversifying exports, and improving the quality of export products, are among the main objectives of the government. A number of new items in the manufacturing and processing sectors have been introduced and higher quality has been achieved through improved methods of handling, transportation, processing and storage.

The value of exports, including border trade, reached K4,228 (US$705 million) in 1993–94. Annual growth was a strong 15.7%, reflecting the development of private sector participation in foreign trade. The shares of major export items are depicted in Figure 8–1. Agricultural and forest products, together, constitute 64% of total exports.

FIGURE 8–1
Exports by Type for 1993–94

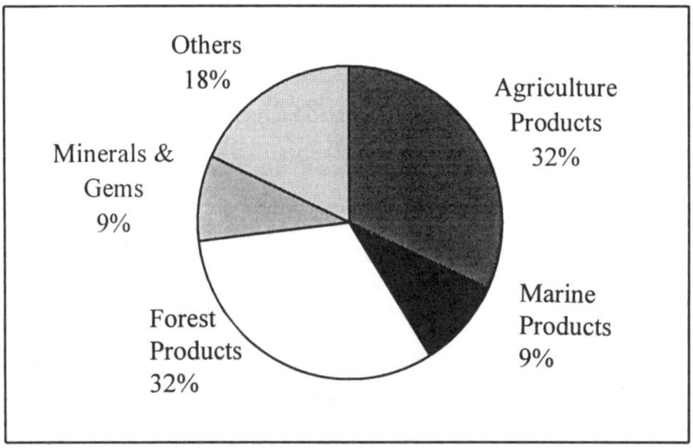

Composition of Imports

Traditional imports have included capital goods, industrial raw materials, spare parts and consumer goods. With the new economic system and trade liberalisation, there have been substantial changes in the pattern of imports. The government has encouraged importation of commodities that contribute to infrastructural development and production sectors. Capital goods and raw materials now constitute about 62% of total imports (see Figure 8–2).

Import and Export Trends

In the short and medium terms, trade patterns are expected to remain unchanged. In the long term, however, with the development of natural resource-based industries and the implementation of economic reforms, export and import patterns are expected to include more semi-manufactured and finished products.

FIGURE 8–2
Imports by Type for 1993–94

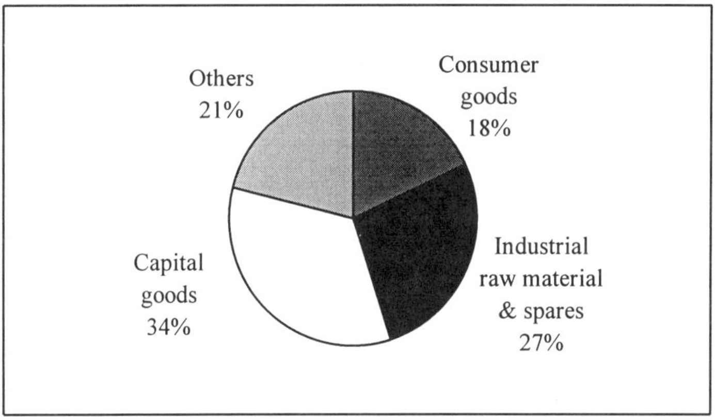

The Trade Community

The government has created a legal framework in the form of the Foreign Investment Law, to encourage and protect foreign government and private investments and participation, in the new economic structure. Local private sector participation also is receiving full support.

Chambers of commerce and joint venture corporations have been reactivated. Since 1988, private citizens are allowed to register as exporters, importers and business representatives. They have lost little time in participating in the new economic environment. The number of exporters, importers, business representatives, partnership firms, limited companies, foreign companies, commodity associations, joint venture corporations and chambers of commerce registered with the Ministry of Trade and Ministry of National Planning and Economic Development, was 12,441 as of April 1995. A breakdown of this total is shown in Table 8–3.

DOING BUSINESS IN MYANMAR

The foreign trade system has been decentralised since May 1976, when the economy was still centrally planned. With decentralisation, state economic enterprises (SEEs) under different ministries, are authorised to engage in their own external trade. They can freely export their products and import what they required. They are exempt from acquiring export-import licences from the Ministry of Trade.

TABLE 8–3
Composition of the Trade Community

Type	Number
Exporters/importers	4,368
Business representatives	1,525
Partnership firms	1,060
Myanmar limited companies	4,927
Foreign companies and branches	457
Joint ventures (Myanmar and foreign)	73
Chambers of commerce	31
Total	12,441

Foreign business enterprises may conduct business in Myanmar in a number of ways:

(i) ***Normal Trade:*** This involves normal commercial transactions, using letters of credit for exports and imports.
(ii) ***Counter-Trade*:** Counter-trade or reciprocal purchase on normal commercial terms can be made freely with private Myanmar companies. However, a counter-trade deal with an SEE can be made only with the approval of the Foreign Exchange Control Committee.
(iii) ***Sale on Consignment Basis:*** Foreign companies can send their commodities to private or public enterprises in Myanmar to be sold

on a consignment basis. Products can be sold either in foreign currency or local currency. If the products are sold in foreign currency, sales proceeds can be repatriated in foreign currency after the payment of commission to the local counterpart and income tax. Products can also be sold in kyats which may be used to purchase Myanmar export products. For US$100 (c.i.f.) of imported goods, the supplier can export US$120 (f.o.b.) of Myanmar products.

(iv) ***Import-First Basis:*** A foreign company can also supply products to a Myanmar company on an import-first basis. With the sales proceeds, the importer can export Myanmar products worth US$110 (f.o.b.) of products imported.

(v) ***Transit Trade:*** Products from a foreign country can transit through Myanmar to a third country. A foreign buyer or seller can appoint a Myanmar private citizen, or an enterprise, or a government entity as a transporter of the transit cargo and pay a 5% commission, a 2.5% customs duty and a 5% service charge, respectively, in hard currency to the Myanmar authorities.

(vi) ***Border Trade:*** With a view to maintaining good neighbour relations, border trade is also allowed. Delivery of goods can be made over borders for normal commercial transactions.

(vii) ***Business Representative:*** A foreign company can appoint a person or an enterprise, registered with the Ministry of Trade, as its business representative in Myanmar.

(viii) ***Establishment of a Foreign Company or Branch:*** Every foreign company or branch of a foreign company must apply for a Permit to Trade from the Ministry of National Planning and Development before being registered with the Registrar of Joint Stock Companies. A foreigner can form a joint venture with a Myanmar citizen or enterprise with a minimum of 35%, or a maximum of 100%, equity.

Licensing Laws

Licensing laws are principally contained in the Control of Imports and Exports (Temporary) Act, 1947 and any amendments are administered by the Ministry of Trade which, from time to time, issues orders, notifications and directives pertaining to export and import matters, including the issuance of licences and permits.

Licensing Authority

The authority to issue export-import licences and permits is delegated to the following organisations: the Directorate of Trade, under the Ministry of Trade; the Border Trade Offices of Myanmar Export Import Services, under the Ministry of Trade; and the Township Border Trade Co-ordination Committees. The Directorate of Trade is authorised to issue export-import licences and permits for conventional and cross-border trade. The Border Trade Offices of Myanmar Export Import Services also are authorised to issue export-import licences for cross-border trade by the normal method. The Township Border Trade Co-ordination Committees, headed by the Chairman of the Township Law and Order Restoration Councils, are authorised to issue export-import permissions for border trade by the border trade method.

Registration

All local and foreign private business enterprises, cooperative societies and joint-venture organisations, carrying out export-import business, are required to register with the Directorates of Trade. Under the Myanmar Companies Act, foreign companies and branches are required to obtain a trade permit from the Ministry of National Planning and Economic Development before they can register as an exporter-importer. The registration and extension fees are K5,000 for one year or K10,000 for three years.

Export-import Licences

Private exporters and importers are required to hold an export-import licence-permit issued by the licensing authorities concerned. The expiry period for those issued by the Directorate of Trade is normally six months from the date of issue, with three-month extensions. Those issued by the Border Trade Offices and Border Trade Co-ordination Committees have an expiry period of three months from the date of issue. They can be extended for one month at a time.

The Ministry of Trade also issues open general licences (OGL), normally for one year at a time, to those organisations doing business with an investment permit issued by the Union of Myanmar Investment Commission. Permission is granted only to those organisations which, by the nature of their business, are required to import frequently, either for capital investment or for business operation purposes. With an OGL, an importer is not required to apply for a licence for every import during the period specified in the OGL. OGLs are issued only for capital investment items imported as foreign capital and raw materials used in the first three years of commercial production.

Permitted Exports

A registered exporter-importer has the right to export all commodities, except rice, rice products and those products prescribed as solely exportable by SEEs. The following 28 categories are prohibited from export via the border areas (see Table 8–4).

TABLE 8–4
Prohibited Exports

Teak	Tin
Petroleum	Wolfram
Gems and jewelleries	Gold
Rice	Diamonds
Arms and ammunitions	Jade
Sea water prawns (frozen)	Chicken, duck, pig, goat and sheep (live or slaughtered)
Ivory	Rubber
Buffalo, cow, elephant, horse and rare species of animals	Zinc
Antiques	Bronze
Cotton wool	Pearls
Leather	Coal
Groundnuts	Tin-scheelite
Fresh water fish/prawns (frozen and dried)	Lead
Silver	Other metals

Permitted Imports

Policy pronouncements on imports emphasise the importance of basic needs for key economic sectors, including agriculture, livestock breeding, fishery, forestry, transportation, manufacturing, mining and so forth. This is reflected in the classification of import items which are divided into two categories:

(i) ***Priority Items:*** Agricultural machinery, farm implements, fertilisers, pesticides, high-yield quality seeds, edible oil, oil and fats for the soap industry, construction stores and building materials.
(ii) ***Optional Items:*** Food and beverages, personal, household and electrical goods.

Importers of optional items are required to import the equivalent value of priority items. For imports not listed in the above two categories, priority items, equivalent to a maximum of one-third in value, have to be imported. No quotas or ceilings are fixed for imports, except for motor vehicles, so long as the requirement to import the prescribed amount of priority items is fulfilled.

Registered exporter-importers can retain 100% of export earnings. There are no quotas or ceiling for exports except textiles which are subject to quotas fixed by the importing country.

Export-Import Taxes and Fees

Reflecting the liberalisation of the new economic order, no licence fee is payable on exports of any commodity including agricultural crops. However, a 5% commercial tax is payable on the customs duty levied on the exports shown in Table 8–5. All imports are subject to licence fees, customs duty and commercial tax. The licence fees are shown in Table 8–6.

TABLE 8–5
Customs Duty on Exports

Commodity	Normal Trade	Border Trade
Rice and broken rice	Kyat 10/metric tonne	Not allowed
Pulses and beans	5%	20%
Maize	5%	20%
Sesame	5%	–
Oil cakes	5%	Not allowed
Leather	5%	Not allowed
Vegetables	5%	20%

TABLE 8–6
Import Licence Fees (kyat)

C.I.F. Value	Licence Fee
Up to 10,000	250
From 10,001 to 25,000	625
From 25,001 to 50,000	1,250
From 50,001 to 100,000	2,500
From 100,001 to 200,000	5,000
From 200,001 to 400,000	10,000
From 400,001 to 1,000,000	20,000
From 1,000,001 and above	50,000

Customs Duty

Customs duty is payable according to a tariff schedule which is based on the assessable value of the imports. This is the sum of the CIF value and landing charges, which are equivalent to 0.5% of the CIF value. Customs duty, together with commercial tax, is collected at the point of entry and at the time of clearance of imported goods. Import tariffs cover 21 sections and 98 chapters, consisting of 1,241 headings and 6,062 sub-headings based on the Harmonised Commodity Description and Coding System. There are currently 22 bands of import tariffs ranging from 0 to 500%. Raw materials and other essential imports are taxed at very low rates while the highest rate is applied to luxury items.

Commercial Tax

Commercial tax is a charge on a wide range of domestically produced and imported goods. Certain items, mostly basic foods and raw materials, are exempt from tax. The tax is levied according to the schedule appended to the Commercial Tax Law. Rates vary depending on the types of goods and services. Non-exempted imports are taxed at 10%, 20%, and 30%, according to the respective schedule. Another schedule represents specific types of food such as cigarettes, liquor, and so forth. which carry tax rates above 30%.

Some imported items, like fertilisers, agricultural machinery and implements, insecticides, and pesticides and medicines, are exempt from paying licence fees, commercial tax and customs duty.

CONCLUSION

Following the adoption of the market-oriented system in late 1988, the government has encouraged both local and foreign private participation in the economy. The Ministry of Trade plays an active role in the process of transformation from a centrally planned economy to a market economy. The Ministry has lowered technical barriers to trade and has simplified export-import procedures. Great opportunities now exist for foreign businessmen wanting to trade with Myanmar.

Chapter 9

Regional Economic Characteristics of Myanmar

BY
CHOO Joon Yong
Joseph SIAH Jong Ping
Jeffrey TEO Cheng Yew

INTRODUCTION

WITH THE RECENT unconditional release of dissident leader Aung San Suu Kyi on 10 July 1995, the ruling State Law and Order Restoration Council (SLORC) took a big step towards political normalcy and economic progress in Myanmar (Reuter, 1995). The human rights issue now should be less of a stumbling block to the receipt of much needed foreign aid and investment. With the door open to democracy and development, foreign businessmen are looking towards Myanmar more than ever as an investment opportunity and truly a land of golden potential (Melzer, 1995).

In line with the theme of economic development, the focus of this chapter is to identify different investment opportunities in Myanmar and the geographical areas where the resources for these opportunities are concentrated. The primary goal of this chapter is to develop an investment map for business. This map serves two purposes. First, it indicates areas where various economic activities are concentrated based on geographic features. Second, it provides some guidance for selecting the most appropriate city as a base for investment operations.

TRADE AND ECONOMY OF MYANMAR

This section describes eight types of economic activity which both represent business opportunities for foreign investments and which are strongly encouraged by the government of Myanmar.

Agriculture

Joint ventures, cooperative societies, private individuals and organisations can be granted the right to utilise cultivatable, fallow or waste land upon application. A term of up to 30 years has been fixed for cultivation and agricultural use, but this period may be extended on negotiation, and in the case of seasonal crops, the lease can continue as long as there is no breach of conditions. Contract farming of annual crops is also possible. Investors are required to bring in seeds, inputs, and appropriate implements, while the Ministry is responsible for organising the farmers to grow the crops and for providing extension services. Government farms (ranging from 500 to 10,000 acres) can be leased for the production and processing of crops.

There is an inexpensive supply of skilled agricultural graduates and inputs that can be coupled with advanced technology, investment (financial and material), and international marketing methods provided by foreign partners. Myanmar prefers joint venture partners to make their contribution in kind, in the form of fertilisers, diesel oil, power tillers and small farm implements, for example. One spin-off from primary agricultural activity is an agro-based industry which both local and foreign entrepreneurs are encouraged to establish. The types of plantations and suitable agro-based activities are listed in Appendix 9–1.

Livestock and Fisheries

Myanmar, being favoured by topographical, climatic and geographical conditions, teams with rich and diverse fishery resources. Factories, fishing vessels and related enterprises, once owned by the state, are being transferred to the private sector through lease or sale. As of 1994, 102 fishing vessels had been sold and 13 factories leased to private companies. There are many ponds, lakes, reservoirs and flood areas suited to fresh water fish cultivation; as well as several rich river sources. Myanmar's continental shelf provides an awesome 228,781 square kilometres and an exclusive economic zone of 486,000 square kilometres for this industry. Vast pasture lands and different climates suited to different livestock, exist in different regions of the country (EUM, 1995, p. 21).

Mining

Since 1988, several government connected joint ventures have conducted feasibility studies, exploration and developed processing plants. Agreements have been signed with Ivanhoe Myanmar Holdings Limited and Roong Siam Mining Myanmar Company Limited of Thailand, and ECI Minerals Pte. Limited of Singapore to develop and market resources within Minywa and Tanintharyi Divisions. The Myanmar Pearl Enterprise has established a joint venture with Niino International Corporation of Japan to install and operate a cultured pearl farm at Pearl Island No. 2 in the Tanintharyi Division. The Myanmar Gem Enterprise has formed a joint venture company with VES Group Company Limited of Thailand to expand existing jewellery production in Myanmar for both export and domestic sale (EUM, 1995, p. 37).

Forestry

Myanmar has several forest types across the country and in different climatic zones. These range from the temperate forests in the snow-capped regions of the north to the deciduous forests in the centre and the tropical rain forests of the southern peninsular. Different qualities of teak grow in abundance in Myanmar which enjoys the largest share of the world teak trade. Teak extraction remains the sole responsibility of the Myanmar Timber Enterprise but the Ministry is looking into processing being undertaken by the private sector (EUM, 1995, pp. 40, 42). Other hardwoods are extracted for both domestic use and export.

Manufacturing

The Ministry of Industry was restructured in late 1988 to reflect the move towards a market-oriented system. Key initiatives included promotion of greater productivity, improved industrial competitiveness and export diversification of manufactured goods. The Ministry has two umbrella departments: the Directorate of Industries (DI) and the Directorate of Regional Industrial Coordination and Industrial Inspection (RICII). The Ministry operates in six different industries (textiles, foodstuffs, ceramics, pharmaceuticals, general maintenance, and paper and chemicals) and directly supervises 94 factories (EUM, 1995, p. 45).

Energy

(i) ***Oil and Gas:*** There are enormous oil and gas reserves in Myanmar, both onshore and offshore. There is exploration by Myanmar Oil and Gas Enterprise as well as international oil companies on production-sharing contracts. The Ministry of Energy awarded licences to 12 international companies for oil and gas exploration between 1989 and 1990. These include licences for reactivating suspended fields (RSF) and increased oil recovery (IOR). There are several other available onshore blocks for exploration and development on a production-sharing basis (EUM, 1995, p. 49).

(ii) ***Petroleum and Petrochemical Sector:*** Domestic demand for fuel is expected to rise substantially. This will be met either by imports or by offering private entrepreneurs the opportunity to share the surplus capacity at the Thanlyin refinery close to Yangon. As Myanmar strives towards building an agro-industrial base, urea fertiliser could be in great demand. The current local production is 1,200 metric tonnes per day, which falls far short of the estimated annual demand of 600,000 metric tonnes. Thus, the government plans to establish more urea fertiliser plants on a joint venture basis by utilising part of the offshore gas reserves as feed stock (EUM, 1995, p. 50).

(iii) ***Electric Power Sector:*** Hydroelectric power plays a vital role in the nation's social and economic development. So high priority has been placed on the development of the electric power sector. The Ministry has taken steps towards installing more gas-fired turbine generators in and around Yangon. Private participation in the generation and distribution of power is being considered (San Khup, 1995).

Construction

Myanmar has much under-utilised land suitable for development. Some of this land is easily accessible, such as that within the Thanlyin Kyauktan Region, a 140-square kilometre area located 16 kilometres from Yangon and 40 kilometres from the sea. Due to its strategic location, the Thanlyin-Kyauktan Regional Development Plan has been formulated. This integrated project is headed by the Singapore consortium Sinmardev (Lee, 1994). To date, basic infrastructure, such as roads, telecommunications, power and water supply, has been planned and some completed.

REGIONAL GEOGRAPHY

Myanmar is a land of varied physical character and seven different regions are prominent: the Arakan Coast, Tenasserim, Western Hills, Northern Hills, Shan Plateau, Dry Zone and Lower Myanmar. Each different region experiences widely differing climatic conditions. The annual rainfall varies from 75 centimetres and less in the central dry zone to 500 centimetres in the coastal regions. The average temperature ranges from 21°C in delta areas to 32°C in the coastal regions. Temperatures can run considerably higher in the central plains during the hot season. Myanmar, most of which is in the tropical region, has a tropical monsoon climate that falls into three seasons: the hot season from mid-February to mid-May, the rainy season from mid-May to mid-October, and the cool season from mid-October to mid-February.

Arakan Coast (Main Town: Akyab)

The western coast north of 18 degrees is cut off from the rest of the country by the Arakan Yomas mountain range. The plains of this narrow coastal strip comprise a series of small and scattered lowlands, mainly delta plains built up by the rivers Mayu, Kaladan, Lemro, Tanlwe and Thade. The largest tract of lowland is in the hinterland of Akyab, the principal town in Arakan. Heavy monsoon rains, torrential downpours, and typhoons frequently cause flooding and soil erosion. Although the dense evergreen forest has been substantially cleared, bamboo thickets cover much of the former forest land. Akyab is the chief port of the Arakan Coast. The port of Kyaukpyu, at the northern tip of Ramree Island, has been developed and it possesses a civilian airport giving it easy links with Akyab and Yangon.

Tenasserim (Main Towns: Moulmein, Tavoy and Mergui)

The panhandle of Tenasserim resembles the Arakan Coast in many physical respects. It is a broken, rocky, island-fringed coast. The Mergui Archipelago, lying off the southern section of the Tenasserim coast, comprises hundreds of islands and islets and most of them are hilly.

Many of these islands are gradually being connected to the mainland through silting. Tenasserim receives very heavy rainfall and the dry season is brief. Rice cultivation is important in the hinterland of Moulmein. Along the coast, there is much fishing from the silt platforms. In the Mergui Archipelago, beches-de-mer and edible birds' nests are collected. Mergui is a fishing and pearling centre. Interest in Tenasserim largely centres upon its mineral wealth. The granitic rocks contain tin and tungsten ores. Mining is not highly developed but there is some exploitation of alluvial deposits. Clearly there is scope for development but future production is likely to be geared to world prices for tin and tungsten (Robinson, 1979, p. 240). A railway runs southwards from Moulmein for about 128 kilometres to the small town of Ye. A main road penetrates as far south as Mergui and the main towns have air-links. But along this coastal province, there is a great dependence upon the sea for transport and communication.

Western Hills (Towns: Mawlaik, Falam and Tiddim)

This so-called hill region embraces the mountain country of the Patkai, Naga, and Manipur ranges in the north, through which run the India-Myanmar frontier, the Chin Hills in the centre and the Arakan Yomas in the south. It is a narrow mountain zone where the ranges are built of folded sedimentaries which have been heavily eroded and trenched by rivers. Cultivation is of the shifting type which has led to the destruction of much valuable forest cover. Maize, millet and hill rice are grown but the quality and the yield of the crops are low. Settlements are of the village type, usually located on the higher slopes and hilltops, partly for defensive reasons and partly because the valleys and foothills are unhealthy and malarial.

Northern Hills (Main Towns: Katha, Bhamo and Myitkyina)

This region comprises the far north of Myanmar which is north of the town of Bhamo. Physically, the region is bordered by high mountains on all sides except for the south, and it consists of the valleys of the rivers Ayeyarwaddy and Chindwin. The region as a whole is wild, undeveloped and sparsely populated. The chief towns are Katha, Bhamo and Myitkyina. Myitkyina is the northern terminus of the railway system. All three towns are linked by main highways and the latter two have air services.

Shan Plateau (Main Town: Lashio)

This region has common boundaries with the Shan States. The Shan are one of the largest tribal groups in the Union and they are related linguistically to the Thais of Thailand. The territory of the Shans is an extensive plateau which lies at an elevation between 900 and 1,200 metres. The climate is temperate and pleasant. Rainfall varies but it is typically between 1,000 and 2,000 millimetres. The natural vegetation is subtropical mixed forest and deciduous forest with some savanna.

The Shans are largely cultivators, some practising fixed, others shifting, agriculture. The crops include rice, millet, yams, tea and tung trees. The Shan plateau offers considerable opportunities for agricultural development. There are important mineral deposits on the plateau. Bawdwin has rich silver-lead deposits with associated zinc and copper ores. Tin and wolframite also exist and there are fine rubies at Mogok on the western edge of the plateau. Lignite deposits can be found in some of the old lake basins (Robinson, 1979, p. 42). Two railways penetrate the plateau; one to Lashio and the other to Taung-gyi. There are several good roads crossing the plateau, and Lashio and Loikaw are served by airfields.

Dry Zone (Main Town: Mandalay)

The dry zone of central Myanmar embraces the lowlands between the Arakan Yomas and the western fringe of the southern Shan State. It consists mostly of undulating lowlands on either side of the Ayeyarwaddy. The notable physical features are the flattish terrain, with light porous soils, and moisture deficiency resulting from less than 1,016 millimetres of annual precipitation. The dry zone of central Myanmar was the earliest centre of true Burmese civilisation. Until the British conquest, this region was the seat of the Burmese state and contained the majority of the people. Seven former capitals are situated here. Of these, the most famous are Pagan, Ava and Mandalay.

This semi-arid region of the middle Ayeyarwaddy basin is the true heart of Myanmar although its population has fallen behind that of the lower Ayeyarwaddy basin. This dry zone depends upon irrigation and dry farming techniques. Water is obtained from small tanks which store some of the run-off from the monsoon rainy season or from wells which tap the water-table of the sandy soils. An irrigation canal system serves about 0.6 million hectares. Most of the irrigated area is devoted to rice production. The other principal crops are sorghum, sesame, groundnuts, cotton, beans and pulses. This region is also important because of its oil deposits. The oilfields of Yenangvat, Chauk and Yenangyaung are found in the south-western part of the region where the Ayeyarwaddy turns south to flow through the lowland corridor between the Arakan Yomas and the Pegu Yomas.

The chief towns are the river ports which serve as collecting and marketing points for the produce of the region. Water transport is the primary method of carriage and communication. Two railways, one following the Ayeyarwaddy valley and the other the Sittang valley, serve the dry zone. The Ayeyarwaddy is the chief transport artery. It is 2,170 kilometres long and it forms a delta 240 kilometres by 210 kilometres as it enters the sea. The town of Mandalay, besides being the major communications centre of the region, is an important administrative and cultural centre.

Lower Myanmar (Main Towns: Yangon, Bassein and Pegu)

Lower Myanmar consists of three sections: the Ayeyarwaddy Delta, the Pegu Yomas and the Sittang Valley. To the west, sandwiched between the Arakan and Pegu Yomas, lies the vast delta expanse of the lower Ayeyarwaddy. This level plain stretches in a gradual unbroken slope over a distance of 288 kilometres from its apex, near Prome, to the sea. There are nine main river outlets but most of the river water passes out through the Eya mouth.

About one-sixth of the area lies below the level of the high spring tides and is mangrove-infested, and a further one-sixth is only about a foot above this level. From Cape Negrais to Elephant Point, the Ayeyarwaddy Delta is 121 kilometres wide. The entire area of the delta is extremely fertile and forms a great alluvial rice-growing region. Bassein, the only large town of the delta apart from Yangon, is the great rice-port of the region.

Eastward from the delta is the Yangon River. At the head of this inlet is Yangon, which is situated 32 kilometres upstream. The population of Yangon is cosmopolitan with large numbers of Indians and Chinese. The Yangon Division has over three million inhabitants and it is the most densely populated region in the country (Win Myint, 1995). River and rail communications have made it an important focal point with over 80% of Myanmar's trade. It is also a centre of industrial development. In addition to its old rice-milling, saw-milling and oil-refining industries, a variety of manufacturing industries, including textiles, pharmaceuticals and engineering, has grown up. Close to Yangon is Syriam, the second main centre of oil refining. The capacity of the Syrian refinery has been increased from 185,000 gallons to 685,000 gallons per day. Separated from the Ayeyarwaddy delta by the Pegu Yomas, is the valley and lowland tract of the Sittang River. Like the Ayeyarwaddy Delta, the plains of the Sittang are fertile, deal with commercial rice cultivation and are densely populated. The old city of Pegu, a former capital, is the chief centre in the south.

A FUNCTIONAL ANALYSIS OF THE ECONOMIC REGIONS

Many areas in Myanmar lack the proper amenities and facilities that businesses require to function efficiently. Other than the two cities of Yangon and Mandalay, which themselves have only a basic infrastructure in place, other parts of Myanmar are difficult to access and have rather poor infrastructure facilities. Although both major cities have airports, only that at Yangon is large enough and adequately equipped to handle international air traffic. Mandalay's airport only caters to domestic flights. In view of these constraints, it is sensible for potential businesses to base their branches, or representative offices, in Yangon or Mandalay.

Agriculture

Myanmar's economy is primarily agricultural. Agriculture employs nearly two-thirds of the population and accounts for 60% of total GDP (EUM, 1995, p. 33). Most of the 8.4 million hectares of arable land are concentrated in the delta region and in the valleys of the Ayeyarwaddy, Chindwin and Sittang rivers. In the south and in the far north, the rainfall is sufficient for cultivation. The main crop grown is rice. The delta region, which is one of the world's leading rice producing areas, has over 2.6 million hectares devoted to rice cultivation. Other crops grown in lower Myanmar are maize, sugar-cane, tobacco and rubber (in the Tenasserim panhandle). Crops grown in the dry zone of upper Myanmar include millet, oilseeds, beans and cotton. They depend on irrigation as rainfall is scanty.

Since cultivation of cereals, edible oil crops, industrial crops, and pulses and beans has increased, farmers require more light agricultural machinery and small farm implements to support crop cultivation. Thus, foreign investors are invited to set up factories to manufacture light agricultural machinery and small farm implements on a large scale in order to meet the demand. These include power tillers, walking tractors, water pumps, sprinklers, threshers, seeders, weeders and dryers (EUM, 1995, p. 33).

Businesses intending to invest in agricultural production should locate in Yangon or Mandalay, depending on the proximity of the specific product cultivation area to the cities. Both of these cities are supported by a good system of rail and sea transport which are important to the delivery of bulk agricultural commodities. Opportunities available in the area of agriculture include the provision of modern farming technology, machinery, equipment, fertilisers, chemicals and animal breeding technology.

Livestock and Fisheries

Animal husbandry is not highly developed, but there are a considerable number of animals being reared. Draught animals, like humped cattle and goats, are kept for ploughing, drawing carts and hauling. In the wetter, marshy environment of the delta, pigs and waterbuffaloes are reared.

Myanmar has a long coastline of 2,832 kilometres and the maximum sustainable yield for fisheries has been estimated at 1.05 million metric tonnes per year (EUM, 1995, p. 21). Less than half of this potential has been exploited. There are two approaches to investing in this sector. The first is through collaboration with local entrepreneurs in a joint venture. The second is by holding pertinent rights and licences. A potential entrepreneur is obliged to provide three out of the following five facilities: cold storage, ice plant, canning factory, fish meal plant and aquaculture. The state provides support to the livestock and fishery sectors by distributing quality livestock, taking preventive and curative measures against animal diseases, distributing quality fingerlings, disseminating modern breeding techniques, and selling fishing gear and implements. In collaboration with foreign companies and local entrepreneurs, the state is producing fish, prawn and fish products.

Clearly, Yangon is the best place to base fishery operations in view of its strategic location at the mouth of the delta. It also has a good port and cargo handling facilities to support the packaging and export of frozen fish products overseas.

Mining

The Ministry of Mines welcomes proposals to form joint ventures with its economic departments. These ventures include cooperatives to conduct feasibility studies, to explore, and to produce various kinds of minerals. Reserves of iron ore are located at Pang Pet which is east of Meiktila. There are rich silver-lead deposits at Bawdwin in the Shan States and considerable tin and tungsten resources in Tenasserim. Gold is found in most of the river gravel deposits of upper Myanmar. White marble is quarried near Mandalay and jade is mined in northern Myanmar. Two state enterprises under the Ministry of Trade oversee the production of metallic minerals while another one deals with industrial materials as well as iron and steel products.

The production of precious stones, like rubies, sapphires, diamonds and jade, is handled by the Myanmar Gem Enterprise. The government has granted permission to investors to sign joint venture contracts with state enterprises concerned with the production of tin concentrate, gold, gemstones and jade. Under these ventures, the minerals produced are shared between the parties (EUM, 1995, p. 20).

The Mogok area in the Mandalay Division is the source of the world's finest rubies as well as a wide variety of other gems like sapphires, garnets, amethysts, zircons, moonstones and lolites. Jade is found predominantly in the Phakant area in Kachin State, which is renowned for its fine quality imperial jade, commercial jade and utility jade.

Precious stones from these areas are sold wholesale at gem emporiums in Yangon on a regular basis to retailers and gem traders. Businesses in the gem and jewellery trade should locate in Yangon to source supplies of precious stones from these emporiums.

Forestry

Forests cover more than 50% of the country's total land area and forestry is one of the main foreign exchange earning sectors. Myanmar produces the bulk of the world's teak. The most important forests from an economic viewpoint are the mixed deciduous forest containing teak, pyinkado and padauk, which are especially well-developed along the Pegu

Yomas and Mu valley of upper Myanmar. Bamboo forests, which offer a great potential as a source for pulp paper, cover large areas of the Arakan.

Forestry is government controlled. The government is particularly keen to attract foreign investment in sawmills, timber processing plants and furniture factories. These are best established in Mandalay to capitalise on the dense forest reserves of upper Myanmar and the Ayeyarwaddy River, which is navigable all year round, allowing logs from the Pegu Yomas to be transported conveniently and cheaply to Yangon. Processing plants might also be constructed in Yangon where the processed wood can be packaged and exported overseas. Lease schemes and buy-back schemes, whereby foreign investors bring in processing equipment, need to be negotiated with the Foreign Investment Commission (FIC).

Manufacturing

There has been little manufacturing in Myanmar beyond traditional cottage industries concerned with textiles, metal and wood. Only recently have there been industrial developments like the Ywama steel mill in Yangon, the Thayetmyo cement factory, the Thamaing jute mill and the brick and tile works at Donyngone. West German loans have financed a glass factory, a fertiliser plant and a textile mill. Recent Singapore investments and joint ventures have also resulted in the construction of a brewery plant, cigarette production plants, and a wood processing plant. Important aid has been received from the United Nations and, with the recent release of Aung San Suu Kyi from house arrest, the U.S., the World Bank and the IMF may provide similar aid.

The Ministry of Industry adopts four methods of economic collaboration with the private sector, namely joint ventures, consignment systems, leases of factory/land and buy-back arrangements. The Ministry of Industry is interested in forming joint ventures with foreign partners, especially in the ceramic, pulp and paper, foodstuff, packing and pharmaceutical industries (EUM, 1995, p. 42). The Ministry has been carrying out structural adjustments to create a suitable enabling environment for industries to grow. Yangon and Mandalay are prime sites for manufacturing plants because of their transport links.

Energy

The Ministry of Energy encourages foreign participation in the joint development of the following hydropower resources: Kun (84 MW, Bago Division), Bilin (240 MW, Mon State), Yeywa (400 MW, Mandalay Division), and Baluchaung No. 3 (48 MW, Kayah State). Both local and foreign investors are encouraged to consider the installation of waste-heat recovery systems to several existing gas turbine power plants as an upgrade to combined cycle operations (EUM, 1995, p. 23).

The Myanmar Oil and Gas Enterprise is responsible for the exploration, production and transportation of crude oil and natural gas. It operates 14 oil and gas fields in the onshore areas. Oilfields occur in a line down the middle of Myanmar and to the north-west and west of the Pegu Yomas. The Myanmar Oil Corporation, the largest of the operating concerns, is owned by the government. Myanmar has invited offers for exploration of 18 offshore blocks along the Thanintharyi and Rakhine coast under a production-sharing agreement basis. Test wells are being drilled in the Gulf of Matroban, financed by Japanese loans. The Yetagun Gas Reserves' development aims to direct sales to neighbouring countries through pipelines. These plans include the manufacture of value added products such as urea, methanol, olefins, power generation and conversion to intermediate products such as LNG for export. Modern technology and expertise are still needed to explore new fields and to revive the oil and gas sector. Markets exist for ancillary products like oil and gas equipment, pipeline construction, machinery and parts (EUM, 1995, p. 23).

Construction

The Ministry of Construction has built the Thanlyin-Kyauktan Industrial Zone to high standards and provided social facilities, commercial complexes, warehousing facilities and other support services. The Ministry of National Planning and Economic Development is negotiating with a Singapore consortium to develop an industrial estate to be built in four phases. Phase one is scheduled to start in 1995 and phase four in the year 2000 (Lee, 1994).

Tourism

Myanmar's rich and diverse cultural heritage means tourism has a great potential for rapid growth. It is currently hampered by inadequacies in transportation, hotels, restaurants and entertainment. There is demand in Bagan, Mandalay and Inle Lake for international class hotels. Bagan could become the top tourist draw with its unspoiled ancient city landscape. At present, most hotel development is taking place in Yangon. There are two projects in Mandalay. Two resort hotels are planned on islands in the south near Kawthaing, and one at the Golden Triangle Area.

The majority of the hotel projects are build-operate-transfer (BOT) developments or joint ventures. These can be 100% foreign-owned or joint ventures with government or local investors. Leases run for 30 years from the date of operation. This can be extended for three 5-year terms. Repatriation of profits is allowed and the law guarantees no nationalisation (EUM, 1995, p. 57). Investment is urgently needed for beach resorts, country clubs, golf courses, shopping, office and entertainment complexes, service apartments, time-sharing apartments and condominiums.

SUMMARY

Although there have been reports of unrest and disputes in the outlying areas bordering the Shan and Kachin states, these are sporadic and appear to be under control. From conversations with Myanmar nationals, it seems that the SLORC have been successful in containing violence. Trade and investment, therefore, should not be affected by disputes.

This chapter has provided a brief overview of eight types of economic activity in Myanmar and a description of each of the country's seven distinct topographic regions. It explored the economic developments within these regions and singled out business opportunities within each of the eight economic activities.

APPENDIX 9–1
Types of Plantations, Agro-based Industries, and Potential Cooperatives in Myanmar

A. **Plantations**
1. Rubber, oil palm and cashew nut.
2. Mango, banana and pineapple.
3. Plantations for horticultural crops (tropical and sub-tropical).

B. **Agro-based Industries**
1. Tomato juice and concentrate.
2. Grape fruit juice.

C. **Cooperatives**
1. Avocado oil.
2. Quick frozen and preserved fruits and vegetables.
3. Edible oil.
4. Animal feed.
5. Cleaning and grading of pulses and beans.
6. Upgrading and expansion of existing vegetable, flower and medicinal plant farms.
7. Mulberry cultivation, cocoon production and silk enterprises.
8. Production of pickled products (bamboo shoots, vegetables and fruits).
9. Production of hybrid seeds and other vegetable and flower seeds.
10. Improvement of quality crumb rubber production.
11. Production of value-added rubber goods (surgical gloves, condoms).

Source: *Myanmar – The Golden Land,* Publication by the Embassy of the Union of Myanmar in commemoration of the 47th anniversary of Independence Day, 1995.

REFERENCES

Country Profile Series – The Union of Myanmar, Singapore Trade Development Board, 1995.

Eliot, J., *et al.*, *Thailand and Burma Handbook*, Trade & Travel Publications Ltd., Hongkong, 1994.

Khin San May, "Economic Role of Mandalay and the Surrounding Regions", Seminar Paper, MBA Business Study Mission to Myanmar, 19 June 1995.

Lee K. C., “Changes in Myanmar’s Policies Spell New Openings for Investors”, *The Straits Times*, 19 September 1994.

Lee S. H., “Straight-talking Business Elite in Myanmar Move into High Gear”, *The Sunday Times*, 30 April 1995a.

Lee S. H., “Doing Business in Myanmar: Singapore’s Gung-ho Traders”, *The Sunday Times*, 18 June 1995b.

Melzer, B., “Land of Pagodas Opens Up”, *The Sunday Times*, 25 June 1995.

Myanmar – The Golden Land, Embassy of the Union of Myanmar, Publication in commemoration of the 47th anniversary of Independence Day, 1995.

Myanmar: A Guide for Businessmen and Investors, Coopers & Lybrand, 1994.

Naw Angelene, “Tourism Development in Myanmar, Visit Myanmar Year, Hotel and Tourism Infrastructure”, Seminar Paper, MBA Business Study Mission to Myanmar, 16 June 1995.

Reuter, “Myanmar Releases Aung San Suu Kyi”, *The Straits Times*, 11 July 1995.

Robinson, H., *Monsoon Asia*, MacDonald & Evan Ltd., 1979.

San Khup, “Macroeconomic Policies with Special Emphasis on Infrastructural Development”, Seminar Paper, MBA Business Study Mission to Myanmar, June 1995.

Win Myint, “Master Plan for Regional Development of Yangon”, Seminar Paper, MBA Business Study Mission to Myanmar, 16 June 1995.

Chapter 10

Master Plan for Regional Development of Yangon

BY
WIN MYINT*

INTRODUCTION

MYANMAR'S ESTIMATED POPULATION in 1993 was 43.13 million with an annual growth rate of 1.88%. The share of rural population has remained at 70–75% since 1973. The urban population of 11 million is distributed in 300 towns including the cities of Yangon and Mandalay. For administrative purpose, Myanmar is divided into seven divisions and seven states. Each state and division comprises a number of districts in which there are townships composed of both urban and rural areas.

The distribution of Myanmar's population is a function of the topography. Population centres greater than 100,000 people are in the delta and central regions of Myanmar, and along major rivers which are transportation arteries.

REGIONAL DEVELOPMENT

Structural reforms and new economic policies which emphasise exports, financial liberalisation and less regulation are accelerating urbanisation

* Director, Department of Housing Settlement and Urban Development, Yangon, Myanmar.

by increasing the flows of goods, people, commodities and information to urban centres and the links between urban and rural areas. The government's physical and economic development policies now take into account the whole human settlement system rather than rural and urban development in isolation. Priority is given to the development of agricultural, infrastructure, tourism and border areas.

Development Programmes in Yangon Region

Yangon division, at 10,171 square kilometres, is one of the smallest of the fourteen states and divisions. It consists of Yangon City and twelve rural townships. Out of the 4.9 million population, 70.5% live in urban areas. Over three million people live in Yangon and the population density is 485 persons per square kilometre. Yangon division is the most densely populated region in the country.

The main industries are agriculture followed by trade, manufacturing and services. Most of the development has been in these sectors. The main improvements have been as follows:

(i) **Agriculture:**
- (a) Increased rice production through the double cropping system.
- (b) Increased production of edible oil for local consumption, and pulses and beans for export.

(ii) **Tourism:**
- (a) Improvements in infrastructure.
- (b) Conservation and reconstruction of cultural heritage.
- (c) Promotion of tourism.

(iii) **Infrastructure:**
- (a) Improvement of passenger facilities at Yangon International Airport (see Figure 10–1).
- (b) Construction of the new Hansawaddy International Airport at Bago.
- (c) Improvement of the Htaukkyant-Bago highway and widening to a six-lane highway.
- (d) Improvements of regional road.
- (e) Expansion of the container yard at Yangon port.
- (f) Construction of a new container terminal at Thilawa port in Thanlyin Kyauktan.

FIGURE 10–1
Yangon-Bago Regional Growth Triangle

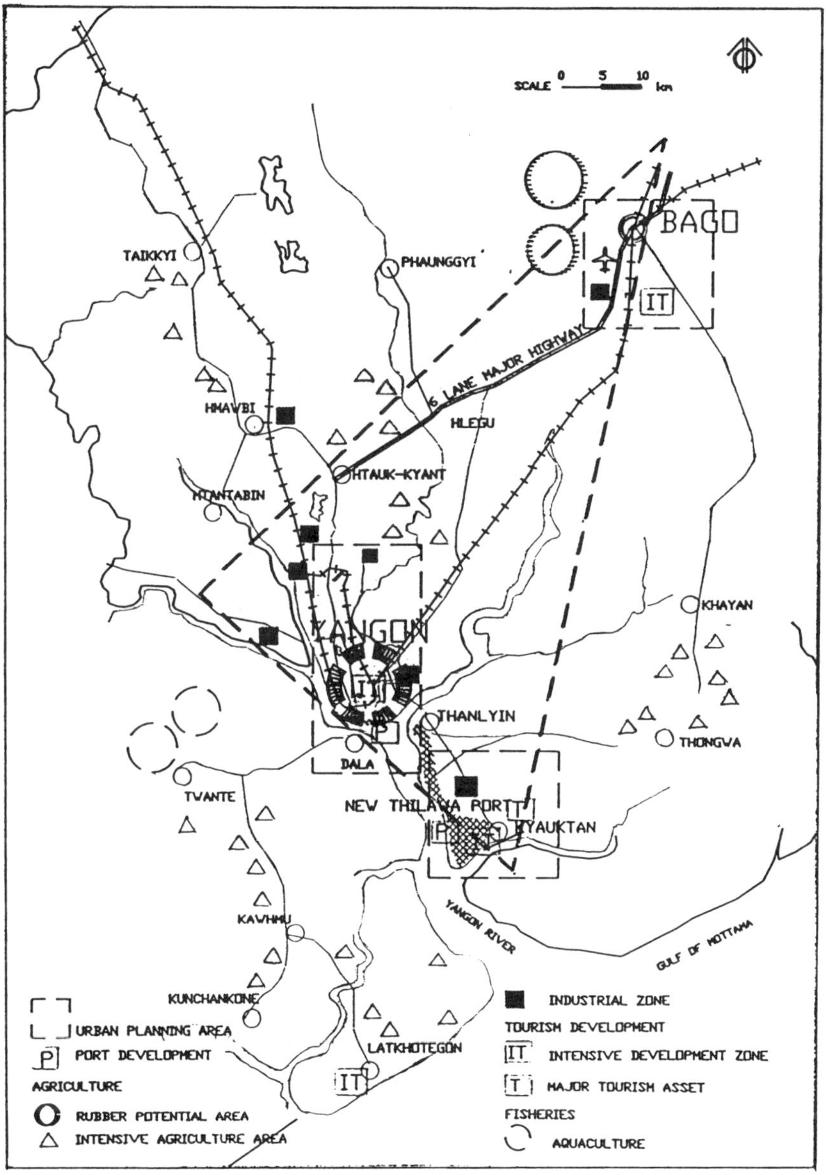

(g) Construction of telecommunication facilities in Yangon and Bago.

(iv) **Manufacturing:**

(a) Establishment of industrial estates and zones.

(b) Privatisation of some government industries.

(v) **Urban Development:**

(a) Site and services projects.

(b) Area development projects within Yangon.

CONCLUSION

Developments in the above five sectors will shape the distribution of employment over the next decade. While Yangon City dominates the most densely populated region of the country, agriculture still plays the greatest role in the regional economy. The other twelve small urban centres play a major role in servicing the rural hinterland and fostering agriculture development. The structural shift in employment from agricultural to non-agricultural sectors has not taken place in Myanmar as it has in neighbouring countries.

In the urban sector, infrastructure development, hotel construction in Yangon and Bago for Visit Myanmar Year, and an increase in investment in services will create new employment opportunities. In addition, there are plans to establish industrial zones around Yangon and Bago for foreign and local investors.

LAW, ACCOUNTING AND TAX

Chapter 11

Corporate and Commercial Laws of Myanmar

BY
TUN SHIN*

INTRODUCTION

THE LEGAL SYSTEM of Myanmar has its roots in, but is not a replica of, the common law legal system. It is a combination of the common law and civil law legal systems. The principles of common law are implanted into codified laws or statutes which are promulgated by the legislature. The codified laws or statutes grew out of the Justinian Code of the Roman era or the Codex Napoleon of Napoleonic times.

Corporate, economic and commercial laws also belong to the fundamentals of Myanmar's legal system. They remained intact for 25 years up to 1988, when Myanmar adopted the market economy system. The State Law and Order Restoration Council (SLORC) put life into these laws and passed new laws for investment and privatisation to encourage and promote foreign investment.

* Legal Advisor, Ministry of National Planning and Economic Development, Yangon, Myanmar.

TYPES OF LAWS

Corporate and commercial laws can be categorised into the following:

(a) The State-owned Economic Enterprises Law.
(b) Investment laws.
(c) Land laws.
(d) Transport laws.
(e) Locus Standii of enterprises and companies, and the laws governing them.
(f) Hierarchy of statutes and other related laws.
(g) Settlement of disputes in corporate and commercial cases.
(h) Economy related laws.

State-Owned Economic Enterprise Law

The Public International Law gives the state absolute sovereignty over its land, sea and air, and inalienable rights over its natural resources. The State-Owned Economic Enterprises Law (1989) exercises rights given by the Public International Law as lex loci of Myanmar. Section 3 gives the government this right. It also empowers state-owned economic enterprises alone to undertake 12 activities. Exemption, or an escape section for non-jurists, is made through Section 4. Under this section, these activities can be given to joint ventures between the government and any other person, or to an economic organisation or to any person, subject to conditions. The *modus operandi* for such permission is made through a notification by the government. Section 4 also serves as a vehicle for privatisation. It gives government the right to allow these activities to operate under the privatisation scheme.

Investment Laws

Myanmar is a country with vast natural resources. One of the first laws promulgated in 1988 was the Union of Myanmar Foreign Investment Law, which has the economic objectives of promotion and expansion of exports, exploitation of high technology, large capital and investment projects which increase employment, energy conservation and enhanced regional development.

The law empowers the Myanmar Investment Commission to grant permits to enterprises with a 35–100% share of foreign capital amounting to US$100,000. Such joint ventures, or 100% investments, are entitled to apply for three-year tax exemption and other tax reliefs. The law also guarantees no nationalisation on expiry of the contract and the right to repatriate profits in foreign currency after paying Myanmar taxes.

The state also encourages domestic investment. The Myanmar Citizens Investment Law (State Law and Order Restoration Council Law No. 4/94, 1994) entitles citizens to the same exemptions and privileges as those granted to foreigners under the Foreign Investment Law.

Land Laws

The main land law of Myanmar is a statute called the Transfer of Property Act (1882). This deals with the definition of transfer, such as sale, mortgage, lease, exchange and gifts. It embodies the basic principles of English Common Law.

The successor to this law is the Transfer of Immovable Property Restriction Law (Pyithu Hluttaw Law No. 1, 1987). This Law prohibits the transfer of property from foreigners to citizens, and *vice versa*. There are exceptions for diplomatic organisations, the United Nations and other organisations or individuals exempted by the ministry concerned. This law does not apply to companies or organisations formed as joint ventures in the interest of the state. In practice, this law does not apply to Myanmar Investment Commission cases.

Myanmar's land is categorised as culturable, fallow and waste. To regulate these lands, the state has formed a Central Committee which citizens can apply to for the use of land up to 5,000 acres. If foreigners are involved, an application can be made to the Myanmar Investment Commission.

Registrar offices, formed under the Registration Act (1909) exist in all parts of Myanmar. These offices keep account of encumbrance regarding immovable property. Notification No. 390 records the rental charged by government departments. Notification No. 593 specifies that the Myanmar Investment Commission has the right to comment on substantial investments lasting more than 30 years. Government departments are to seek such comments.

Transport Laws

Charter parties use the classic Lloyds form for time charters, voyage charters and demise charters. These forms use the principles of common law. Carver's Carriage by Sea, Scrutton on Charter Party and Ivarmy's Carriage of Goods by Sea are all used in Myanmar. The Carriage of Goods by Sea Act enforces the Hague Rules or the Convention for Unification of Certain Rules of Bill of Lading (Brussels, 1923). Shipping lawyers know the importance of the Bill of Lading Act (1856) which gives the cause of action directly from consignee to the ship owner. This is almost a replica of the English Bill of Lading Act. The registration of ships is governed by the Myanmar Registration of Ships Act (1841). Originally designed for the registration of ships owned by Myanmar citizens in the Myanmar Registry, this act was amended in 1986 to give registration to ships that are made on Charter by Demise or Bare-Boat Charter to a Myanmar citizen or authorised organisation. The Sea-going Vessels Navigation Convention Act (1952) gives effect to the Brussels Convention on Collision of Ship or Salvage (1910).

Myanmar ratified the Chicago Convention (1944) and the Convention for International Civil Aviation Organisation (1948). Air services agreements are based on the Bermuda pattern. The Aircraft Act (1934) and Aircraft Rules (1937) cover aircraft navigation. The Aircraft Rules were amended by State Law and Order Restoration Council Rule No. 1/94, to permit the issuance of air operators' certificates to joint venture airlines incorporated in Myanmar. Two joint venture airlines have been incorporated.

Loss of life, and damage or loss of cargo, baggage or luggage come under the Carriage by Air Act (1935). This gives domestic legal effect to the Convention for the Unification of Rules Relating to International Convention for Carriage by Air, popularly known to aviation lawyers as the Warsaw Convention of 1929. Textbooks on air law, like Bin Cheng's The Law of International Air Transport, Shawcross and Beaumout on Air Law, McNair's The Law of the Air, and others, are widely used in Myanmar.

The Law of Carriage by Land derives from common law. Two principle acts are the Carriers Act (1865) and the Railway Act (1890).

Locus Standii of Enterprises and Companies

I have often been asked about contracts with State-Owned Economic Enterprises (SEE) and sovereign immunity. Sovereign immunity is a concept in public international law which gives immunity to a state from the claims or commercial jurisdiction of courts of law.

Whether a SEE can invoke sovereign immunity is best understood by studying how these enterprises are formed in Myanmar. A SEE is formed as a corporate body that has complete legal personality in the Myanmar legal system. It is not the state itself and it cannot invoke sovereign immunity. It is a commercial enterprise. It has the right to sue and be sued as a company. There are many examples of arbitration between a SEE and other individual parties.

There are two types of document that give locus standii to SEEs. The first type is the law which forms the enterprise. A good example is the Myanmar Airways Act, promulgated in 1953 by Act No. 39. This act formed Myanmar Airways, an enterprise under the Ministry of Transport. Another example is the 1964 Myanmar Five Star Shipping Corporation Law, known as the Revolutionary Council Law No. 2 (1964). This gives legal standing to the Myanmar Five Star Line. Under such acts or laws, an enterprise is given the *locus standii* to be a legal person that has a right to sue or be sued.

Another type of enterprise is formed under a notification from a ministry. The ministry concerned issues a notification for the formation of an enterprise or directorate. An example is the notification issued by the Ministry of Hotels and Tourism for the formation of the Myanmar Hotels and Tourism Service. The Ministry of National Planning and Economic Development issued the notification for the formation of the Directorate of Investment and Company Administration with the Department of Companies or Company Registrar as one of its departments.

Besides SEEs, joint ventures, foreign companies operating in Myanmar and partnerships, are also products of the new market economy system. Joint ventures can be formed either under the Foreign Investment Law or outside this law. Joint ventures with the state are formed under the Special Company Act (1950). The Myanmar Companies Act is the procedural law that covers the formation of all types of companies. It is based on the India Act VII (1913). The basic principles are the same as the Singapore Company Act. Partnerships can be formed with two to 20 persons. A partnership is not a corporate body. It is governed by the Partnership Act (1932). Its registration is optional. There is also sole proprietorship in Myanmar for which no registration is required. Foreign companies have to obtain a permit from the Ministry of National Planning and Economic Development. The Capital Structure Committee reviews applications for permits.

The Hierarchy of Statutes and Other Related Laws

Under the hierarchy of laws in Myanmar, first come acts which were formed from the time of the British annexation up to 1962. These are statutes passed by the legislature. After 1962, statutes are called laws. A law has the same legal effect as its predecessor, the act. Acts or laws are statutes in the common law sense. Below statutes, are rules or procedures which derive from acts or laws. Next, for detailed enforcement of laws or acts and rules, there are regulations. Finally, there are notifications, which are normally issued by the ministry concerned, and they are normally at the bottom of the ladder. However, in certain exceptional cases, legislature makes a certain notification with the force of law. An example is Notification No. 1 (12 December 1991) which formed the Central Committee for the Management of Culturable Land, Fallow Land and Waste Land. Notifications having the force of law are rare.

The Settlement of Disputes in Corporate and Commercial Cases

The settlement of disputes clause in commercial contracts serves as a *modus vivendi*, which is the mode of settlement when disputes arise. The Arbitration Act, promulgated as the Myanmar Act IV (1994), is the main procedural law for arbitration in Myanmar. This law is based on the English Arbitration Act (1950). The appointment of arbitrators, supervision by the Court for their removal, the award, the enforcement of award in the civil court and appeal from an award to the supreme court are all mentioned in this act.

In the first schedule, there are implied conditions of an arbitration agreement. This schedule is deemed to be part of the agreement between parties for arbitration. Besides the Arbitration Act, there is the Arbitration (Protocol & Convention) Act (1939), which gives domestic legal effect to the Protocol on Arbitration Clauses (The Geneva Protocol of 1923). This protocol is part of the act in the first schedule. In the same way, the Convention on the Execution of Foreign Arbitral Awards was given legal effect in the second schedule of this act. This protocol is called the Geneva Protocol (1927). The convention is known as the Geneva Convention of 1923.

Myanmar is currently considering whether to accept international arbitration and the United Nations Commission on International Trade Law System, the International Chamber of Commerce System, the International Centre for Settlement of Investment Disputes (Washington Convention) and the New York Convention.

Economy Related Laws

The Contract Act (1872), based on the India Act IX (1872), has the same principles that one finds in the law of contract in Singapore. Its principles include the promise, proposal, acceptance, consideration, factors, tendering to defeat contractual liability, such as incapacity, misrepresentation, duress and undue influence, illegality, privity, discharge, remedies, contingent contract and agency.

For investment contracts, two offices have jurisdiction: the Attorney General's Office and the Directorate of Investment and Company Administration under the Ministry of National Planning and Economic Development, which serves as a secretariat to the Myanmar Investment Commission. The Attorney General's Office vets contracts when state enterprises are involved. They mainly deal with legal policy, standard legal clauses and legal principles. The legal division of the Directorate of Investment and Company Administration is responsible for private contracts between private citizens and foreigners, or investment contracts between citizens. It also gives legal advice to foreign lawyers and foreign investors.

Intellectual Property laws derive from Indian Intellectual Property Laws. In Myanmar the Registration Act (1909) was followed by the Registration Manual (1946). In this manual, article 18(f) specifies the registration of the trade marks, giving them legal effect. The legal effect starts after registration. The Copyright Act (1914), India Act III (1914), Patent & Design Act of Myanmar and India Act V (1945) are designed to protect copyrights and patents. These are similar to the laws of Singapore which share the same legal family.

CONCLUSION

Many of the principles of the Myanmar legal system and, in particular, the commercial and corporate laws, are based on the principles of the common law system and legal family. The laws presented are pillars of the Myanmar market economy system.

Chapter 12

Myanmar's Foreign Investment Law

BY
KOH Hui Chuan
Ken ONG
YAP Soo San
Zainal Abidin MAHMOOD

INTRODUCTION

ONE OF THE most important tasks for Myanmar today is the promotion of economic development. Since taking over power in September 1988, the State Law and Order Restoration Council (SLORC) discarded the central planning type of economic management and adopted a market-oriented policy. The overall objective of Myanmar's development policy at present is achieving development that combines economic growth with the preservation of the environment (Myat Thein, 1995). Towards that end, a Short-term Plan (1992–93 to 1995–96) has been drawn up and implemented. The key objectives are to set up production in agriculture and to increase export earnings, including foreign exchange earnings from services, with a targeted average annual growth rate of 5.1% (San Khup, 1995).

With the country opening up to foreign investors, and with a view to successfully implementing a new economic policy, new laws, regulations and procedures have been enacted. One of the most important reforms is the promulgation of the Foreign Investment Law (November 1988) to induce direct foreign investment .

This chapter covers various ways in which a foreign investor can enter Myanmar and the related procedures for incorporation. It also deals with foreign investment in relation to the country's economic plans. The final section evaluates some of the issues raised.

FORMS OF ORGANISATION AND PROCEDURES FOR INCORPORATION

Foreign investors may incorporate their businesses in the following forms:

(i) Sole proprietorship.
(ii) Partnership.
(iii) Limited liability company.
(iv) Joint venture.
(v) Branch of a foreign company.
(vi) Representative office.

A sole proprietorship, a partnership and a limited company can be wholly-owned by foreigners.[1] If it takes the form of a joint venture, then the capital contribution from the foreign partner(s) must be at least 35% of the total capital. A foreign company that is incorporated outside Myanmar but has an established place in the latter would be considered a foreign branch. Finally, anyone outside Myanmar can appoint a citizen or an economic organisation of Myanmar as a business representative.

If a company is incorporated without the involvement of a state enterprise, then it will be governed by the Myanmar Companies Act. On the other hand, if a company involves a state enterprise, then it will be incorporated under the Special Company Act. The provisions of the Myanmar Companies Act will still apply in this instance, so long as there are no agreements to exclude them.

Every foreign company or branch which has been granted a "Permit to Trade" is required to bring capital into Myanmar in foreign currency acceptable to the Myanmar Foreign Trade Bank. For this purpose, the Capital Structure Committee will fix, for each foreign company or branch,

---

1 Singapore, Ministry of Trade, *Doing Business in Myanmar – The Myanmar Companies Act Provisions Relative to a Foreign Company*, 2nd Edition, June 1990, p. 22.

the amount of capital required for business in Myanmar determined on a uniform, reasonable and acceptable basis. Under the section entitled "Capital to be brought into Myanmar" of the Myanmar Companies Act, the minimum amount of capital which must be physically brought into the country in an acceptable currency, in respect of foreign companies, are the following equivalents:

(i) K1,000,000 for an industrial company (including trading and services).
(ii) K500,000 for a trading company (including services).
(iii) K300,000 for a services company (services only).

The amount of authorised capital registered determines the registration costs. This is stated in Annexure 7 (Table of Fees) of the Myanmar *Companies Act.*

The process of registration usually takes approximately one month to complete. If the parties are local companies, then they are governed by the Myanmar Citizens Investment Law. If any of the parties are foreign partners, then they come under the Foreign Investment Law. They are required to apply for a "Permit to Trade" from the Myanmar Investment Commission which is subject to Cabinet approval. The Cabinet also will consider the State-owned Economic Enterprises Law for ventures that are restricted by the state (see Appendix 12–1 for the restricted list).

Upon approval, the Commission issues a trade permit and notification. A joint venture involving a state enterprise is formed under the Special Company Act. Otherwise, it is registered under the Myanmar Companies Act. The incorporation certificate and notification is issued by the Ministry of National Planning and Economic Development. The incorporation procedures for the registration of a company are shown in Figure 12–1.

THE FOREIGN INVESTMENT LAW

The Myanmar Foreign Investment Law is the first of its kind since the Revolutionary Council came to power in 1962. It was formulated ten weeks after the military takeover in September 1988 (Mya Than, 1990). When it was released in November 1988, it constituted a historically significant step towards a free market system by allowing foreign investors into the country after 26 years of closed-door policy. The Foreign Investment Law is significant because it is the symbol of an "open door policy". Moreover, it is remarkable that the SLORC could produce such a liberal law within a few weeks of coming to power (Mya Than, 1990).

FIGURE 12–1
Flow Chart on Incorporation Procedures for the Registration of Companies

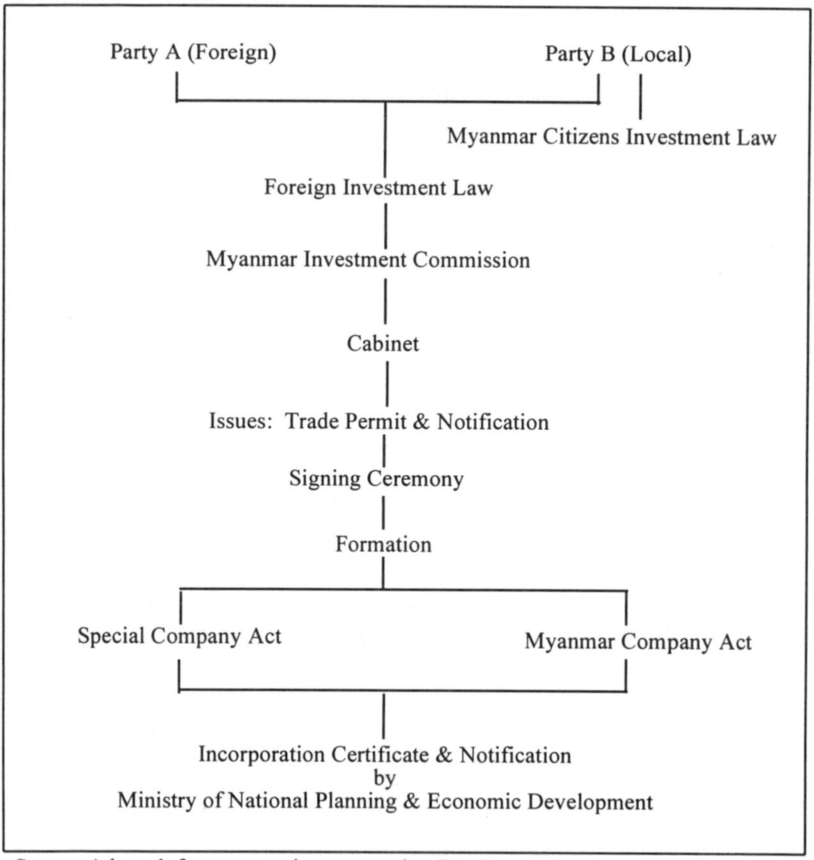

Source: Adapted from a seminar paper by Dr. Tun Chin, Legal Advisor to the Ministry of National Planning and Economic Development, entitled "Corporate and Commercial Laws of Myanmar", presented in June 1995 to the NTU MBA Business Study Mission in Yangon.

The objectives of the Foreign Investment Law are:

(i) the promotion and expansion of exports;
(ii) the exploitation of natural resources which require heavy investment;
(iii) the acquisition of high technology;
(iv) support and assistance for production and services involving large capital;
(v) the expansion of employment opportunities;
(vi) the development of projects which save energy consumption; and
(vii) regional development.[2]

Under this law, two types of foreign participation are permitted: 100% foreign-owned companies and joint venture companies in which foreign equity must amount to a minimum of 35%. As mentioned earlier, foreign investors may form a proprietorship, partnership, limited liability company or joint venture with or without a private or state partner.

A foreign investor who invests and operates under the new law has the right to enjoy economic benefits in the form of tax incentives and reliefs. Income tax exemptions are allowed for a period of at least three years. There is a provision for income tax exemption on profits if they are retained in a reserve fund and reinvested within one year. Expatriates are subject to the same income tax as Myanmar citizens.

Under Chapter 10 of the Foreign Investment Law, foreign investors have the following rights:

(i) Accelerated depreciation in respect of machinery, equipment, buildings, or other capital assets used in the business (Paragraph 21c).
(ii) Deduction of expatriates' income payable to the state from the assessable income (Paragraph 21e).
(iii) Deduction of research and development expenses carried out in Myanmar from the assessable income (Paragraph 21g).
(iv) The carry forward and offset of losses for up to three consecutive years from the year in which the loss is sustained and within two

---

2 Myanmar, Union of Myanmar Foreign Investment Law – Procedures and types of economic activities allowed for foreign investment, January 1995.

years immediately following the enjoyment of exemption of relief from income tax (Paragraph 21h).

There is also provision for relief from income tax of up to 50% on the profits from the exports of the company (Paragraph 21d). Furthermore, exemptions on import duties and other internal taxes are provided for imported machinery, equipment, materials, and so forth, during the period of construction, and in the case of raw materials, for the first three years of operation after the construction (Paragraph 21, i, and j).

The new law also guarantees that no enterprise is nationalised during the term of contract or during an extended term (Paragraph 22 of Chapter 11).

ECONOMIC PLAN

In an effort to stimulate the economy, a short-term economic plan was drawn up in 1992, covering the period 1992–93 to 1995–96. Its main aims are to step up production and exports so as to achieve rapid economic recovery and to speed up the development process. Priority is given to the development of productive sectors such as agriculture, livestock and fishery. Emphasis is also placed on enhancing manufacturing, mining and energy production by more effective utilisation of current capacities. A series of reforms have been implemented in these sectors over the last six years to transform the economy into a free-market system.

Need for an Overall Long-term Economic Plan

The Foreign Investment Law appears to be a short-term measure designed to obtain "quick returns" in foreign exchange rather than as a basis for a long-term plan to attract foreign direct investment from which the country can benefit through the transfer of technology, managerial and marketing skills. A long-term industrialisation plan seems lacking.

One result of the short-term plan, which allows the exploitation of natural resources, has been the selling of rights to extract resources such as fishery and forestry products. The government started conducting operations in these areas with Thai, Japanese, Malaysian, Singaporean and Korean partners soon after the Foreign Investment Law was promulgated. Selling fishing and logging rights may be a quick way of earning foreign currency, but there is a danger of draining the country's resources if systematic controls and management procedures are not in place. The short-term plan may not attract much substantial foreign investment until Myanmar's long-term plans are clearer.

Need for Better Incentives

Myanmar faces keen competition from neighbouring countries which also are trying to attract foreign investors. Table 12–1 summarises and compares the incentives offered to investors in South-east Asia and China. Those offered by Myanmar are quite attractive but some countries seem to have more to offer. For example, the tax incentive appears to be less attractive in Myanmar than in China or Cambodia. Myanmar offers a tax holiday of three years starting from the commencement date while China offers a tax holiday of two years starting from the first profit-making year and, thereafter, a 50% tax reduction for the following three years. Cambodia offers tax holidays of up to eight years. Myanmar may have to provide more than its competitors in order to attract more foreign investors.

Need for Reduction in Bureaucracy

Under the present trade regime, there has been a considerable increase in the number of local and foreign companies. However, their activities are limited by restrictions, regulations, bureaucratic hurdles and "discretionary measures" (Mya Than, 1993). Control may increase further following the report of a government Commission set up to review the investment environment. The Commission has recommended that foreign companies and joint ventures have to work with the state bank or the state insurance company. Such restrictions could send a message to potential foreign investors that SLORC intends to practise extensive control and active participation in the economy.

Need to Reconcile Official and Unofficial Exchange Rates

The Foreign Investment Law states that foreign currency shall be transferred at the prevailing official rate of exchange (Paragraph 26 of Chapter 13). This definitely has an adverse effect on potential foreign

TABLE 12–1
Summary of Comparative Investment Incentives

Investment Incentives	PRC	Lao PDR	Vietnam	Cambodia	Myanmar	Indonesia	Malaysia	Philippines	Singapore	Thailand
Basic rights and guarantees										
Guarantee against expropriation	x	x	x		x	x	x	x	x	x
Guarantee against losses due to:										
a. Nationalisation	x	x	x	x	x	x	x		x	x
b. Damage caused by war	x					x	x			
c. Inconvertibility of currency		x	x			x	x		x	
Remittance of foreign exchange earnings and payments	x	x	x	x	x	x	x	x	x	x
Repatriation of capital	x	x	x	x	x	x	x	x	x	x
Protection schemes and priorities given to investors and aliens										
Employment of aliens	x		x		x	x	x	x	x	x
Patent protection	x					x	x	x	x	x
Government loan preference							x	x	x	x
Protection against unjust competition										
a. Import competition						x	x	x		x
b. Government competition								x		x
c. Local competition						x		x		x
Real estate ownership by aliens	x	x					x		x	x

TABLE 12–1 (cont'd)

Investment Incentives	PRC	Lao PDR	Vietnam	Cambodia	Myanmar	Indonesia	Malaysia	Philippines	Singapore	Thailand
Exemptions from taxes and tariffs										
Capital gains tax	x		x	x	x		x	x		x
Corporate income tax	x		x	x	x	x	x		x	x
Taxes on imported capital goods	x		x	x	x	x	x	x		x
Taxes on imported raw materials	x		x	x	x	x	x	x	x	x
Taxes on royalties	x		x		x		x		x	x
Withholding tax on interest on foreign loans (tax credit)	x		x	x			x		x	x
Other taxes and fees	x		x	x	x	x	x	x	x	x
Deductions from taxable corporate income										
Accelerated depreciation allowance	x				x	x	x		x	x
Carry forward of capital allowance during relief period					x		x	x	x	
Carry forward of loss	x				x	x	x	x	x	x
Export allowance/deductions					x		x	x	x	x
Deduction of organisation expenses	x				x		x	x		x
Deduction of preoperating expenses	x				x			x		x
Deduction of reinvested profits			x	x	x			x		
Investment allowance						x	x		x	

TABLE 12–1 (cont'd)

Investment Incentives	PRC	Lao PDR	Vietnam	Cambodia	Myanmar	Indonesia	Malaysia	Philippines	Singapore	Thailand
Tax credits										
Investment tax credits							x		x	
Tax credit on domestic capital equipment							x	x		
Other tax credits	x						x	x		x
Extension of Incentive availment period	x		x	x	x		x		x	
Special Incentives										
To multinational companies								x		
To exporters	x		x		x		x	x	x	x
To offshore banking units							x	x	x	
Other laws granting benefits to foreign investors	x	x	x		x		x	x	x	x
Assistance to Investors										
Joint venture brokerage	x	x	x		x	x	x	x	x	x
Technical assistance	x						x	x	x	x
Application/other requirement processing	x	x	x	x	x	x	x	x	x	x

Sources: 1. Mya Than, "The Union of Burma Foreign Investment Law – Prospects of mobilising foreign capital for development?", in *Myanmar Dilemmas and Options, The Challenges of Economic Transition in the 1990s.*

2. Asian Development Bank, *Subregional Economic Cooperation – Initial Possibilities for Cambodia, Lao PDR, Myanmar, Thailand, Vietnam and Yunnan Province of the People's Republic of China*, February 1993.

x = Applies in this country.

investors. The official rate currently stands at 6 kyats to US$1 while the unofficial rate can reach 120 kyats to US$1. The kyat, therefore, is overvalued 20 times. This has led to a dual currency economy which causes price distortion and inflation. Foreign investors constantly face major currency headaches.

With the official exchange rate, Myanmar domestic wages offer no comparative advantage over neighbouring countries which export the same commodities. Local manufacturers find that they are not protected because of the low "real" import duty. Thus, it becomes more profitable to import instead of investing in manufacturing. The currency overvaluation is a serious drawback to trade and adjustments are necessary to eliminate the hindrances that it constitutes to the expansion of trade. If there is to be an "official" exchange rate, then it must be a market responsive rate.

Need for Clarification of Ambiguous Terminologies and Sentences

In stating the basic principles for foreign investments, the Law uses broad terms such as "heavy investment", "high technology" and "large capital" (Paragraph 4 of Chapter 3 of the Foreign Investment Law). These terms need to be defined in detail for foreign investors.

For example, in Vietnam, the term "transferred technology" is defined in Article 41 of the Decrees for the Implementation of the Law on Foreign Investment in Vietnam as follows:

(i) The technology transferred to a joint venture shall be one necessary and suitable for the joint venture to produce significant socio-economic effects or to increase the competitive strength of its products in the international market;

(ii) The transferred technology has to meet one of the following requirements:
  - (a) it must be capable of bringing about a considerable improvement in the appearance and quality of products and an increase in output;
  - (b) it must be capable of creating new products which Vietnam urgently needs or of producing import substitutes; and
  - (c) its application will result in a considerable saving in terms of raw materials and energy.

In Paragraph 6(b) of Chapter 4 of the Myanmar Foreign Investment Law, it states that the enterprise is subject to other existing laws of the state without spelling out which laws apply. This needs to be clarified since investors want to know whether extensive bureaucratic processes are involved in investing in Myanmar. In addition, the Investment Law does not specify priority sectors for foreign investors, although it can be deduced that extraction export and high technology industries would be given priority.

The reason for such ambiguities could be because the law was promulgated too soon after the SLORC took power. On one hand, it may be that the coverage is unspecific and wide in order to permit flexibility when assessing foreign capital projects. On the other hand, it leaves too much room for interpretation by potential foreign investors.

The issue of notifications[3] seems to be the answer to clarifying the law. Although they are at the bottom of the hierarchy of laws, they have been extensively used in the past few years since the promulgation of the Foreign Investment Law to make important additions (see Appendix 12–2). Our impression is that the government is positive and prepared to consider any proposal for foreign joint ventures that will benefit the country. Even if they are controlled presently under Section 3 of the State-owned Economic Enterprise Law, the government certainly is able to enact new laws and/or prescribe procedures via notifications to support their implementation. What is desired, however, is the attachment of a list of relevant notifications to the Foreign Investment Law and, also, a list of the places where the law can be purchased.

Need for Reconciliation Between Objectives and Realistic Possibilities

One of the objectives of the Foreign Investment Law is to seek high technology investment. However, for a country like Myanmar which currently has a low skilled labour force, it may not have the technical base necessary to support such investments. It is also unlikely that

---

[3] A notification is an Administrative Order issued by a Ministry or sometimes by a Directorate. They are empowered to do so by either rules or inherent powers of an organisation. Sometimes, the legislature issues such notification and in these cases it has the status of laws. This is an extract from a telefacsimile message of 30 June 1995 from Dr. Tun Shin, Legal Advisor to the Ministry of National Planning and Economic Development, in response to our queries of 26 June 1995.

foreign companies with advanced technology will invest in Myanmar rather than Singapore or other neighbouring countries that have a more established technical base. In addition, with the inadequate infrastructural support, foreign companies would seem better off in neighbouring countries that have better support utilities. Thus, Myanmar has to reassess its objectives in view of the current situation.

Liberal Formation of Organisation

Potential foreign investors will have to grapple with the decision as to what type of organisation they should register. Should they enter the market as sole proprietor, wholly-owned subsidiary, joint venture or something else? Presently, Singapore's investments in Myanmar are in the form of joint ventures, wholly-owned subsidiaries and representative offices. Most of them are on a joint venture basis (see Table 12–2). We recommend that potential investors from Singapore first explore the possibility of joint ventures because local partners provide the benefit of familiarity with their own environment including culture, social and financial variables. This intimate knowledge of local conditions facilitates the smooth running of business operations.

TABLE 12–2
Types of Foreign Investment in Myanmar by Singapore Investors (As of 31 August 1992)

Type	No. of Projects	Foreign Capital
Wholly foreign-owned enterprise	5	N.A.
Joint venture with:		
a. State enterprises	19	N.A.
b. Private/semi-private enterprises	3	N.A.
c. Cooperative societies	1	N.A.
Production sharing enterprises	20	N.A.
Total	48	N.A.

Source: Asian Development Bank, *Subregional Economic Cooperation – Initial Possibilities for Cambodia, Lao PDR, Myanmar, Thailand, Vietnam and Yunnan Province of the People's Republic of China*, February 1993.

It is beneficial to foreign investors if the joint venture partner is a state enterprise since exemptions from compliance with some of the provisions of the Myanmar Companies Act can be requested. For instance, one can pay the tax on the proceeds of sales in local currency rather than in foreign currency. Moreover, it will be easier to seek assistance from other ministries should foreign investors encounter any obstacles, as the directors of the state enterprise will have good connections or rapport with these ministries. While foreign investors are not allowed to invest in certain industries (see Section 3 of the State-owned Economic Enterprise Law in Appendix 12–1) such as the extraction of teak, pearls, jade and precious stones, a ministry may allow foreign investors to invest in these industries as empowered under Section 8(6) of the Myanmar Companies Act. These privileges are not given to foreign investors if the joint venture partner is not a state enterprise.

Foreign investors unable to find any suitable local partner can invest by setting up a wholly-owned subsidiary on the condition that the return from this investment is high. However, should the risks be too great in terms of the high costs of investment, establishment of a representative office might be considered.

Proposed Amendments to the Myanmar Companies Act

In order to enhance the investment climate in Myanmar, the following amendments to the Myanmar Companies Act are proposed:

(i) **Minimum Amount of Capital:** Any amount of investment that is brought in by foreign investors should be encouraged. Thus, Section 3 of the Myanmar Companies Act entitled "Minimum Amount of Capital" should be abolished. By doing so, it will generate more investment flow into the country.

(ii) **Submission of Financial Statements:** It is stipulated in Section 3 of the Application Procedure that foreign investors need to submit the financial statements of the company for the last two years. This implies that the government is only interested in companies that are well-established in the market. This section may prevent individuals with great entrepreneurial skill and business ideas from establishing their businesses in Myanmar. Thus, the government may forego some excellent potential investments.

It can be argued that these two requirements by the Myanmar government are to prevent unscrupulous foreign investors from exploiting the current burgeoning economy. By doing so, the government probably is assured that foreign investors are committed and are able to meet their financial requirements.

Reduce the Duration for Registration of Companies

Assuming all documents are in order, it takes about one month to complete the registration of a company.[4] Perhaps the time taken to approve the registration could be reduced to less than one month as this may deter foreign investments. This can be done by reviewing the application procedures and the necessity of requiring certain information from the investors.

CONCLUSION

From the issues raised here, Myanmar should seek investments in low technology, export-oriented, and labour-intensive industries that are no longer available in high income countries, such as Singapore, where labour costs are high. Some multinational companies, as well as local companies, are moving out of Singapore. Myanmar has a competitive advantage in terms of wages. Employment opportunities are greater in low technology than in high technology investments. Myanmar could produce consumer goods to substitute imports which are presently consuming the country's limited foreign exchange. There seems to be a huge market for consumer goods like televisions, washing machines and refrigerators. Perhaps it would be wise to encourage foreign investors to produce such goods, using the large pool of labour, rather than seeking high technology investments which currently seem to be beyond the means of Myanmar.

It is also the desire of every developing country to accelerate the pace of development once its doors are opened. Myanmar, with the promulgation of flexible foreign investment laws, must give equal attention to any foreign investment proposal which promises the longer term objectives of transfer and training of skills to people in the technical, productivity, quality and management areas. However, this must be done in tandem with the political need to create employment

---

4 This is an extract from a telefacsimile message of 30 June 1995 from Dr. Tun Shin, Legal Advisor to the Ministry of National Planning and Economic Development in response to our queries of 26 June 1995.

and wealth in the country. This may not result in immediate short-term returns in foreign exchange since there is little likelihood that the country can leapfrog into high technology industry.

APPENDIX 12–1
List of Activities Restricted Under Section 3 of State-Owned Economic Enterprises Law

(i) Extraction of teak and sale of the same.
(ii) Cultivation and conservation of forest plantations.
(iii) Exploration, extraction and sale of petroleum and natural gas.
(iv) Exploration and extraction of pearls, jade and precious stones.
(v) Breeding and production of fish and prawns.
(vi) Postal and telecommunications services.
(vii) Air and railway transport services.
(viii) Banking and insurance services.
(ix) Exploration and extraction of metals and export of the same.
(x) Electricity generating services other than those permitted by law.
(xi) Manufacturing of products relating to security and defence prescribed by notifications.

APPENDIX 12–2
List of Notifications

Two important notifications relating to the Foreign Investment Law include:

(i) Notification No. 11/88 issued by the government for the formation of the Union of Myanmar Foreign Investment Commission and which prescribes the procedures relating to the Union of Myanmar Foreign Investment Law (7 December 1988).
(ii) Notification No. 1/89 issued by the Foreign Investment Commission which published the types of economic activities allowed for foreign investment (30 May 1989).

Other laws and notifications relating to foreign investment promulgated in the past few years are as follows:

(i) The State-owned Economic Enterprises Law 31 March 1989, identifies areas of economic activity that will be solely undertaken by the state. However, Section 4 provides for the formation of joint ventures between the state economic enterprises and local or foreign entrepreneurs or organisations for reserved activities beneficial to Myanmar.
(ii) Rules relating to the State-Owned Economic Enterprises Law, Notification No. 15/89, 6 December 1989.
(iii) The Private Industrial Enterprises Law, 1990, which aims to consolidate and promote large, medium and small scale private industries.
(iv) Procedures Relating to the Private Industrial Enterprise Law, Notification No. 23/91, issued by the Ministry of No. 1 Industry, 1 February 1991.
(v) Myanmar Hotels and Tourism Law, 23 October 1993, aims to promote and develop the hotel and tourism industry and to generate foreign exchange earnings from such services.
(vi) Procedures relating to the Myanmar Tourism Law, Notification No. 36/90, issued by the Ministry of Trade 31 December 1990.

REFERENCES

Doing Business in Myanmar – The Myanmar Companies Act Provisions Relative to a Foreign Company, 2nd Edition. Ministry of Trade, Singapore, June 1990, p. 22.

Duncan Freeman, "The life and death of a joint venture in China", *Asia Law and Practice*, August 1994.

"Investment in Myanmar (Burma): Obstacle Course", *Business Asia*, 14 March 1994.

Mya Than, "The Union of Burma Foreign Investment Law – Prospects of Mobilising Foreign Capital for Development", in *Myanmar Dilemmas And Options, The Challenges of Economic Transition in the 1990s*, eds. Mya Than and Joseph L.H. Tan. Asean Economic Research Unit, Institute of South East Asian Studies, 1990.

Mya Than, "Myanmar Places its Bets on the Free Market Economy", *Business Times*, August 1993.

Myat Thein, "Socio-economic and Cultural Background of Myanmar", Seminar Paper, MBA Business Study Mission to Myanmar, 16 June 1995.

San Khup, "Macro-Economic Policies with Special Emphasis on Infrastructural Development", Seminar Paper, MBA Business Study Mission to Myanmar, 16 June 1995.

Chapter 13

The Accounting Environment in Myanmar*

BY
Jasmine KOH
LEK Lee Eng
Sujata RAMAKRISHAN
AW Kah Wai

INTRODUCTION

THE OBJECTIVE OF this chapter is to provide potential investors with a comprehensive insight into the five main aspects of Myanmar's accounting environment namely, accounting regulation, corporate reporting, audit practices, accounting firms and professional development.

Regulatory power is vested with two bodies: the Registry of Companies (pursuant to the Myanmar Companies Act) and the Myanmar Accountancy Council (pursuant to the Myanmar Accountancy Council Law). The former also controls the disclosure requirements for financial reporting. Presently, there are no official Myanmar accounting standards. The primary sources of accounting principles are the United Kingdom and international accounting bodies. Although it is mandatory for companies to have audits, there are no official auditing standards

* We wish to thank Mr. Yap Chee Meng, Partner, KPMG Peat Marwick; Mr. Reggie Thein, Partner, Coopers & Lybrand; Daw Theingi Tin, Registrar of Companies, Myanmar; U Tin Win, U Tin Win Group, Myanmar; Mr. Cheah E Fun, Managing Director, Myanmar-Inotech Ltd.; and U Saw Thein, General Manager, Myanmar-Inotech Ltd.

and guidelines. Generally, practice appears to follow the British and the U.S. standards.

Currently, foreigners and foreign accounting firms are prohibited from practising in Myanmar. However, in line with the increasing number of Singapore firms investing in Myanmar, most of the "Big Six" international firms have established a referral service with local accounting firms in Myanmar. This aligns financial reporting with Singapore's standards and facilitates consolidation of accounts.

Information on the status of accounting was obtained from a wide range of sources including the Registry of Companies, the Myanmar Accountancy Council, public accounting firms, commercial firms and academics. Extensive interviews were held with selected representatives from each of these sources in an effort to have investors understand the present accounting practices and regulations in Myanmar.

THE ACCOUNTING REGULATORY FRAMEWORK

The Registry of Companies is an organisation within the Ministry of National Planning and Economic Development (see Figure 13–1). It is responsible for the administration of the Myanmar Companies Act of 1914 (subsequently amended), which is based on the Indian Act VII of 1913 (adopted from the United Kingdom). The Myanmar Companies Act was established to regulate the creation, operation and reporting requirements of companies in Myanmar. The Registrar of Companies is vested with the power to charge any person found guilty of non-compliance with the requirements of the Act.

The Myanmar Accountancy Council plays the role of "watchdog" and works towards the advancement of accountancy in Myanmar. Members of the Council are appointed by the government. The structure of the Council is shown in Table 13–1.

The Council was formed under the Myanmar Accountancy Council Law, 1972 (subsequently amended). Its role includes giving advice to government departments on matters concerning accounting; conducting, managing and supervising training courses in accounting; and taking action against public accountants who are negligent in their duties or violate the code of professional ethics. The Council also issues the Certified Public Accountant (CPA) certificate to candidates passing the CPA examinations and completing their apprenticeship service.

FIGURE 13–1
The Regulatory Framework

State Law and Order Restoration Council
|
Ministry of National Planning and Economic Development
|
Directorate of Investment and Company Administration
|
Registry of Companies

State Law and Order Restoration Council
|
Auditor General
|
Myanmar Accountancy Council

TABLE 13–1
Structure of Myanmar Accountancy Council

Position	Role
The Auditor General.	Chairman
Citizen members of the accountancy profession, not exceeding ten in number.	Members
Suitable citizens, not exceeding four in number.	Members
A person assigned by the Chairman.	Secretary

The Myanmar Accountancy Council is not a standard setting body. At present, Myanmar has not established any accounting standards. However, plans are being made to set up a professional accounting body (very much like the ICPAS in Singapore) in 1996. This body will consider the formulation of accounting standards and maintain an appropriate standard of reporting for companies operating in Myanmar.

DISCLOSURE REQUIREMENTS FOR CORPORATE REPORTING

The Myanmar Companies Act

Based on the regulatory framework outlined above, the financial reporting requirements for companies operating in Myanmar are laid down in the Myanmar Companies Act. Some of the major features are outlined below.

Maintenance of Records

A company incorporated under the Act is required to maintain proper accounts in respect of:

(a) all sums of money received and paid;
(b) all sales and purchases of goods; and
(c) all assets and liabilities.

The books of the accounts shall be kept at the registered office of the company or at such other place as the directors think fit, and shall be open to inspection by the directors during business hours (Section 130). The company must also maintain registers of:

(a) members;
(b) directors, managers and managing agents;
(c) charges to record the assets; and
(d) debentures.

Preparation and Reporting of Annual Statutory Accounts

The Act also details the disclosure requirements of the statutory accounts which generally follow the United Kingdom. A summary of the capital and liabilities of the company, disclosing particulars of liabilities and assets and how the value of the assets have been determined, is required. The balance sheet is to be in the form marked F in the Third Schedule of the Act. The profit and loss account is to include details of remuneration paid to directors and agents, bad debts, depreciation and provision for taxation, among others. The financial statements must be accompanied by a director's report and an auditor's report (Section 132).

Annual general meetings (AGM) must be held within 18 months of incorporation and, subsequently, once every year at intervals not exceeding 15 months. All public companies must send a copy of the balance sheet and profit and loss account, with a copy of the auditor's report, to the registered address of every member of the company at least 14 days before the AGM. Directors of the company are required to present a balance sheet and profit and loss account at the AGM (Section 131).

Within 21 days after the AGM, all public companies are required to file an annual return with the Registrar of Companies (ROC). This return must set forth:

(a) the meeting date of the AGM;
(b) details of the capital structure of the company;
(c) a list of the amount due on mortgages;
(d) information on shareholders; and
(e) a list of directors and managers.

It is not a legal requirement for private companies to submit their accounts to the ROC. However, since the profit and loss statement is prepared for income tax purposes, private companies are encouraged to file their statements with the ROC on a voluntary basis.[1]

Presentation of Financial Statements

The presentation of financial statements is prescribed under the Companies Act. As mentioned earlier, there are no official standards in Myanmar, unlike Singapore, which officially adopts its Statements of Accounting Standards (SAS) from International Accounting Standards (IAS). Foreign enterprises and joint ventures usually adopt the standards of their country of origin.[2]

Currency

All figures in the accounts must be quoted in kyats. Each asset, liability, revenue or cost resulting from a transaction denominated in foreign

---

1 Source: Daw Theingi Tin, Registrar of Companies, June 1995.
2 Source: U Tin Win, June 1995.

currency is to be recorded in kyat at the official rate in effect on the date the transaction occurred. Monetary assets and liabilities are translated using the closing rate on the balance sheet date.

Accounting Year

The Income Tax Law requires all accounts to be completed by 31 March of each year. Thus, the financial year is from 1 April to 31 March.

Language

The financial statements can be written in English or Burmese.

Foreign Branch Companies

Foreign branch companies are required to file the following information with the registrar annually:

(a) the balance sheet of the head office incorporated outside Myanmar;
(b) a statement of share-holding by shareholders' nationality; and
(c) other supplementary statements if required.

Joint Venture with State-Owned Companies

Copies of the financial statements must be sent to the relevant government ministries and departments. For example, Myanmar-Inotech submits quarterly statements to the Ministry.

Income Tax Law

All financial statements, together with the income tax return, must be submitted to the Internal Revenue Department (under the Ministry of Finance) by 30 June of each year.

The Dual Currency Problem

As of June 1995, the official exchange rate was US$1 to 6 kyats while the open market exchange rate was around US$1 to 100 kyats. The huge disparity between the official and open-market rate has serious ramifications for financial reporting. For example, U.S. capital brought into the country as an initial investment would be understated when converted to kyats at the official rate. Thus, a major currency translation adjustment is usually required when consolidating the accounts of a Myanmar subsidiary with the parent company's accounts.

Some companies maintain two sets of books, one in kyats for statutory reporting and the other in U.S. dollars for reporting to the parent company. For example, one major CPA firm[3] adopts the practice of converting expenses in U.S. dollars to kyats using the official rate while converting expenses in kyats using the open-market rate. This prevents the U.S. dollar reports from being distorted.

For a trading company, the distortion normally is corrected if the trading cycle (i.e., both the import and export cycle) is completed within the reporting period. To illustrate, imports converted at the official rate would understate the cost of sales, but this is offset by the understated export sales in the same year. Thus, the net impact of the dual currency problem on the bottom line profit figure is minimised.

Can the objective of financial reporting in Myanmar be said to be firm-oriented (i.e., to present a "true and fair" view of the firm) or macroeconomic oriented (i.e., tax-driven)?

Due to the dual exchange rate system, some companies believe that the financial statements are not meaningful from their perspective because they merely satisfy statutory and tax requirements. However, this view may change with the increased inflow of foreign investments and the planned establishment of an international stock exchange. These factors may lead to the unification of the official and open-market exchange rates. It is likely that the development of formal accounting standards and audit requirements may follow.

AUDIT PRACTICES

Under Section 131 of the Companies Act, all incorporated companies are required to have their accounts audited. An auditor practising in Myanmar must be a Certified Public Accountant and a practising accountant.[4] Only citizens who are registered as qualified accountants are eligible for an audit licence which authorises them to perform

---

3 Source: U Tin Win, June 1995.

4 Source: The Myanmar Accountancy Council Law.

statutory audits. The audit licence has a duration of one year and must be renewed annually. Most auditors in Myanmar do not form partnerships and they usually practise on a proprietorship basis. Therefore, they sign accounts in their own names. Though the usual trend is for auditors to work alone, most of the groups handling the large accounts of joint ventures and foreign subsidiaries have tended to form partnerships because of the excessive workload involved in the audit. But these partnerships are restricted to the larger audit firms.

There are no official auditing standards and guidelines. Auditing practices conform with those in Britain and the U.S. as a rule.

Appointment of Auditors

Under the Companies Act, every company must appoint one or more auditors, qualified for appointment under the Myanmar *Accountancy* Council Law, to report to the shareholders on the company's financial statements. The first auditor of the company must be appointed by the Board of Directors. Subsequent appointments must be made by members at the Annual General Meeting (Section 144). Where a state-owned enterprise[5] has an equity share in a company, the auditor is appointed by the Ministry of National Planning and Economic Development under the advice of the Auditor General.[6]

Audit Opinion

Under Section 145 of the Act, the auditor should express a "true and correct" view on the financial statements. This means that the accounts are checked 100%. This is more severe than the true and fair view practised in other countries such as Britain, the U.S. and Singapore. In Myanmar, the auditors must express an opinion on the following matters:

(i) whether or not they have obtained all the required information and explanations;
(ii) whether or not the balance sheet and the profit and loss account are drawn up in conformity with the provisions of the Myanmar Companies Act;

---

[5] A state-owned enterprise means the government has more than a 50% interest.
[6] Source: U Tin Win, June 1995.

(iii) whether or not the balance sheet and the profit and loss account exhibit a true and correct view of the company's affairs; and
(iv) whether the books of accounts have been properly kept by the company.

The requirement of a 100% check of the accounts and the expression of a "true and correct" view are followed for local accounts since the volume of transactions is not very large. In the case of joint ventures, there is a large number of transactions. Thus, auditors conduct test procedures on a sample and, therefore, only a "true and fair view" on the financial statements is expressed.

Extent of Interest in Client's Firm

To meet the postulates of integrity, objectivity and independence, an auditor should have limited interest (both financial and otherwise) in the client's business. Section 144(5) provides details on the extent of such interest so that independence is seen in appearance and in fact.

An audit file in the office of U Tin Win was examined to determine the documentation procedures and the audit procedures that were performed in an audit. The client was a foreign subsidiary of a company in Singapore. The accounts of the parent company are audited by a "Big Six" audit firm in Singapore. Audit procedures and documentation were carried out per the guidelines issued by the latter so as to facilitate consolidation. There is no standardised audit programme. However, the local accounting firm uses an informal checklist to make notes of the work done.

ACCOUNTING FIRMS

There are more than 20 local accounting firms in Myanmar and most of them are based in Yangon. Typically, the accounting firms have one or two practising accountants. Usually, account assistants are hired to ease the workload. The number of assistants varies with the time of year but it usually peaks around 31 March. An average accounting firm with about three partners employs approximately 30 to 40 audit assistants.

Of all the accounting firms, six major ones can be identified.[7] They are listed in descending order of size in Table 13–2. The Hla Tun Group is the firm most favoured by the government. It is often the nominated accounting firm for joint venture companies involving the government.[8] Investors entering into a joint venture arrangement with the Myanmar government are advised to retain the nominated accounting firm.

TABLE 13–2
Major Firms

Firm	Particulars
Hla Tun Group (Principal : Hla Tun)	53/55 Maha Bandoola Garden Street Yangon P.O. Box 175 Tel: 71495 or 72810 Fax: 86744
Tin Win Group	97, 36th Street Kyauktada Township Yangon Tel: 78596 Fax: 96755 or 26979
Khin Su Htay	615R Pyay Road Kamayut, Yangon Tel: 30416
Win Thin	161 Konzeolan Street (1st Floor) Yangon Tel: 73417
Finance Accounting Management and Trading Co. (Principal : U Kyee Myaint)	444 Strand Road Lanmadaw, Yangon Tel: 75772 or 81008
Daw San Aye	No. 9 Sunaram Park Yangon Tel: 58914

Section 12 of the Myanmar Accountancy Council Law of 1972, prohibits foreigners and foreign accounting firms from operating in Myanmar. In view of this restriction, most international accounting firms have established, or are in the process of establishing, a referral service with local accounting firms in Myanmar. The referral service allows

7 Source: Daw Theingi Tin (Registrar of Companies), June 1995.
8 Source: U Saw Thien, General Manager, Myanmar-Inotech Ltd., June 1995.

foreign-based firms in Myanmar to be audited by a preferred Myanmar accountant. Table 13–3 shows some of the international accounting firms and their corresponding affiliated Myanmar accounting firms.

TABLE 13–3
Local Affiliations

Local Firm	International Firm
Hla Tun Group	Coopers and Lybrand Arthur Anderson
Khin Su Htay	Peat Marwick
Tin Win Group	Ernst and Young

Apart from auditing, the major accounting firms in Myanmar provide tax, bookkeeping and consultancy services. Table 13–4 shows typical audit fees charged by the major accounting firms.[9] On average, it takes about one month to audit a medium-sized firm.

TABLE 13–4
Structure of Audit Fees

Size of Client	Local	Foreign
Small Firm	K5,000	US$1,000
Medium-sized firm	K30,000-50,000	Partner: US$300/hr.
Large-sized firm	K100,000	Assistants: US$150/hr.

PROFESSIONAL DEVELOPMENT

The Myanmar Accountancy Council (MAC) is the professional accounting body in Myanmar. As of 1994, available data shows 198 registered members. Out of this membership, 73% are in public

9 Source: U Tin Win and Tin Win Group, June 1995.

accounting and 27% are from government, academia, commercial, industrial and other sources.[10]

Entrance into the accounting profession is strictly controlled by the authorities. At Yangon University, only the top 100 graduates from the Bachelor of Commerce degree programme are eligible for training to become an accountant.[11] Graduates who elect to enter the accounting profession are required to serve two years of internship (articleship) either with the Central Accounts Office (the accounts office of the government) or with a local accounting firm. Upon completion, one must pass the Registered Accountant examination administered by the MAC.

The Myanmar Accountancy Law of 1994 stipulates the conditions under which a person may apply for registration as a Certified Public Accountant:

(i) A person must be a Myanmar citizen, and
(ii) possesses an accountancy certificate or a degree in accountancy from an overseas university recognised by the MAC, or
(iii) have obtained a pass in the Registered Accountant examination and completed the articleship, or
(iv) be registered as an accountant under the Myanmar *Accountancy Law* of 1972.

In order to become a practising accountant, one must apply to the MAC for a Certificate of Practice after registering as a Certified Public Accountant.

The salary of a practising accountant working for a local accounting firm is approximately US$300 to US$500 per month. A management accountant working for a local firm earns between US$50 to US$150 per month.[12] An accountant working with the government earns between US$30 to US$40 per month. However, this low salary often is offset by other incentives such as free housing and transportation.

---

[10] Source: Foo See Liang, *Survey of the Accounting Profession and Practices in East Asia*, Nanyang Technological University, School of Accountancy and Business, December 1994.

[11] Source: Daw Khin Thein Yi, Professor and Head of Department, Department of Applied Economics, Institute of Economics, Yangon University, June 1995.

[12] Source: U Tin Win and Tin Win Group, June 1995.

The ethics, duties and rights of an accountant are prescribed by the Myanmar Accountancy Law of 1994. The duties of the practising accountant are stipulated under Section 18, professional ethics under Section 19, and rights under Section 20. The law is enforced by the MAC.

Of interest under Section 19, are several issues involving the professional ethics of a practising accountant. First, such a person is prohibited from advertising directly or indirectly and soliciting accountancy work. Secondly, demanding fees based on a percentage of profits is prohibited. Third, duties must be performed with due professional care.

Non-compliance with the law is punishable. A three-member inquiry committee investigates conduct. A five-member disciplinary committee passes judgement based on the findings of the inquiry committee. The punishment ranges from a formal warning to cancellation of the Certificate of Practice.

One may file an appeal to the council within sixty days from the date on which judgement is passed by the disciplinary committee. The Council may confirm, set aside or alter the judgement passed by the disciplinary committee, or order a new inquiry. Any judgement made by the Council is final and conclusive.

SUMMARY AND CONCLUSION

Overall, the accounting environment in Myanmar is simple. The existing accounting infrastructure is based on colonial practices. Over the years, not much has been done by way of amendments and there have been no official promulgations. There are broad guidelines in place with respect to the accounting framework but specific accounting requirements are absent. As stated earlier, international accounting standards and auditing standards are followed as a matter of general practice.

The impetus for formalising and establishing a comprehensive accounting framework might arise from several factors. First, the increased exposure and influx of foreign companies into Myanmar may create the demand. Second, increased foreign investment and the establishment of a stock exchange requires the development of formal accounting standards. Third, international public accounting firms that have formed strategic alliances with local accounting firms may influence change. Finally, foreign companies require effective controls and standard auditing procedures.

Public accountants currently in Myanmar, especially those in the larger accounting firms, are highly educated and have been involved in accounting and auditing practices along international lines. However, they represent the older generation in Myanmar. The younger generation, on the other hand, lacks international exposure and understanding due to the closed-door policies of the last three decades. There is much that remains to be done to educate and provide the younger generation of CPAs with the requisite tools to compete in the global arena.

Chapter 14

Business Ventures in Myanmar: Taxes and Economic Incentives

BY
A. Kumara PATHY
Raymond KOK Seng Hun
LIM Chwee Heng

INTRODUCTION

THE PROMULGATION OF the Myanmar Foreign Investment Law (FIL) in November 1988 ushered in a new era, with the ultimate aim of improving the economy.

This chapter provides an overview of taxes related to doing business in Myanmar and the incentives that are offered through the FIL. The taxes can be classified into income tax, profit tax and commercial tax.

Income tax is applicable to all incomes while profit tax deals with other profits not covered by the income tax. The commercial tax is a form of consumption tax. It is applicable to imported or domestically produced goods and to services such as entertainment, restaurants and others. In addition, there are also stamp duties, lottery duties and so forth.

As far as tax incentives are concerned, the main source is the FIL. It is intended to boost the economic level of the country and is tailored around export-oriented business activities. The benefits range from tax holidays of up to three years for earned income to exemption on customs duty, and lower tax rates payable for foreign employees. To qualify for the benefits, investments must involve at least one of the following: promotion and expansion of exports, exploitation of natural resources, acquisition of high technology, support and assistance of production, or services involving heavy capital and regional development.

TAXATION IN MYANMAR

Myanmar income tax law is set forth in the Income Tax Law of 1974 and supplementary legislation. Other principal taxes are prescribed in separate legislation including the Profit Tax Law of 1976, the Commercial Tax Law of 1990, amendment of the Commercial Tax Law of 1991, the Myanmar Stamp Act of 1935, and the Court Fee Act of 1937. New legislation or proposals to amend existing legislation may be approved by the State Law and Order Restoration Council.

The Internal Revenue Department, which is under the Ministry of Finance and Revenue, administers one direct tax via the commercial tax and four indirect taxes: income tax; profit tax; the state lottery; and stamp duties.

INCOME TAX

Scope

This tax is applicable to profits and gains from business activities. The profit of a trade or business generally means the surplus created when receipts exceed expenditures. Under the tax law, a receipt may be taxable as income even though there is no element of profit or gain. The general rule is that all income is taxable unless expressly exempted.

Application of the Law

The income tax law applies to the following types of taxpayers and classes of income:

(a) State-economic enterprises;
(b) Cooperative societies;
(c) Foreigners and foreign organisations engaged under special permission in state sponsored enterprises;

(d) Income from salaries;
(e) Non-resident foreigners;
(f) Income earned abroad by non-resident citizens;
(g) Companies;
(h) Resident foreigners;
(i) Partnerships or joint ventures formed between, or with, (a), (b), (c), (e) and (h) above.

Resident Versus Non-resident

For income tax purposes, a foreigner or foreign organisation is classified into "resident" or "non-resident". A "resident foreigner" is defined as follows:

(i) In the case of an individual, a foreigner who lives in Myanmar for not less than 183 days during the year of assessment.
(ii) In the case of a company, a company formed under the Myanmar Companies Act or any other existing Myanmar law, wholly or partly, with foreign shareholders.
(iii) In the case of an association of persons other than a company, an association formed wholly or partly with foreigners and where control, management and decision-making of its affairs are situated and exercised wholly in the Union of Myanmar.

A foreigner or a foreign organisation not resident in Myanmar are classified as non-resident.

Tax Charge

A resident foreigner or a resident citizen is subject to tax on all worldwide income. In the case of an enterprise operating under the Foreign Investment Law, tax is payable only on income derived from sources within Myanmar. A non-resident foreigner is subject to tax on all income from sources within Myanmar at the rates specifically prescribed for non-residents.

The tax is charged on total income which can be from a profession, business, property or other sources disclosed or undisclosed. Income from salary and capital gains are assessed separately. In computing the net profit of a business, all expenditures incurred for the purpose of earning income, and the capital asset depreciation on plant, machinery, equipment, buildings, vehicles and furniture, can be used as deductions. The exceptions are capital expenditures, personal expenditures, expenditure and salary payments to non-income accruing activities.

Tax Rate

Net income, or net profit, after deducting permissible expenditures and allowances, is taxed at the rates shown in Table 14–1.

TABLE 14–1
Tax Rates for Different Incomes

Types of Taxpayer or Income	Tax rate
Companies formed in Myanmar under the Myanmar Companies Act or any other existing Myanmar law.	30 %
Income earned abroad by non-resident citizens.	10%
Income earned abroad by non-resident citizens remitted into Myanmar.	5%
Co-operative societies are taxed at progressive rates.	3%–30%
On income from "salaries" other than income of non-resident foreigners, the tax is computed as per Table 14–3.	3%–30%
Capital gains (No tax is payable on such gains where the value of sale, exchange or transfer of the capital asset does not exceed K50,000.)	10%
Capital gains for non-resident foreigners.	40%
On total income of non-resident foreigners (including non-resident foreign organisations such as a branch of a foreign company).	35%, or rate in Table 14–3, whichever is greater
State economic enterprise.	30%
Enterprise operating under the Myanmar Foreign Investment Law.	30%
Foreign organisations engaged under special permission in a state-sponsored project, enterprise or any undertaking.	30%
Individual foreigners engaged under special permission in a state-sponsored project, enterprise or any undertaking.	20%
Other income, including property income, business income, income from other sources and undeclared income.	3%–50%

Loss Offset

Where a taxpayer sustains a loss in a year for certain categories of income, other than capital gains, he is entitled to offset the loss against the profits of other income categories in that same year. No loss can be carried forward to the following year.

Shipping

A non-resident foreigner who carries on business as an owner, or as charterer of a ship, is liable to pay tax for each trip on income that accrues or arises in Myanmar. A rate of 5% of the total freight receipts earned for the carriage of passengers, livestock and goods from Myanmar ports, is deemed to be the net income and it is taxed at the rate applicable to non-resident foreigners. The master of the ship or the ship's agent, if there is an agent in Myanmar, then must file a return of income and pay taxes before the departure of the ship. A tax clearance certificate must be given to the Post Officer for such departures.

Summary on Income Tax

Income tax is a tax on profit and gains. It covers most income from business, professional activities and salaries. Foreign companies incorporated in Myanmar are treated as residents and taxed at the rate of 30% on income accruing or arising inside and outside Myanmar; in other words, tax is on worldwide income. However, firms incorporated overseas, and registered locally as branches, are treated as non-residents. Their income accruing and arising in Myanmar is taxed at the minimum non-resident rate of 35% or at graduated resident rates (3–50%), whichever yields the higher amount of tax (see Tables 14–2 and 14–3).

TABLE 14–2
Tax Rates for Residents

From (kyat)	To (kyat)	Tax Rate
1	5,000	3%
5,001	10,000	7%
10,001	20,000	10%
20,001	35,000	15%
35,001	50,000	20%
50,001	75,000	25%
75,001 and above		30%

Foreign businesses engaged in government projects are taxed at 30%, whereas foreign individuals engaged in government projects are taxed at 20%. Foreign individuals on salaried incomes are taxed from 3–50%. If the employer pays the employee's taxes, tax on a tax basis of assessment is adopted. Relatively speaking, resident status gives a better tax rate. For example, for capital gains, residents are taxed at 10% whereas non-residents are taxed at 40%. For an income of K50,000, the tax rate is 20% and 35% for residents and non-residents, respectively. At an income of K75,000 and above, it is 30% and 45–50% for residents and non-residents, respectively.

TABLE 14–3
Tax Rates for Non-resident Foreigners

From (kyat)	To (kyat)	Tax Rate
1	5,000	3%
5001	10,000	10%
10,001	15,000	15%
15,001	20,000	20%
20,001	30,000	25%
30,001	40,000	30%
40,001	50,000	35%
50,001	70,000	40%
70,001	100,000	45%
100,001	150,000	48%
150,001 and above		50%

PROFIT TAX

This tax also is considered as a tax on income. Taxable income that is not covered by the Income Tax Law is subject to tax under the Profit Tax Law.

Tax Rate

The minimum income subject to tax is K8,001. Taxes are payable according to income levels which range from 2.4–48.9%.

Capital Gains

Any person with taxable capital gains is required to file a return of income within one month of the sale, exchange or transfer of the capital asset. The assessment on capital gains must be made within the respective income year. The rate of tax is a flat 10% of the capital gain but the tax payable is not to exceed one-half of the amount remaining after deducting K50,000 from the value of the sale, exchange or transfer of the capital asset. No tax is payable if the value of the sale, exchange or transfer of the capital asset within a year is less than K50,000.

Summary on Profit Tax

Profit tax covers those cases that do not fall under the income tax category. Taxpayers are typically individuals who are resident citizens. The tax is charged for income above K8,000 and it is payable according to the income level. The assessment procedure is almost the same as that for income tax.

COMMERCIAL TAX

Application

The Commercial Tax Law was promulgated in March 1990 and replaced the Commodities and Service Tax Law. Certain items previously taxable under the Profit Tax Law (i.e., the import of goods, entertainment and production of salt) are now covered by the new Law instead of the Profit Tax Law. The new Law came into effect from the financial year 1990–91 and it applies to the public, co-operative and private sectors.

Charge of Tax

The commercial tax is a turnover tax levied on goods and services. This tax is charged on a wide range of goods, either domestically produced or manufactured, or imported into the country. Certain items of goods, mostly basic foods and raw materials, are exempt from tax. The types of services liable to tax include the transport of passengers, entertainment, trade and operation of hotels, lodgings, restaurants, cafes and foodstalls, and so forth.

Tax Rates

For the cooperative and private sectors, no tax is payable if the annual turnover is less than the amount not liable to tax. Tax is levied according to the schedules appended to the law. The rates of tax vary according to the types of goods and services (see Table 14–4).

TABLE 14–4
Tax Rates for Goods and Services

Types of Goods and Services	Tax Rates
Wheat grain, vegetable, animal feed, books, milk powder, petroleum and other basic daily requirements.	None
Ice, bread, grease, dyes, charcoal, chemical products, teak log, magazines, marble, sports equipment.	10%
Glassware, coffee powder, raw rubber, cotton goods, cement, construction materials, telecommunication equipment, plastic materials, commercial vehicles.	20%
Sweets, teak conversion, leather products, silk fabrics, passenger vehicles, office machinery, furniture, electrical appliances.	30%
Cigarettes, fuel/petrol, liquor, beer, pearls, jade and other precious stones.	60–225%
Railway and other land transport services, waterways, airways.	8%
Entertainment business.	15–30%
Trading business (purchase and sale of goods).	5%
Hotel, food and beverage businesses.	10%

With the exception of trade, tax is imposed as an ad valorem single-stage tax at the point of sale by the producer or manufacturer for domestically produced or manufactured goods, and at the point of import (collected together with customs duty) for imported goods.

Summary on Commercial Tax

A commercial tax is payable on goods imported or produced within Myanmar, trading, sales and services. Certain items of goods, mostly basic food and raw materials, are exempt from this tax. Tax rates on most imported and domestic goods range from zero to 30%. For other goods, like cigarettes, beer and wine, the tax goes up to 225%.

OTHER TAX CONSIDERATIONS

Import/Export Licence Fees

An import licence is required for all imports. Import licence fees range from K250 to K50,000 based on the assessable value of goods. An import licence has a validity of six months and it may be extended on payment of the prescribed fees. An export licence is required for exports. However, no export licence fees are payable except for the export of logs.

Customs Duties

Custom duties on imported goods are payable according to the Myanmar tariff schedules based on the assessable value of goods. The custom duties payable on imports are noted in Table 14–5.

TABLE 14–5
Custom Duties for Imported Goods

Types of Goods	Rates
Textiles.	5–300%
Machinery, instruments, apparatus and appliances.	15–75%
Transport equipment.	5–500%
General household articles.	50–200%

Under Section 23 of the Sea Customs Act, certain exemptions of duties are allowed by the state. For example, agricultural products, water pumps, pumping machinery, pipes and insecticides, are exempt from import tariffs with effect from January 1993.

In the case of joint ventures or firms set up under the foreign investment programme, the Foreign Investment Commission may authorise the exemption of duties as provided by Sections 22 and 23 of the Foreign Investment Law of 1988.

With regard to exports, an *ad valorem* duty of 5 to 10% is levied on oilcakes, pulps and cereals, raw hides, skins, and bamboo. A specific duty of K5 to K10 per tonne is levied on certain varieties of rice.

Claims for Drawback

When goods imported into Myanmar are declared drawback at the time of importation, and when these goods are re-exported under claims for drawback, there is a reimbursement of seven-eighths of the import duty that was paid provided everything is in accordance with the prescribed conditions.

Deductible Taxes

Property taxes, resource royalties and rentals, stamp duty, and commercial tax on imported goods, are treated as part of goods acquired.

Inventory Valuation

Normal inventory valuation based on cost, market, or net realisable value, is accepted for tax purposes but the method must be consistent from year to year.

Reasonable Expenses

Expenses that are not of a personal nature, are considered reasonable, and are incurred solely and exclusively for the business, usually are allowed as deductions for tax purposes.

TAX ADMINISTRATION

Tax payments

Income for the year is estimated and tax is paid quarterly, in advance, at the end of June, September, December and March. On the final assessment, if the liability exceeds the tax instalments, then an interest penalty of 5 to 10% is imposed. Tax assessment is based on the previous year's income. The tax year begins on 1 April and ends 31 March of the following year. All accounts must be brought up to 31 March, and tax returns must be filed before 30 June of the same year.

Employers have to submit two returns. One is the "Monthly Statements of Salaries and Income Tax Deductions" which has to be filed together with the income tax payment within one week of tax deductions. The other is the "Annual Statement of Salaries and Income Tax Deductions" which has to be brought up to 31 March and filed by 30 June each year. Late returns are subject to a penalty of 5 to 10%.

Tax period

The Myanmar Income Tax Law requires all accounts to be brought up to 31 March each year. Corporations and individuals may not adopt different year-ends. For salaried persons, income tax payments are deducted, in advance, based on estimated income.

Tax Reliefs

Foreign sources of income earned by a resident corporation are included in taxable income and subject to Myanmar income tax. Credits are not allowed for any foreign tax paid on overseas income. There is only one double taxation treaty and that is with the United Kingdom.

INVESTMENT INCENTIVES

The aim of the Foreign Investment Law is to attract more foreign capital into the country. The government has offered investment incentives and guarantees to foreign investors and it has eased restrictions on foreign enterprises.

Fiscal Incentives

Foreign investments in the production of goods and services are exempt from income tax for a period of three consecutive years (tax holiday), inclusive of the year of commencement. In cases where it is beneficial to the state, exemption or relief from income tax for a further reasonable period is possible depending upon the success of the enterprise in which the investment is made.

Tax on income generally refers to profits and gains, or surplus, where receipts exceed expenditures. However, Chapter 2, Section 2.1, of the Income Tax Law states that a receipt may be taxable as income even though it may not contain an element of profit or gain. The general principle is that anything which can properly be described as income is taxable unless it is expressly exempted.

There is relief from income tax on profits if they are maintained in a reserve fund and reinvested within a year after the reserve fund is established. This feature is to encourage companies to retain income in the business.

Companies are allowed to use accelerated depreciation for machinery, equipment, buildings, or other capital assets used, at a rate approved by the Investment Commission. The rate is applied to the original cost for purposes of income tax assessment. This allows companies to take advantage of lower taxable income. There is an allowance for research and development expenditures which are necessary and carried out within the country.

Exported goods are exempt from income tax on 50% of the exported profits. This is consistent with the basic principle of promoting the expansion of exports. Investments in the manufacturing sector can save the business income tax if products are exported.

Companies are allowed to pay income tax on behalf of foreign employees and they can deduct such payments from taxable income. This is an incentive for investors to import the necessary expertise required for their business. Companies also are allowed to pay the income tax of foreign employees at the rates applicable to citizens residing within the country. This can mean a savings of up to 30% on income tax payable. Residents are taxed at 5 to 30% while non-residents are subjected to a flat 35%, or the rates shown in Table 14–3, whichever is greater.

Companies can carry forward and offset losses for up to three consecutive years from the year in which the loss is sustained for those losses occurring within two years immediately following the exemption or relief from income tax. Clearly, this is an advantage for companies not able to recoup the cost of investment within the tax holiday period.

There is relief from custom duties or other internal taxes on machinery, equipment, instruments, machinery components, spare parts, and material imported and used for construction. These savings can amount to as much as 500% of the duty or 200% of the commercial tax. Investments in infrastructure projects and buildings, such as hotels and resorts, can realise substantial benefits.

There is relief from custom duties or other internal taxes on raw materials imported for the first three years of commercial production following the completion of construction. This is advantageous to investments in the manufacturing sector.

Companies are subject to tax on all income derived from sources within and outside the country. But for those enterprises operating under the FIL, taxes are payable only on income derived from sources within the country.

Non-fiscal Incentives

Sections 22 and 23 of the FIL guarantee that an economic enterprise formed under a permit shall not be nationalised during the contract term, or during the extended term, or on expiry of the contract term. The share of profit of foreign investors, legitimate balance of salary and other lawful income (after tax and other deductions), may be transferred abroad in foreign currency through the Myanmar Foreign Trade Bank at the prevailing rate of exchange. In case of termination and/or dissolution of an enterprise, the repatriation of funds may be allowed in foreign currency at the prevailing rate of exchange.

Other Reliefs

Dividends received are exempt from income tax and they are not treated as part of the total income of the recipient. To avoid tax cascading, input tax can be offset against output tax. The tax paid by a registered producer or manufacturer, for the import of partly finished goods (used as raw materials) for the production or manufacturing of products, can be credited against the tax payable on the sale of the finished products. Where the partly finished goods are locally purchased from another registered manufacturer or producer, the tax paid by the producer or manufacturer on sale of these goods can be credited against the tax payable on sale of the purchaser's finished products. Certain goods, mostly basic food and raw materials which are locally produced or imported, are exempt from commercial tax.

Qualifying Under the FIL

The government's priority in inducing foreign investment lies in the primary sector for industries which have high value added and are export-orientated. Foreign capital is important to the development of Myanmar. Basically, investments which involve promotion and expansion of exports, exploitation of natural resources, acquisition of high technology, and regional development are highly encouraged.

CONCLUSION

Taxes and incentives are important considerations in an investment decision. Like most countries, these matters are complex and the relevant benefits and advantages must be thoroughly understood. In Myanmar, the FIL provides an array of possibilities depending on the type of investment and the resident status of the business.

REFERENCES

Khin Maung Oo, "Trade Regime and Doing Business in Myanmar", Seminar Paper, MBA Business Study Mission to Myanmar, 16 June 1995.

Myanmar: A Guide for Businessmen and Investors, Coopers & Lybrand, 1994.

Procedures and Types of Economic Activities for Foreign Investment, The Union of Myanmar Foreign Investment Law, 1995.

Spotlight on Business, Ernst & Young, October 1994, pp. 2–7.

Tin Min, "Banking and Monetary System in Myanmar", Business Opportunities Conference on Myanmar, Yangon, September 1993.

Tun Shin, "Corporate and Commercial Unions of Myanmar", Seminar Paper, MBA Business Study Mission to Myanmar, 16 June 1995.

MANUFACTURING AND SERVICES

Chapter 15

Myanmar's Manufacturing Sector

BY
GOH Yu Min
Ernest HO
Christopher LEE
TAN Lay Eng

INTRODUCTION

MANUFACTURING IN MYANMAR is in its infancy. This sector contributed only 10.7% of GDP in 1994–1995. Manufacturing and processing activities have not taken advantage of Myanmar's large pool of literate people nor the rich source of raw materials like wood and fisheries. However, this is changing. The government has identified manufacturing as a key pillar of economic growth. Coupled with the adoption of an open door and market-oriented policy, the government is strongly supporting initiatives in this potentially lucrative sector. The necessary logistics and infrastructure are being put in place, and fiscal and financial incentives are being offered to investors. It is not surprising, therefore, that manufacturing has captured a significant share of foreign investment over the last few years. Singapore companies are among the more aggressive investors with ten manufacturers already firmly established.

With rich natural resources and a high literacy level, the government realises that many business opportunities exist for foreign investors. Since 1988, significant changes in policy have been made which benefit the manufacturing sector directly or indirectly. Some of the more significant are the following:

(i) Abandoning the price controls policy for rice and other basic commodities in September 1988.
(ii) Establishing the Foreign Investment Law in November 1988. This law allows foreign investors to establish either wholly foreign-owned enterprises or joint ventures. It also guarantees no nationalisation and permits the repatriation of profits.
(iii) Revoking the 1965 Law for the Establishment of a Socialist Economic System in March 1989.
(iv) Enacting new laws to abolish state monopolies in many industrial branches and allowing co-operatives and private entrepreneurs (both domestic and foreign) to engage in the production and trade of most industrial goods.
(v) Endorsing the Private Industrial Enterprise Law in November 1990 to enable the establishment of small, medium and large scale enterprises and to promote industrial enterprises.
(vi) Enacting the Cottage Industries Law in October 1991. This is intended to promote small scale industries which use natural resources as their main raw materials.

These changes have allowed the Myanmar government to tap into the export market and generate foreign exchange earnings which, in turn, allow the government to fund various projects for improving the infrastructure and related facilities, a critical factor in attracting foreign investors in manufacturing. The remainder of this chapter reviews the present state of the manufacturing sector and examines a number of viable business alternatives.

PRESENT STATUS

The volume of import and export trade in Myanmar has been increasing rapidly since 1988–89. It was K5.6 billion in 1988–89 and reached a peak of K14.3 billion (provisional) in 1994–95 (Myat Thein, 1995). The export value by type of commodity is given in Table 15–1.

Exports consist of textile products, leather, cement, some basic pharmaceutical products, petrochemical products and animal feed products. Agricultural and forest products together constituted about 64% of total exports in 1993–94. Most of these products are exported in their natural (unprocessed) form. For example, forest products are exported as logs and sawn timber, and minerals are exported in the form of base metal and ores. There are opportunities for processing these prime resources into semi-finished or finished products provided the resources are not protected by government regulations.

TABLE 15–1
Export Value by Type of Commodity
1985–86, 1987–88 and 1993–94 (in million kyat)

Type of Commodity	Export Value (million kyat)		
	1985-86	1987-88	1993-94
Agricultural products	1,131.0	453.5	1,358.0
Animal & marine products	99.8	76.3	368.3
Forest products	1,051.0	754.3	1,356.8
Minerals and gems	205.9	225.0	364.5
Others	78.4	146.1	780.5
TOTAL	2,566.1	1,655.2	4,228.1

Source: Ministry of Planning and Finance, Review of the Financial, Economic and Social Conditions for 1989-90.

A trade deficit of K3.9 billion (provisional) in 1994–95, has put the government under pressure. A sustainable industrial sector is needed to keep the economy growing and investments in the manufacturing sector are encouraged. It is hoped that the development of this sector can enhance the value of exports and reduce reliance on imports.

In the first four-year economic plan, covering fiscal years 1992–93 to 1995–96, manufacturing is one of five key sectors (the others are agriculture, livestock, fishery and mining) targeted for further development. Data on the performance of this sector in terms of gross domestic product (GDP) for recent years is provided in Table 15–2. Despite strong government support to develop this sector, there has been no corresponding increase in its GDP share. Between 1989 and 1995, the sector's GDP share fluctuated within a narrow range, from 10.7 to 13.4%.

Further analysis of this sector indicates that it is relatively primitive and geared towards fulfilling the basic domestic needs of the people. Among the more common products manufactured are food, beverages and clothing. This is understandable because Myanmar has been isolated from the world for decades. In fact, food and beverages production generates more than three-quarters of the gross manufacturing output and about 40% of total manufacturing value. There is a potential market for food and beverages as most of these are produced by state-owned enterprises and there are not enough different brands to satisfy consumer needs.

TABLE 15–2
Performance of Industry
(As at 1985–86 Constant Producers' Prices)

Year	Value (million kyat)	% of GDP	Growth Rate
1985–86	7,054.7	12.6	
1986–87	6,592.2	11.9	-6.6
1987–88	6,221.8	11.7	-5.6
1988–89	5,138.4	10.9	-17.4
1989–90	5,914.9	12.1	+15.1
1990–91	6,232.2	12.4	+5.4
1991–92	6,341.5	12.7	+1.8
1992–93	7,063.6	12.9	+11.4
1993–94	7,772.1	13.4	+10.0
1994–95*	6,628.6	10.7	-14.7

* provisional
Source: Ministry of Planning and Finance, Review of the Financial, Economic and Social Conditions for 1994–95 and earlier issues.

Other principal manufacturing activities involve the processing of primary products, including agricultural produce, industrial raw materials and petroleum refining. Clothing and textiles also offer an opportunity for manufacturing diversification. For example, the central markets of Yangon and Mandalay displayed the same items and offered limited choice. Commonly used household items, such as towels and blankets were mostly imported from China and higher quality cloth items from Indonesia. Although most people wear longhi and slippers, the national dress, there is a trend for the younger generation to buy items like jeans, trousers and shoes which seems irreversible as the country opens up to external influences.

Since 1989, foreign investment has been rising. It increased from US$200 million in 1990–91 to US$1,055 million in 1992–93, and to

US$2,599 million in 1994–95, when about 6.7%, or US$175.30 million, was channelled into manufacturing. In fact, direct foreign investment in manufacturing projects outnumbered all other sectors with 50 projects out of a total of 134 (see Table 15–3).

TABLE 15–3
Foreign Investment by Sector from 1992 to 1995

Sector	1992–93		1993–94		1994–95	
	Number of Projects	Amount (US$ million)	Number of Projects	Amount (US$ million)	Number of Projects	Amount (US$ million)
Agriculture	1	2.69	1	2.69	1	2.69
Manufacturing	28	94.82	30	95.96	50	175.30
Fisheries	9	87.59	9	87.59	14	246.32
Oil and Gas	20	381.09	20	381.09	23	1,420.62
Mining	10	155.35	10	155.35	13	182.20
Hotels and Tourism	20	332.38	20	332.38	30	570.38
Transport	1	1.00	1	1.00	3	2.30
TOTAL	89	1,054.92	91	1,056.06	134	2,599.81

Source: Myanmar Business, "Myanmar: An Economy in Transition", Vol. 1, No. 1, April 94 and Thun Shin, "Corporate and Commercial Laws in Myanmar", Seminar paper, MBA Study Mission to Myanmar, 16 June 1995.

Although manufacturing and processing accounted for only 10.7% of GDP in 1994, the potential for growth seems strong. Several factors support this proposition:

(i) Cheap labour costs (K2,000 to 2,500 per month).
(ii) A large pool of literate workers which makes training easy.
(iii) A quality workforce.
(iv) An abundant supply of natural resources.
(v) Plenty of land.
(vi) Strong government support and incentives.
(vii) A relatively untapped domestic market, especially for everyday items.

Potential investors should be aware that manufacturing technologies are very outdated and there are virtually no supporting industries (i.e., manufacturers of machinery, equipment, parts and components).

Equipment and parts required for manufacturing processes normally are imported.

TYPES OF MANUFACTURING ENTERPRISES

This section examines the main forces driving the manufacturing sector. They can be broken down into four categories in terms of ownership.

(i) State-owned enterprises
(ii) Co-operatives
(iii) Private companies
(iv) Foreign companies

State-Owned Enterprises

The majority of industrial establishments in Myanmar are large state-owned enterprises employing thousands of people. They contribute about 40% to the total industrial production value. They produce items ranging from industrial machinery and equipment, agricultural and dockyard equipment, to daily household items. A significant number use technologies that are obsolete and require capital investment.

Enterprises are grouped under either Ministry of No. 1 Industry or Ministry of No. 2 Industry. There are eight manufacturing enterprises under the Ministry of No. 1 Industry. These enterprises produce goods such as textiles, garments, foodstuff, beverages, pharmaceuticals, soap and toilet goods, among others. Ministry of No. 2 Industry owns the Myanmar Heavy Industries and Technical Services Enterprises. The former produces items such as tyres, motor vehicles, pumps and electrical appliances. A summary of the products produced between April 1991 and March 1994 is shown in Table 15–4.

Most state-owned factories utilise less than 50% of their capacity. The government is keen to attract foreign investment to renovate and modernise their factory facilities and to maximise production capacity. The government plans to gradually privatise these enterprises. A number of foreign joint ventures have emerged between foreign companies and state-owned enterprises. Examples include the Myanmar Seafood Pte. Ltd., a joint venture between a Singapore company and Myanmar

Seafood, and Daewoo Garment factory, a joint venture between Daewoo of Korea and Myanmar Textile.

Cooperatives

Cooperatives form a very small percentage of the industry establishment. Their numbers have been decreasing in recent years.

TABLE 15–4
Products Produced by the Ministry of No. 2 Industry between April 1991 and March 1994

Products	Quantity	Products	Quantity
Tyres	176,627	Heavy motor vehicles	451
Light motor vehicles	1,147	Bicycles	8,865
Water pumps	7,199	Power tillers	854
Tractors	608	Light bulbs	458,081
Tube lights	2,343,606	Dry cell batteries	12,642,869
Transformers	132	Electric motors	1,853
PVC electric wire reels	90,177	Electric power meters	25,467
Domestic electrical appliances	620,851	Car batteries	14,396
Power generators	355		

Source: Khin Maung Oo, "Trade Regime and Doing Business in Myanmar", Seminar paper, MBA Study Mission to Myanmar, 16 June 1995.

Private Enterprises

There is a large number of local private enterprises in the manufacturing and processing sector. These establishments are mostly small family businesses or cottage industries. Approximately 95% of them employ less than ten workers each and they are usually friends and relatives. They are engaged primarily in the production of simple consumer goods and contribute 50% to the total industrial production value of the country. This is more than the production value of state-owned enterprises.

The private enterprises appear more productive than state-owned companies and there is great potential for small scale foreign investment in these enterprises. The synergy here comes from matching foreign marketing expertise and technology with the knowledge and skills of the local labour force.

Foreign Companies

This group of investors plays a major role in shaping the manufacturing and processing sector in Myanmar. They will have a significant impact on quality and efficiency. Also, they will bring modern machinery, management skills and improvements to existing and new factories. The contribution to production value from this group will continue to increase.

SINGAPOREAN COMPANIES IN MYANMAR

As at mid-March 1995, Singaporean companies had invested US$293.35 million in 23 projects in Myanmar, as shown in Table 15–5. Only Thai companies had more projects, valued at US$398.91 million. In dollar terms, Singaporean companies ranked fourth after the United Kingdom, France and Thailand. The U.K. and France have substantial investments in oil and gas exploration projects. The biggest single investment is in the vast offshore gas project financed by a consortium including Total of France and Unocal Corporation of the U.S.

TABLE 15–5
Top Ten Foreign Investment Countries

Country	Number of Projects	Approved Amount (US$ Million)
United Kingdom	10	632.21
France	1	465.00
Thailand	25	398.91
Singapore	23	293.35
United States	13	226.27
Japan	5	101.14
Holland	2	83.00
Austria	1	71.50
Malaysia	7	69.57
Hong Kong	16	63.44

Source: Myanmar Investment Commission, 1995.

Most of Singapore's investments in Myanmar are in hotels, fisheries and manufacturing. A list of Singaporean companies in Myanmar's manufacturing sector is shown in Appendix 15–1. Most investments are joint ventures with state-owned enterprises. Those with private enterprises are generally small and, as a result, there is no published information about them. The consulting group GSK International has clients who are doing business or are actively seeking new business opportunities with private enterprises in Myanmar. They can be a good source of information for potential investors.

MANUFACTURING AND PROCESSING OPPORTUNITIES

Activities that may attract foreign investors are those that take advantage of the Myanmar's abundant raw materials. Three promising areas are the manufacturing and processing of timber, textiles and copper-related products. These ventures require partnership with a state-owned company under Ministry of No. 1 Industry.

Export Markets

(i) ***Manufacturing and Processing of Timber Products:*** Myanmar has an abundance of timber like teak, hardwoods and bamboo. It has the largest share of the world teak trade with an annual yield of about 0.6 million cubic metres. These resources require modern technology to extract and process into valuable end products.

(ii) ***Manufacturing and Processing of Textile-Related Products:*** The textile industry is highly labour-intensive. Myanmar's large pool of workers, therefore, makes this another potential area for foreign investment, although fabrics are not available locally and have to be imported. The end products in this instance would be mass produced apparels like jeans, shirts and blouses for worldwide distribution.

Relatively cheap and plentiful labour dampens productivity initiatives. Foreign investors can improve productivity through new processes or more advanced equipment and machinery. For example, Daewoo Garment Pte. Ltd. has a daily production rate of only six garments per person.

Daewoo Garment is 55% owned by Daewoo and 45% owned by the Myanmar government. The set-up cost for this venture was about US$7 million. Breakeven is expected to be reached in two years.

A viable method for small investors in the garment industry is contract manufacturing. Myanmar had an economically inactive population of 11.4 million in 1990 (*Statistical Year Book*, 1993). This accounts for 42% of the population, aged ten years and above, who are neither students nor pensioners. Most of these people are females doing housework or other chores in suburban areas and villages. Low wages, poor transportation, job scarcity and looking after the home, are the more common reasons for not seeking a job. Since most females already have some basic sewing skills, it is easy to re-train them for commercial work.

These individuals can form the basis of a skilled workforce for garment making especially if high quality is not required. Investors can organise labour through community leaders, providing them with materials and samples. Workers can be paid by piece rate. Such an arrangement can benefit both parties. For workers, transportation problems are eliminated. For investors, overheads associated with factory production are reduced.

(iii) ***Manufacturing and Processing of Copper-Related Products:*** Myanmar's total estimated copper ore deposits are 310 millions tonnes, found in Salingyi Township and in Letpadaung. The No. 1 Copper Mine situated in Salingyi Township produces about 8,000 tonnes of ore per day, which can be processed into end products like cables. While imported heavy machinery is required to process the copper into cables, the costs of this is offset by low labour costs. Consequently, production costs are lower and the industry competitive compared to countries like Malaysia. Investors should note that copper extraction and processing is presently dominated by a Canadian company, Ivan Hoe, which has exclusive mining rights in one of the two major mining areas.

Domestic Markets

Myanmar is in the infancy stage of consumerism. For example, while beverages and food products are available, variety is lacking and brand name recognition is non-existent. Thus, there are opportunities for manufacturers to introduce modern food technology, and to create indigenous brand names for packaged beverages and canned foods. This is viable with a domestic population of nearly 43 million.

There are opportunities for markets of daily necessities like umbrellas, bicycles, towels and so forth. Higher technology products like televisions and VCRs can also find strong domestic demand, although brand loyalty is already a reality and difficult to break. This is evident in the way Toshiba dominates the television market. Domestic markets have their own particular risks and the marketing strategy associated with locally produced products must be evaluated very carefully.

OPERATING ISSUES

In this section, some of the common operating issues are addressed. Key issues can be divided into the manufacturing process (i.e., pre-production, production and distribution stages) and those that may indirectly impact investment (i.e., government policy, cultural issues and foreign policy). Figure 15–1 summarises the framework used in discussing these issues.

Pre-Production Stage

(i) ***Availability of Industrial and Commercial Land:*** Land designated for industry and commerce is owned by the government and is generally available for business purposes subject to the Transfer of Immovable Property Registration Law of 1987.

The maximum lease is for 30 years. An extension for an additional 20 years is possible based on the attractiveness of the investment to the government. For example, the development of hotels is in line with the government's initiative to promote tourism and, as a result, likely to receive extensions. The uncertainty of an extension, however, discourages high capital outlay for buildings (and heavy equipment) since there is no way to ensure that relocation will not be an issue after 30 years.

Rent for land in 1995 was US$2.00 and up per square foot. The jointly owned Daewoo-Myanmar Government textile factory for instance, is paying US$2.50 per square foot for uncovered space and US$5.00 per square foot for the factory (i.e., covered space).

FIGURE 15–1
Operating Issues for Manufacturing and Processing

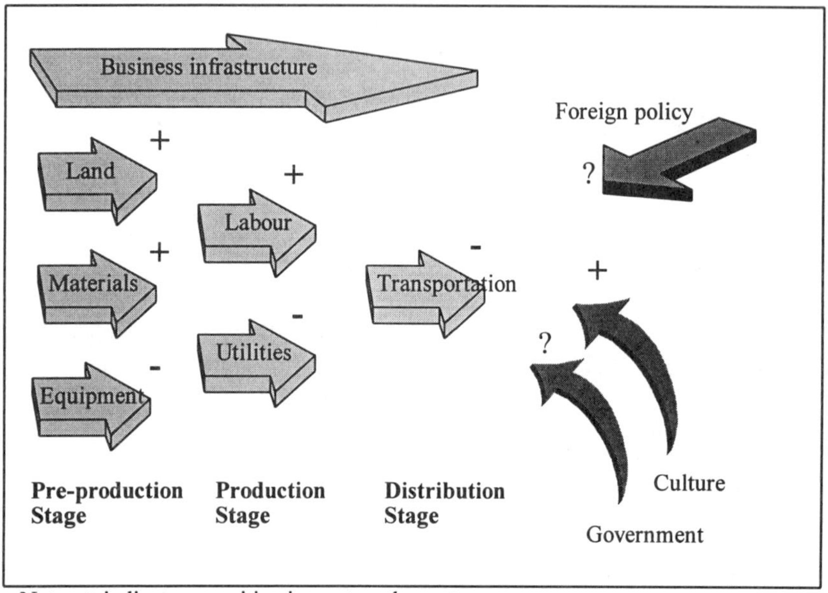

Note: + indicates a positive impact on the sector.
- indicates a negative impact on the sector.
? indicates an uncertain impact on the sector.

The government has designated several areas as industrial zones which benefit from better infrastructure, such as roads, rail, port facilities and so forth. Within Yangon, the light industry zone (e.g., Mingaladon Industrial Zone) is located in the north-western area while the heavy industry zone (e.g., Dallah Industrial Zone) in the south-western area.

The most recent and most notable development is the Thanlyin-Kyauktan industrial zone, which is about one-hour drive south-west of Yangon. This zone occupies some 140 square kilometres (about one-fifth the size of Singapore). In fact, the development of the Thanlyin-Kyauktan industrial zone is similar to that of Singapore's Jurong industrial zone in the 1960s. The former is being undertaken by Sinmardev, a Singaporean consortium, comprising RSP

Architects, Planners & Engineers and a specialist contractor. Over the next two decades, a cluster of five satellite towns housing a population of one million people will be developed in this zone.

The ready availability of land for industrial and commercial use is a positive factor in considering investments in manufacturing and processing.

(ii) ***Forestry, Agricultural and Mineral Raw Materials:*** Myanmar has vast amounts and a huge variety of natural resources. For example, most of the forested areas are still untouched, presenting opportunities for forestry-related manufacturing like timber processing, paper processing and furniture making. Myanmar also has substantial deposits of minerals like copper and tin. The country's long coastline makes fishery-related industries attractive as there is an abundance of marine life.

The availability of raw materials implies less reliance on imported raw materials for manufacturing and processing. This translates into lower operating and materials cost.

(iii) ***Old and Outdated Machinery and Equipment:*** Many of the existing factories are using old and outdated machinery and equipment. Such production assets are unproductive, at best, and useless in the context of modern production techniques. Machinery and equipment must therefore be imported. Import duties on machinery and equipment range from 25 to 200%. Under the Foreign Investment Law, a company may be exempted or given relief from customs duty and/or other internal taxes on imported machinery and equipment (which includes components, spare parts and materials used during the period of construction) for the first three years of production following the completion of construction. The company may also claim relief or exemption on imported raw materials. The Foreign Investment Law also allows a company to use accelerated depreciation methods for machinery, equipment, buildings or other capital assets used in the business, based on the original value for income tax assessment.

Production Stage

(i) ***Literate Workforce:*** Myanmar has a well-trained workforce available for most basic industrial activities. In 1992–93 the workforce was estimated to number 16.5 million of which 40% was skilled. Each year, the universities, institutes and colleges produce on average 30,000 graduates. In addition, some 8,000 people are trained in agricultural, vocational and technical institutes. An estimated 78% of the Myanmar population is functionally literate and bilingual (in English and the Myanmar language).

Because of this foundation, training of workers and skills upgrading is much easier. Conversations with foreign employers and Myanmar employees suggest that English is generally well-understood. Employers stated that the attitudes of workers were excellent in terms of learning new skills and exhibiting diligent work habits.

A Myanmar factory worker earns around K2,000 to K2,500 per month. Trained engineers earn from K3,000 to K5,000 per month. These wage rates are extremely low. Although government fixes wages, recent high inflation (33% in 1993–94, 22% in 1992–93 and 29% in 1991–92) implies that wages are likely to rise soon.

Labour laws allow for a 44- to 48-hour work week in the manufacturing sector. This translates into a 5½- to 6-day week.

(ii) ***Utilities:*** Electricity is supplied by the Myanmar Electric Power Enterprise (MEPE). Sources of electricity include hydroelectricity and diesel-powered generators. Electricity tariffs are US 8 cents per unit. Power failures are frequent occurrences, even in the capital city of Yangon, and industries that depend on a reliable or continuous supply of power must plan for this contingency. Most firms choose to bring in their own diesel-powered generators. The rationing of fuel for use in private generators is not a problem for foreign investors because the government grants requests for additional fuel.

Water is also managed by the government. The supply is not reliable. Some firms dig their own artesian wells to ensure a reliable supply of water.

Distribution Stage

(i) ***Transportation:*** Domestic transportation is available in the form of rail operated by Myanmar Railways, sea operated by Myanmar Five Star Line which owns a fleet of 21 vessels, and air. Four airports in the cities of Yangon, Mandalay, Bagan and Heho are in operation. In addition, the government is working on an extensive road and highway system.

Yangon, the primary international port, handles over 90% of the sea-borne trade. Yangon port caters for both break-bulk conventional cargo (the majority) and container cargo. Myanmar Five Star Line has representative offices in Britain, Japan and Singapore. It also has agents in Australia, Bangladesh, China, Hong Kong, India, Indonesia, Malaysia, Pakistan, South Korea, Thailand and the U.S. In addition, eight other foreign shipping lines operate into Myanmar. These include Nippon Yusen Kaisha Line (Japan), Eastern Car Liner Ltd. (Japan), Bangkok Container Line Co. Ltd. (Thailand), Lian Huat Shipping (Singapore) and Foong Sun Shipping Pte. Ltd. (Singapore).

Six international airlines operate to Myanmar including Myanmar Airways International, Thai International, Silk Air (Singapore), and Aeroflot (Russia) (*Business Times*, November 1994).

Rail transportation between Mandalay and Yangon takes two days. Inland water transportation takes ten days. Roads are generally in good condition in Yangon and other cities. Beyond the cities though, roads are often single-lane, in need of maintenance and generally not suitable for large container trucks. A container load from Mandalay to Yangon costs US$200 one way. Six-lane highways are being developed to serve the Yangon-Bago-Thanlyin growth triangle. Completion is expected by 1998.

Deep sea port facilities are not available in Yangon, which can only accommodate vessels of up to 10,000 tonnes. An alternative deep sea port at Thanlyin, one of the points in the above mentioned growth triangle, will be able to accommodate vessels of up to 20,000 tonnes. Port operations are generally satisfactory with under ten days needed to retrieve cargo and one working day to deposit cargo.

Other Factors

Understanding the “do’s” and “don’ts” of doing business in Myanmar is important. Giving money or gifts for favours – for example, for “expediting” the processing of applications or “opening” doors to key decision makers – is not practised in Myanmar, unlike in some countries where such “greasing” is necessary to get things done. This attitude stems from strong, predominantly Buddhist values which advocate virtues like sincerity and honesty. In fact, one thing that clearly stands out is how "above board" businessmen's operation appear to be in Myanmar. While keen on making a good living, Myanmar businessmen will not compromise their values, prompt distrust or, even worse, breach a contract.

(i) ***Government Policy:*** Realising the futility of blocking out the rest of the world, SLORC has adopted an open door policy since 1988. Economic liberalisation has encouraged direct foreign investment. The government has introduced laws and policies to bring in much needed foreign dollars, most notably the Foreign Investment Law (see earlier chapter).

(ii) ***Foreign policy:*** The U.S.'s response to reported human rights violations has led to a freeze on substantial foreign aid. As a result, agencies like the World Bank, the International Monetary Fund, and traditional donor nations like Japan, have not been inclined to offer aid to Myanmar. However, following the recent release of Aung San Suu Kyi, Japan has indicated that an aid package will be forthcoming. Foreign aid is likely to continue being withheld until Myanmar improves its human rights record to the satisfaction of the U.S.

Myanmar was invited to the ASEAN meeting of foreign ministers in Brunei in July 1995. In 1994, it was invited to the meeting in Thailand. Membership of ASEAN represents great economic potential for Myanmar.

(iii) ***Exchange Rate:*** The great discrepancy between the official exchange rate (6 kyat to US$1) and the unofficial, open market rate (110 kyats to US$1) poses considerable problems for investors.

CONCLUSION

Myanmar offers considerable investment opportunities in the manufacturing and processing sector. Major assets are its abundant natural resources and land, and plentiful semi-skilled labour force. Investment in high technology production is an area which warrants careful consideration. Although there may be abundant labour to assemble parts and components, obtaining supplies of high technology equipment, machinery and raw materials for the manufacturing process can be a barrier to potential investors. Moreover, given the military's strong involvement in the government and outside pressure from developed countries regarding Myanmar's human rights record, the situation may not be ready for heavy capital investment. It would be prudent for investors to start off small in both export and domestic business ventures, with relatively low levels of capital input.

For small investors, our advice is simple: scan the market needs of the population at large. There are plenty of opportunities in mass-market consumer products. Do not wait too long or the advantage of starting early will be lost.

For bigger investors, our advice is more conservative. Form a joint venture with state-owned enterprises, or reliable and more established private enterprises. Choose opportunities that can tap into the inexpensive labour force and abundant natural resources. Start early before labour costs are forced up by competition. Work towards a breakeven situation in approximately five years.

APPENDIX 15–1
Singaporean Companies in Myanmar (in the Manufacturing and Processing Sector)

Name of Company Partners	Product and Activities	Form of Organisation	Amount of Investment (US$m)
Gold Star Ltd. -Cho Cho Trading Co. Ltd. -Transicom Singapore Pte. Ltd.	Production and marketing of animal feeds	Limited Company (Joint venture)	0.250
Myanmar-NC Woodwork Co. Ltd. -Myanmar Metal Industries -NC Woodwork and Construction Pte. Ltd.	Production and marketing of wooden doors, parquet flooring, construction parts, furniture components made of wood other than teak	Limited Company (Joint venture)	0.766
Myanmar-ACE Metal Industries Co. Ltd. -Myanmar Metal Industries -Ace Pressure Weld Int'l Pte. Ltd.	Production and marketing of steel and steel products, steel fabrication and ship breaking	Limited Company (Joint venture)	2.476
Myanmar Motor Limited -Ministry of Trade -Century Motors (S) Pte. Ltd.	Reconditioning of used motor vehicles. Servicing, repair and renovation of motor vehicles	Limited Company (Joint venture)	0.425
Myanmar Singapore United Tobacco Co. Ltd. -Myanmar Foodstuff Industries -Singapore United Tobacco Pte. Ltd.	Production and marketing of cigarettes, tobacco products and export trading	Limited Company (Joint venture)	1.500

APPENDIX 15–1 (cont'd)

Name of Company Partners	Product and Activities	Form of Organisation	Amount of Investment (US$m)
Myanmar Yaung Chi Oo Co. Ltd. -Myanmar Foodstuff Industries -Yaung Chi Oo Trading Pte. Ltd.	Production and marketing of beer and soft drinks	Limited Company (Joint venture)	6.320
Rothmans of Pall Mall Myanmar Pte. Ltd. -The Union of Myanmar Economics Holding Pte. Ltd. -Rothmans Myanmar Holding Co. Ltd.	Manufacturing and sale of cigarettes	Limited Company (Joint venture)	3.690
Myanmar ECI Joint Venture Co. Ltd. -No. 3 Mining Enterprise -ECI Minerals Pte. Ltd.	Production and marketing of drilling mud barite powder	Limited Company (Joint venture)	3.232

REFERENCES

"A Long Way to Go for Myanmar", *Asian Business*, February 1995.

"Behind the Facade in Burma", *Asian Wall Street Journal*, March 1995.

"Blazing Trails in the Backwoods", *Asian Business,* December 1992.

"Bottling Profits in Burma", *Asian Business*, September 1992.

"Burma's Economic Reforms Begin to Produce Results", *Asian Wall Street Journal*, February 1992.

"But Will the Flag Follow Trade", *The Economist*, 8 October 1994.

"Changes in Myanmar's Policies Spell New Openings for Investors", *The Straits Times*, 19 September 1994.

Country Profile Series – The Union of Myanmar, Singapore Trade Development Board, 1995.

"Day of the Generals", *Asiaweek,* April 1994.

Doing Business in Myanmar, Ernst & Young, 1994.

"First Shots in a Photo War", *Asian Business*, October 1992.

"Follow the Lion King", *Myanmar Business,* October 1994, Vol. 1, No. 7.

"Funny Money", *Asian Review,* April 1994.

"Give Private Firms a Role and Make Users Pay, ADB Urges", *The Straits Times*, 20 April 1994.

"Investing in Asia's Transitional Economies", *Business Times*, November 1994.

Investing in Myanmar, KPMG Peat Marwick, 1994.

Khin Maung Oo, "Trade Regime and Doing Business in Myanmar", Seminar Paper, MBA Study Mission to Myanmar, 16 June 1995.

"Making it Legal", *The Economist*, 22 January 1994.

Mya Than and Joseph L.H. Tan, *Myanmar Dilemmas and Options*, The Challenges of Economic Transition in the 1990s, ASEAN Economic Research Unit, Institute of South-east Asian Studies, 1990.

Myanmar (Burma), The Economist Intelligence Unit Limited, EIU Country Report, 3rd quarter, 1994.

"Myanmar: An Economy in Transition", *Myanmar Business*, Vol. 1, No 1, April 1995.

Myanmar: A Guide for Businessmen and Investors, Coopers & Lybrand, 1994.

Myanmar Business, Vol. ,1 No. 8, 2 November 1994.

"Not Quite Indonesia", *The Economist*, 28 January 1995.

"Ripe for Rape", *The Economist*, 15 January 1994.
"SLORC's Pie in the Sky", *Asian Business*, August 1992.
"SLORC's Way to Capitalism", *Asian Business*, February 1995.
"The Golden Triangle's New King", *The Economist*, 4 February 1995.
Thin Maung, *Investment Opportunities in Myanmar*, Proceedings on Business Opportunities Conference on Myanmar, September 1993.
Thun Shin, "Corporate and Commercial Laws in Myanmar", Seminar Paper, MBA Study Mission to Myanmar, 16 June 1995.

Chapter 16

Myanmar's Banking and Financial System

BY
MYAT KYAW*

INTRODUCTION

THE UNION OF Myanmar introduced the market-oriented economic system in the latter part of 1988 after the State Law and Order Restoration Council (SLORC) assumed power. Various reform measures were undertaken in accordance with the new market-oriented economic system. The most important one was the Foreign Investment Law, enacted in November 1988. Salient features of the law include non-nationalisation, a tax holiday for three years and 100% foreign ownership.

To match the economic reforms, the financial system needed to be restructured. Thus, new bank laws namely, the Central Bank of Myanmar Law, the Financial Institutions of Myanmar Law, and the Myanmar Agricultural and Rural Development Bank Law were promulgated in 1990. Rules and regulations pertaining to these laws also were issued. In exercising these laws, the financial system was reformed.

The banking structure in Myanmar consists of the Central Bank of Myanmar, 4 state-owned

* Director, Central Bank, Ministry of Finance, Yangon, Myanmar.

banks, 15 domestic private banks, 26 representative offices of foreign banks, a state-owned finance company and a state-owned insurance institution.

THE BANKING SYSTEM

The Central Bank of Myanmar

The Central Bank of Myanmar Law confers upon the Central Bank of Myanmar broad powers to operate with relative independence and to exercise supervisory and regulatory authority over a wide range of financial institutions, both state-owned and privately owned. The Central Bank sets the central bank rate, capital adequacy ratio, reserve requirements, liquidity ratio and minimum cash margins, which are all uniformly applicable to financial institutions.

The Central Bank is responsible for acting as adviser to the government on economic matters, issuing currency, acting as a banker to the government as well as to the financial institutions, formulating and implementing monetary policy, managing the reserves of the state, implementing exchange rate policy, controlling foreign exchange transactions, licensing, inspecting, supervising and regulating financial institutions. The Central Bank is administered by a Board of Directors consisting of a Governor, a Deputy Governor and five Directors. The Governor and Deputy Governor are appointed for a term of five years on a full-time basis, whereas the term for other members is fixed at four years on a part-time basis.

State-Owned Banks

State-owned banks include the Myanmar Economic Bank, the Myanmar Foreign Trade Bank, the Myanmar Investment and Commercial Bank and the Myanmar Agricultural and Rural Development Bank.

(i) ***The Myanmar Economic Bank (MEB)*** is governed by the Financial Institution of Myanmar Law. The MEB provides nationwide commercial and development banking services through a network of 277 branches and 50 other offices. It accepts demand deposits, time deposits and savings deposits as well as issuing saving certificates, and provides different types of loans to co-operatives, commercial and industrial enterprises, and individuals. It acts as the agent of the Central Bank of Myanmar for the currency chest operations throughout the country. It is also responsible for maintaining the state fund account of government departments and state economics enterprises. MEB branches handle Foreign Exchange Certificates issued by the Central Bank to promote tourism in the country. The buying and selling of foreign currency is handled by licensed branches. MEB branches in six townships handle foreign currency amounts for border trade. The MEB is planning to enlarge the scope of its business from domestic to international banking.

(ii) ***The Myanmar Foreign Trade Bank (MFTB)*** is governed by the Financial Institutions of Myanmar Law. It conducts most foreign exchange transactions for the state sector as well as for the co-operative and private sectors. The MFTB renders the following banking services:

(a) accepting deposits in kyats and foreign currencies;
(b) issuing, accepting, discounting, buying, selling and collecting all securities, including bills of exchange;
(c) all matters relating to letters of credit;
(d) buying and selling travellers' cheques and foreign currencies;
(e) all matters relating to international fund transfers and bank guarantees; and
(f) making status enquiries and reports on local and foreign firms and banks.

The MFTB performs international banking operations through a correspondent network of over 124 foreign banks in 58 countries.

(iii) ***The Myanmar Investment and Commercial Bank (MICB)*** is governed by the Financial Institutions of Myanmar Law. It operates as a commercial, investment and development bank for local and foreign investors, joint venture companies, local and foreign business enterprises, and individuals. Both domestic and foreign banking services are provided. It has a branch in Mandalay. The functions of MICB include the following:

(a) accepting demand and time deposits;
(b) lending or advancing money for the short term or long term with security or otherwise;

(c) providing foreign banking services such as opening bank accounts in foreign currencies, remittance facilities, buying and selling foreign exchange, encashment and sale of travellers' cheques, credit cards, import and export letters of credit, and bills;
(d) providing guarantees for credit and business performance; and
(e) financing existing or new businesses.

The MICB undertakes international banking operations through its correspondent network of 122 banks.

(iv) Governed by the Myanmar Agricultural and Development Bank Law, the ***Myanmar Agricultural and Rural Development Bank (MARDB)*** provides seasonal, short-term and long-term credit to farmers through a nationwide network of 14 regional offices, 167 branches and 46 agencies. It also provides loans to agricultural, livestock and rural socio-economic enterprises, co-operatives, private individuals and private enterprises. Under a programme to develop border and national areas, and to eradicate narcotic drugs, the bank provides loans with concessionary interest rates. The bank launched a rural savings programme in October 1993 to encourage farmers and the rural populace to save their surplus income at the bank. They are allowed to borrow development loans up to four times their savings deposits.

Domestic Private Banks

In accordance with the new banking laws enacted in 1990, 15 domestic private banks have been granted licences since May 1992. All of them are operating successfully. They are:

(a) Myanmar Citizens Bank Ltd.
(b) First Private Bank Ltd.
(c) Co-operative Bank Ltd.
(d) Yadanabon Bank Ltd.
(e) Myawaddy Bank Ltd.
(f) Yangon City Bank Ltd.
(g) Yoma Bank Ltd.
(h) Myanmar Oriental Bank Ltd.
(i) Myanmar May Flower Bank Ltd.

(j) Tun Foundation Bank Ltd.
(k) Kanbawza Bank Ltd.
(l) Prime Commercial Bank Ltd.
(m) Asian Yangon International Bank Ltd.
(n) Myanmar Universal Bank Ltd.
(o) Asia Wealth Bank Ltd.

Each domestic private bank is managed by a board of directors composed of experienced personnel. Private banking business is growing very fast with deposits totalling about K5.8 billion and loans of K4.2 billion over the last three years.

Four of these private banks namely, Myanmar Citizens Bank, Co-operative Bank, Myawaddy Bank and Yangon City Bank, are licensed to deal in foreign exchange. Three domestic private banks – Yoma Bank, Myanmar Oriental Bank and Myanmar May Flower Bank – are permitted to issue credit cards in local currency.

Finance Company

The ***Myanmar Small Loans Enterprise*** is a state-owned finance company that deals in small loans business.

Insurance Institutions

The Myanmar Insurance Law was enacted in July 1993 to facilitate wider coverage of the insurance business. At present, Myanmar Insurance is the sole state-owned insurance institution in Myanmar. It underwrites various classes of insurance, including life, marine, aviation, fire, engineering, third party liability, motor, oil and gas, travel and health insurance. It has a very comprehensive reinsurance programme with internationally reputable and renowned reinsurers. Insurance can be effected in a freely convertible currency. Thus, if a premium is paid in a freely convertible currency, then the claim would be met with the same currency.

Representative Offices of Foreign Banks

Permission to open representative offices in Yangon has been granted to 26 foreign banks from 12 countries (at June 1995). They include the following:

(i) **Singapore**
- The Development Bank of Singapore Limited
- United Overseas Bank Limited
- Keppel Bank of Singapore Limited
- Oversea-Chinese Banking Corporation Limited
- Overseas Union Bank Limited

(ii) **Thailand**
- The Thai Military Bank Limited
- Siam City Bank Limited
- Thai Farmers Bank Limited
- Bank of Ayudhya Public Company Limited
- Bangkok Bank Public Company Limited
- Krung Thai Bank Public Company Limited

(iii) **Malaysia**
- Malayan Banking Berhad
- Public Bank Berhad
- Bank of Commerce (M) Berhad

(iv) **Indonesia**
- Panin Bank International Inc., Nauru

(v) **France**
- Banque Indosuez
- Banque Nationale de Paris
- Banque Francaise du Commerce Exterieur
- Societe Generale

(vi) **Cambodia**
- Global Commercial Bank

(vii) **Hong Kong**
- Hongkong and Shanghai Banking Corporation Limited

(viii) **Bangladesh**
- Arab, Bangladesh Bank Limited

(ix) **Japan**
- The Bank of Tokyo Limited

(x) **United Kingdom**
- Standard Chartered Bank (U.K.)

(xi) **Netherlands**
- ABN AMRO BANK NV (Netherlands)

(xii) **Canada**
- The Bank of Nova Scotia

THE FINANCIAL SYSTEM

Reform in Financial Management

A new state financial management programme was introduced in 1989. Under this programme, the state fund account (SFA) was created whereby all the administrative organisations and state economic enterprises (SEEs) deposit their receipts. Expenditures are paid by funds from the SFA according to budget allocations. Local bodies can operate with their own funds in accordance with their respective city development laws. Under the new financial management programme, previous domestic bank credits of SEEs were converted into government equity so as to relieve the debt burden of SEEs. As a result, the financial position of SEEs has improved significantly.

Tax Reform

To restructure the tax and tariff systems in line with the economic system, the following measures have been undertaken:

(i) Amendments to the Tariff Act 1953, in connection with border trade export tariffs.
(ii) Amendments to the Income Tax Law and the Profit Tax Law in 1989 to allow tax holidays for newly established economic enterprises.
(iii) Promulgation of the Commercial Tax Law in 1990, in place of the Commodities and Services Tax Law, to broaden the tax base by including private sector production and service activities.
(iv) Further amendments to the Income Tax Law, Profit Tax Law and Commercial Tax Law in 1991 to promote investment and maintain price stability.
(v) Revision of stamp duties and court fees to reflect present prices.
(vi) Enactment of a new Tariff Law in 1992 to replace the Tariff Act, 1953.
(vii) Introduction of the harmonised system of import classification, effective from 1 April 1992 for the modernisation and standardisation of tariffs in line with international practices.
(viii) Streamlining procedures in the collection of tax and improvements in tax administration with technical assistance from the UNDP and IMF.

(ix) Reform of customs formalities by cancelling non-tariff barriers and taking measures to prevent delays in clearing imports.

Interest Rates Reform

In order to promote savings, interest rates were raised from 8 to 10% on savings deposits and from 10.9 to 12% on savings certificates in July 1992. The Central Bank rate was raised from 11 to 12.5% in January 1995. Based on the Central Bank rate, the minimum deposit rate is fixed at not less than 3% below this rate and the maximum lending rate is set at not more than 6% above this rate. Thus, commercial banks are free to set their rates anywhere between 9.5 and 18.5%.

Monetary Developments

The rate of monetary expansion stood as high as 34.6% in 1993 and fell to 19.8% in 1994. It rebounded to 35.9% in 1995. This development can be traced to the increase in bank credits to the state and private sectors. To arrest the trend of monetary expansion, the MARDB introduced the Rural Savings Mobilisation Scheme which will contribute towards supplementing the Saving Bank Law by mobilising savings. These efforts have shown encouraging results. Savings rose from K23,339 million in 1993 to K30,240 million in 1994. Despite the dampening effects of these savings, inflation remained high at 33.7% in 1994. It decreased to 22.3% in 1995. The Central Bank began issuing three to five-year bonds from December 1993. Initially, this was to absorb the excess currency in circulation in the economy and, subsequently, to contribute towards development of a capital market. As of March 1995, bonds amounting to K97.5 million were issued.

Balance of Payments

There was a noticeable improvement in the external sector where the balance of payments showed a surplus of K558.1 million in 1994–95, based on provisional data, as compared to a deficit of K214.0 million in 1993–94. This improvement was achieved by the inflow of grants and direct foreign investment, despite a higher deficit in the trade and current accounts. In other words, the surplus in the capital account exceeded the deficit in the current account.

Exchange Arrangements

The currency of Myanmar is the kyat. It is pegged to the SDR at K8.50847 = SDR 1. The buying and selling rates of the kyat against the Deutsche mark, the French franc, the Japanese yen, the pound sterling, the Swiss franc, and the U.S. dollar, as quoted by the Myanmar Foreign Trade Bank, are determined on the basis of the daily calculations of the value of these currencies against the SDR. Buying and selling rates for other currencies, such as the Singapore dollar, Italian lira, Hong Kong dollar, and Netherlands guilder, are determined on the basis of appropriate cross rates in different money markets of various geographical regions.

Foreign Exchange Certificates

Since February 1993, the Central Bank of Myanmar has issued foreign exchange certificates (FECs) in denominations of 1, 5 and 10 units. One unit is equivalent to US$1. These are for the convenience of tourists, in particular, and foreign currency account holders in general. FECs are exchangeable with U.S. dollars, pounds sterling or with acceptable travellers' cheques. FECs can be used by both residents and non-residents for various types of payment within Myanmar. Tourists entering Myanmar are required to exchange a minimum of US$300 for 300 FECs. These cannot be reconverted on departure from Myanmar. However, unused FECs exchanged in excess of 300 FEC units can be reconverted on departure on presentation of the FEC vouchers at the exchange counters. As of 31 March 1995 a total of 65 million FEC units were issued out of which 58 million were deposited with banks.

Exchange Control

Exchange control is administered by the Central Bank in accordance with instructions from the Ministry of Finance and Revenue. Travellers may bring in up to US$2,000 of foreign currency without declaration. Amounts above that must be declared.

Right to Transfer Foreign Currency

Under the Foreign Investment Law, a person who has brought in foreign capital can transfer the following:

(i) foreign currency entitlement;
(ii) net profits after deducting taxes and provisions; and
(iii) foreign currency permitted for withdrawal by the Foreign Investment Commission which may include the value of assets on the winding up of business.

Foreign employees can transfer their salary and lawful income after deducting taxes and other living expenses incurred by them or their families.

Chapter 17

Banking and Finance in Myanmar*

BY
FOO Tiang Weng
GOH Yew Hong
TAN Ai Tong
THAM Yong Hwa

INTRODUCTION

THE EFFECTS OF nationalising banks in 1963 and isolating the country since the military coup of 1962, brought Myanmar's banking system to a halt for nearly 30 years. The antiquated banking system today needs a complete overhaul to meet the needs of current economic activity. A stable and efficient financial and banking infrastructure is imperative for Myanmar's growing economy and external trading activities.

Currently, foreign banks only can open representative offices in Myanmar. Project and trade financing appear to be two lucrative areas for foreign banks. Further opportunities may arise if, and when, Myanmar allows foreign banks to form joint ventures with local banks or even open branch offices. However, the time frame for these events is unknown.

HISTORICAL BACKGROUND

The Union Bank of Myanmar was established in February 1948 to take over the central banking

* We wish to thank Dr. Ng Kah Wah for his comments on this chapter and Mr. John Teoh, Oversea-Chinese Banking Corporation Limited Myanmar Representative, for his information.

functions of the Yangon branch of the Reserve Bank of India. Until 1963, the Myanmar banking system consisted of the Central Bank, a state-owned commercial bank, a state-owned agricultural bank, an industrial development bank and 24 private commercial banks of which 14 were foreign-owned.

After nationalisation of all banks in 1963, arrangements were made to pool the financial resources of the state-owned financial institutions including banks. In 1969, all financial institutions were consolidated into one monolithic bank, namely the People's Bank, which engaged in all banking activities as well as insurance business. In 1976, this monolith was reorganised into the Union of Myanmar Bank (later known as the Central Bank of Myanmar, CBM), the Myanmar Economic Bank (MEB), the Myanmar Foreign Trade Bank (MFTB), the Myanmar Agricultural and Rural Development Bank (MARDB), and the Myanmar Insurance Corporation (MIC).

FINANCIAL REFORMS

In late 1988, financial reforms were initiated in line with moves towards a market-oriented economic system. New banking laws were enacted in July 1990; the new Savings Bank Law in July 1992; and the Myanmar Insurance Law in 1993.

Myanmar has taken some initial steps towards financial reform, including plans to establish a stock exchange, to reorganise existing banks, to create new areas of specialisation for joint ventures in banking, and to allow foreign banks to operate in Myanmar. Since the rules and regulations for setting up a joint venture bank are not explicit, all foreign banks currently in Myanmar operate as representative offices.

The government wants Myanmar's banks to be more efficient, competitive and flexible. Recent legislation has aimed to create a more market-oriented environment. Banks are now required to provide advisory services to their clients in addition to accepting deposits, providing loans and financing trade more efficiently.

In October 1993, a rural savings scheme was introduced to enable farmers to save their earnings and borrow money. This is an initial step in developing rural banking.

Since 1988, the government has made various changes to increase tax revenue. There is the *Commercial Tax Law* of 1990 to broaden the tax base; the new *Tariff Law* of 1992 to replace the *Tariff Act* of 1953; and the introduction of the Harmonised System of Import Classification. As a result of these changes, tax revenue increased from K4.4 billion in 1987 to K10.3 billion in 1992.

On the fiscal front, because of various revenue measures including expansion of the tax base and tougher enforcement of tax collection, the overall budget deficit as a percentage of GDP declined from 8% in 1990–91 to 6% in 1992–93.

On the banking side, the Central Bank of Myanmar Law, the Financial Institutions of Myanmar Law and the Myanmar Agricultural and Rural Development Bank (MARDB) Law, were enacted in July 1990 to develop the financial system and improve the efficiency of financial activities in harmony with new economic policies. The Small Loans Department was separated from the Myanmar Economic Bank in 1992 and set up as a finance company called the Myanmar Small Loans Enterprise. Interest rates on savings deposits and saving certificates were raised from 8 to 10% and from 10.9 to 12%, respectively, in July 1992. Because of these measures, savings increased substantially in 1992 and 1993. In January 1995, the Central Bank rate was raised from 11 to 12.5%. Encouraged to expand their credit facilities to the private sector to support increased economic activities, there has been a significant increase in bank credit to the private and cooperative sectors.

The rate of monetary expansion stood at 34.6% in 1993; fell to 19.8% in 1994, and rebounded again to 35.9% in 1995. To arrest such a trend in monetary expansion and to mobilise savings, the MARDB introduced the Rural Savings Mobilisation Scheme in 1993 to supplement the Savings Bank Law. Savings increased from K23.339 billion in 1993 to K30.240 billion in 1994. The inflation rate was reduced from 33.7% in 1994 to 22.3% in 1995.

To absorb excess currency in circulation and to contribute towards the development of a capital market, the Central Bank began issuing three- to five-year bonds in December 1993. There are no restrictions on purchasing these bonds which pay semi-annual interest of between 10% (for three-year bonds) per annum and 10.5% (for five-year bonds) per annum. As of March 1995, K97.5 million worth of bonds were issued (Myat Kaw, 1994).

The Myanmar Insurance Law was enacted in July 1993 and new types of insurance such as oil and gas insurance, education insurance and health insurance were introduced. Insurance income increased substantially as a result of these measures.

Exchange control is administrated by the Controller of Foreign Exchange under the guidance of the Exchange Control Board through the MFTB in accordance with instructions from the Ministry of Planning and Finance.

The currency of Myanmar is the Myanmar kyat. The import and export of kyat are prohibited. The kyat is not negotiable abroad. All external payments are subject to authorisation. All export proceeds and invisible receipts must be declared to the MFTB.

FOREIGN EXCHANGE MANAGEMENT

A series of exchange liberalisation measures have been introduced during the transformation to a market-oriented economy. All exchange earnings of foreign and local enterprises can be used for imports or other purposes. Under the Foreign Investment Law, a person who has brought in foreign capital can transfer the following:

(i) Net profits after deducting all taxes and provisions.
(ii) Salaries of foreign personnel after deducting taxes and other living expenses.
(iii) The foreign currency entitlement of individuals.
(iv) The foreign currency permitted for withdrawal by the Foreign Investment Commission which may include the value of assets upon winding up of the business.

Foreign Exchange Certificates (FEC) have been issued for the convenience of foreigners visiting Myanmar since February 1993. FECs are denominated in units equivalent to US$10, US$5 and US$1 and are valued at 1,000, 500 and 100 kyats respectively. Foreign visitors are obliged to convert US$500 into FECs. Their aim is to enhance Myanmar's foreign exchange earnings and to make it more convenient for tourists to carry out transactions. Tourists can reconvert unused FECs back to their original currency upon departure provided they have used at least 300 FEC units. Foreign currency in excess of US$2,000 brought into Myanmar has to be declared upon arrival. It is illegal for Myanmar nationals to handle foreign currencies other than FECs and they are not permitted to have overseas bank accounts. As of 31 March 1995, 65 million FEC units were issued and 58 million units have been deposited with banks.

Foreign currency account holders can use their foreign exchange to buy imported goods and to make payments for imported goods and services. Because of these measures, the number and amount of foreign currency deposits have risen in recent years.

As mentioned earlier, only the MFTB, the MICB, some branches of the MEB at the border areas and four domestic private banks are allowed to handle foreign currencies.

CAPITAL MARKET

At present, there is no capital market in Myanmar. However, initial steps have been taken to explore the possibility of establishing a capital market, specifically with Daiwa Securities of Japan (*Business Times,* December 1994). A team of Myanmar personnel has completed its training in this area in Japan. The opening of a stock exchange in early 1996 seems premature.

FINANCIAL INSTITUTIONS OF MYANMAR LAW

The Financial Institutions of Myanmar Law was enacted on 4 July 1990 to promote a financial system to support the effective implementation of the open door economic policy. The Law provides for the establishment of financial institutions, whether state-owned, jointly owned by the state and private interests, or privately owned. It specifies the functions, duties and powers of financial institutions, and the regulatory provisions to be observed by financial institutions.

Under this law, financial institutions in Myanmar are classified into the following groups:

(ii) ***Commercial Banks.*** These engage primarily in the collection of demand deposits with chequing privileges, time deposits having terms of not more than one year and short term credit operations.

(ii) ***Investment or Development Banks.*** These accept time deposits with terms exceeding one year and finance fixed or working capital with terms that match the resources collected by such banks or funds provided by the government.

(iii) ***Finance Companies.*** These engage primarily in financing the purchase of goods or services with funding other than deposits from the public.

(iv) ***Credit Societies***. These engage primarily in financing individual members for consumption, production, or commerce, using funds collected in members' accounts.

Permission to operate in Myanmar as a financial institution with foreign capital, a branch of a foreign bank or a representative office of a foreign financial institution, may be granted by the Central Bank in accordance with the provisions of the Law (Sections 12, 13 and 14). A financial institution licence may be granted by the Central Bank based on the application form and feasibility study. A feasibility study must spell out and identify the following:

(i) The market for the services to be performed and demonstrated interest on the part of the community to be served;
(ii) The money resources required and how they are to be acquired;
(iii) The anticipated profit to be gained by the proposed institution;
(iv) The qualifications and technical competence of the management; and
(v) The types of financial services that the applicant is going to undertake.

The paid-up capital of financial institutions must be in cash and deposited with the Central Bank and is to be released only upon conclusion of the licensing process. Accordingly, 25% of its profits must be set aside in a general reserve account until it reaches 100% of paid-up capital. A financial institution must not choose a name which misleads the public regarding the true nature of the shareholders or activities.

The Central Bank must grant or deny the licence within three months from the date of receipt of the application. Within 15 days from the date when the licence is granted, the financial institution must pay the Central Bank a licence fee amounting to 0.1% of the initial paid-up capital. The Central Bank must determine the minimum capital requirements for new institutions, relying on their proposed location and financial activities.

The transfer, in one or more transactions of any block of shares representing more than 15% of the capital of a financial institution, requires the prior sanction of the Central Bank. Similarly, any establishment of branches, agency offices and other similar offices of the financial institutions, or change in location of branches, agency offices and other similar offices, requires the prior sanction of the Central Bank.

The relationship between the risk-weighted assets, and the capital and reserves of a financial institution, must not exceed ten times. Financial institutions must not lend more than 10% of their capital plus reserves to a single individual, an enterprise, or an economic group. None of their ten largest debtors, including economic groups, are to account for more than 30% of the total loan portfolio. The total amount lent to personnel by a financial institution must not exceed 5% of capital. The Central Bank may require the financial institution to have an audit committee consisting of three members appointed by the shareholders.

FINANCIAL SYSTEM AND WEAKNESSES IN CURRENT BANKING

Despite liberalising the financial sector from a mono-bank system, the growth of the financial sector remains impeded. The demonstrations of 1964, 1985 and 1987, remain as a social stigma which has destroyed the "banking habits" of households and arrested the development of Myanmar's domestic banking environment. There still is resistance to saving or to depositing money in the banking system due to the lack of confidence in the local currency.

Declining deposit rates resulting from high annual inflation rates also contributes to low public savings. Savings and lending rates offered by the banks are controlled at levels below the inflation rate. In early 1995, when the official annual inflation rate was 38%, banks were not permitted to charge more than 18.5% for loans or pay less than 9.5% for savings. The expanding budget deficit of the country is financed by increasing the money supply (M1) which further exacerbates inflationary pressure. Thus, money creation via credit has been capped and loans are restricted to between 30% and 50% of the collateral value (*Far Eastern Economic Review*, February 1995).

An added obstacle to a higher national savings rate is the large disparity in the two-tier exchange rate (i.e., official versus unofficial). This keeps non-convertible local kyats away from the banking system.

Within the dual exchange rate, there are four currency exchange systems in the market, each having a different rate pegged against the U.S. dollar. These systems are the FECs, U.S. dollars, local bank transfers and overseas bank transfers. The rate differentials vary between 5% and 15%, with the lowest rate attached to FECs and the highest rate attached to overseas transfers. Business transactions in the country remain largely cash based, because of these discrepancies. Cheques are seldom used. Businesses with insufficient foreign exchange tend to resort to barter and countertrade as a consequence.

To date, foreign banks have only set up representative offices in Myanmar. Their main task is collecting economic data and scouting for loans that have to be booked offshore (Trade Development Board, April 1995).

OPPORTUNITIES IN THE BANKING AND FINANCIAL INDUSTRY

Myanmar is endowed with rich natural resources. She has abundant supplies of labour, agricultural land, fishery, forest and mineral resources. Much of these remain unexploited. The opening economy coupled with a rudimentary banking industry presents enormous opportunities for foreign banks. In 1994, the banking and finance sector contributed 0.1% to GDP (*Asian Review*, April 1994). The presence of a legal framework for foreign participation, created by the Central Bank of Myanmar Law and the Financial Institutions of Myanmar Law, makes it easier for foreign banks to assess risks and opportunities in Myanmar. However, the banking sector is likely to remain closed to foreigners until domestic banks become strong enough to compete.

Project Financing

Myanmar is a relatively undeveloped country and most of her resources are still under-exploited. With the opening up of the economy, there is an urgent need to develop infrastructural projects. Myanmar is short of funds and has high external debts (US$4,850 billion in 1991–92, or about 87 times GDP). Domestic enterprises face difficulties in raising capital to develop or extend their businesses.

With no capital market to attract foreign funds, the only channel for foreign funds is through direct investment in the form of wholly-owned companies or joint ventures. Foreign banks can act as an intermediary between entrepreneurs and providers of funds. Representative offices in Myanmar can identify profitable ventures and use the bank's international network to source for funds. Representative offices typically perform the following activities:

(i) Act as a liaison between bank HQ and clients.
(ii) Provide credit/risk checks on projects and partners.
(iii) Monitor the progress of projects.

However, foreign banks need to consider several factors when undertaking project financing in Myanmar. First, there are restrictions on land transfers to foreigners which reduces collateral for bank loans. Usually, the local partner contributes land while the foreign partner provides capital and expertise. Foreign banks should limit loans to their first tier customers who are able to offer guarantees. Second, projects should earn foreign exchange to benefit from the incentives provided under the Foreign Investment Law.

Trade Financing

Myanmar's foreign trade has increased steadily since 1988. Total trade in 1993–94 was US$1,840 million, almost double that of 1989–90. In particular, imports grew from US$510 million in 1989–90 to US$1,176 million in 1993–94, an increase of 130% (*Asian Review*, April 1994).

Currently, an importer is required to open a foreign exchange account at a bank in order to apply for an import licence from the Directorate of Trade. An irrevocable letter of credit has to be opened by the importer at the bank. Trade financing of imports can be profitable for foreign banks because it offers revenue from fees for the issuance of letters of credits, foreign exchange earnings and interest income through trade financing.

In the case of exports, an irrevocable letter of credit has to be opened at the Myanmar Investment and Commercial Bank by the buyer through a correspondent or acceptable bank. Thus, there are fewer opportunities for foreign banks in this area.

General Considerations

Foreign banks wishing to set up representative offices in Myanmar should not assume that all the supporting infrastructure is in place. For example, there is a shortage of quality office space and it is difficult to obtain telephone lines. There may be frequent power failures, resulting in a loss of communication links. A visit to Myanmar to determine the cost involved is, of course, imperative before establishing a presence.

CONCLUSION

Given that foreign banks only are allowed to open representative offices in Myanmar, project financing and trade financing appear to be two lucrative possibilities. Further opportunities will arise when Myanmar allows foreign banks to form joint ventures with local banks and open branch offices. However, the time frame for these events are unknown. There are already 26 foreign banks with representative offices in Myanmar (see page 193 for a list), new entrants wishing to do business in Myanmar need to set up representative offices quickly if they wish to be around when Myanmar eventually opens up the banking sector to foreign bank participation.

REFERENCES

Asian Review, April 1994, pp. 6–8.

Country Profile Series: The Union of Myanmar, Singapore Trade Development Board, April 1995.

"Daiwa to Help Myanmar Develop Capital Markets", *Business Times*, 1 December 1994.

"Economics Guru", *Far Eastern Economic Review*, 16 February 1995, p. 52.

"Exchange Rate Realignment: How and When?", *Myanmar Business*, 3 August 1994.

"Listening Post", *Far Eastern Economic Review*, 16 March 1995.

Myat Kaw, "Myanmar Banking and Financial System", Seminar Paper, MBA Business Study Mission to Myanmar, 16 June 1995.

Mya Than, "Myanmar Places its Bet on Free Economy", *Business*

Times, 4 August 1993.

Myat Thein, "Monetary and Fiscal Policies for Development", *Far Eastern Economic Review*, 16 February 1995, pp. 53–58.

Win Myint, "Master Plan for Regional Development of Yangon", Seminar Paper, MBA Business Study Mission to Myanmar, 16 June 1995.

Chapter 18

Marketing in Myanmar

BY
BIN Hee Jum
Kenneth KWOK
LAU Kok Chiang
THEN Joon Boo
YAP Kuan Sze

INTRODUCTION

THIS CHAPTER HIGHLIGHTS marketing information pertinent to Myanmar. It also describes the marketing experiences of several companies, including two which have been doing business in Myanmar for more than a decade. Myanmar's culture, very strong multi-tier family ties, the predominantly Buddhist faith and low per capita income and wages, necessitate a marketing strategy different from other countries. Opportunities exist but first mover advantages are fast disappearing with growing global competition.

A marketing plan can operate at two levels. At the strategic level, broad marketing objectives and strategy, based on an analysis of the current market situation and opportunities, are developed. At the tactical level, specific marketing plans for the period, for advertising, merchandising, pricing, channels, service, and so on, are outlined. This chapter attempts to highlight marketing information gathered from several sources which can aid potential business entrants in both their strategic and tactical marketing plans. The chapter does not recommend specific domestic marketing strategies for families of products and services but, rather, it focuses on successful and unsuccessful marketing experiences of companies that have conducted business in Myanmar. Some emphasis is given to the marketing of consumer goods because of the experiences of the companies interviewed.

Published material on broad national statistics, favoured investment policies and political developments are readily available. Even the worldwide Internet contains many opinions on political developments in Myanmar. However, there is little published material on "marketing" in Myanmar. What are people like in Myanmar? What does the market demand? How are products and services sold? It would appear that only costly first-hand experience and difficult-to-arrange interviews with Myanmar businessmen can reveal answers to these questions. More specific opportunities and threats facing local companies are still shrouded in mystery. This chapter attempts to reveal some information on these issues in the context of the modified "value creating and delivery sequence" marketing framework of Lanning and Michaels (1988) shown in Figure 18–1.

CHOOSING THE VALUE

The first phase, choosing the value, represents the "homework" that must be done before any product exists. Information is provided here so that a market can be segmented, an appropriate target market identified, and the appropriate positioning selected.

The Macro Environment

The macro environment, such as demographics, education, language and religion, provides a very broad basis for market segmentation. Some of these details are shown in Table 18–1.

The People of Burma

In the social hierarchy of Myanmar, Buddhist monks, followed by the elderly, receive the most respect. A Burmese family, however impoverished, will do its best to care for elderly, handicapped or sick relatives, even those quite distantly related. Homes for the aged are homes for those who have no one to care for them.

FIGURE 18–1
The Value Creation and Delivery Process

Choosing the Value			**Providing the Value**		**Communicating the Value**			
Customer Segmentation	Market Selection/ Focus	Value Positioning	Products/ Services Availability	Pricing	Distributing	Salesforce	Sales Promotion	Advertising

Education is worthy of great respect, regardless of whether one has gainful employment or not. Proud parents of university graduates line their living room walls with photos of their offspring in their graduation caps and gowns. A foreign degree generally is regarded as superior to a local degree or diploma. Among the professions, doctors and teachers are accorded high esteem. Doctors who practise for monetary fees alone are abhorred; it is believed that they should be accommodating enough to accept fees in kind, like bags of rice or cans of cooking oil. Relatives and close friends of doctors are generally "looked after" free of charge. Those who are wealthy are also held in high esteem, particularly if they contribute to the welfare of the less well-off. It is all right for a person to be poor as long as he tries to live a morally good and honest life.

TABLE 18–1
Selected Macro Environment Data

Population (1994)	• 44.2 million people. • 135 national groups with Bamars comprising 68.9%.	
Education (1994) (Number of students)	• Primary School • Middle School • High School • Universities and Colleges	6,257,000 1,211,000 317,000 346,000
Language Spoken	• Predominantly Burmese and English. • Ethnic languages also. • (English is well-spoken by many aged 45+)	
Religion	• Buddhist: 89.4%. • Christians, Muslims, Hindus and Animists: 10%.	

Sources: *EIU Country Report*, 1995; *Investing in Myanmar*, 1995; Coopers and Lybrand, 1994.

Buddhism is the predominant religion. A deeply rooted Buddhist belief of the people is "karma" (fated), and that everything that happens to oneself, both good and bad, is due to past deeds in this life and former lives. The Myanmar people are generally cheerful, fun-loving, happy-go-lucky, modest and easily contented. Family ties are strong and multi-tier families living under one roof are common. The highly respected community, predominant Buddhist beliefs and strong traditional family values will have a strong impact on any marketing strategy.

Market Opportunities and Threats

Many consumer product companies use two criteria to judge the potential of a new market; one is population and the other is per capita income. Assessing the potential of the Myanmar market is facilitated by the statistics shown in Table 18–2.

TABLE 18–2
Per Capita GDP, Wage Rates, Inflation and Imports

Per Capita GDP for 1994	K7,862. (US$1,310 at 6 kyats per US$ or US$71 at 110 kyats per US$).
Labour	• Minimum wage for an unskilled worker in the state sector is K20 for an eight-hour day. • Average worker earns US$15–20 per month • Engineer/Accountant US$30–40 per month* • General domestic helper US$15 per month*
Consumer Price Inflation	• 1992: 22%. • 1993: 32%. • 1994: 27%.
Primary Imports	Vegetable oils and fats, petroleum products, iron and steel, machineries, electrical appliances, transport equipment, textile yarn and fabrics, medicinal and pharmaceutical products, and miscellaneous food preparations.

* approximations from interviews

Sources: *EIU Country Report*, 1995; *Investing in Myanmar*, 1995; Coopers and Lybrand, 1994.

Although the average monthly salary of a worker is US$15 to US$20, many people save to buy consumer goods. A typical colour television which costs about US$300 is somehow affordable and they are selling well. It seems that there are opportunities for electronic consumer goods and computer hardware/software. Some apparel items, such as shirts, sell (or even rent) well. However, the traditional clothing of longyi (sarong) and sandals (slippers) either signify a huge market potential for western clothing, such as jeans and shoes, or no market at all.

The greatest threat to new entrants in developing a market is the highly established border trade with neighbouring countries such as China, Thailand and India. Many goods flow overland into Myanmar, through common borders, at very competitive prices. Parallel imports would represent the greatest threat to brands which have been established and built up over the years by distributors. In addition, the enforcement of copyright is uncertain.

Customer Segmentation

At a basic level, customers in Myanmar can be segmented into two main categories, namely age group and geographical location. Further segmentation is possible depending on the products to be marketed. During the market analysis phase, more precise customer segmentation can be developed through surveys.

Broad segmentation enhances the awareness of potential marketers. Geographical segments can be divided into rural and urban areas, with the latter being more densely concentrated and the former being spread out. This difference will affect the method of distribution and promotion used. One must be prepared to spend more money for promotion and distribution if the product is targeted at rural consumers. Also, urban populations tend to consist of a smaller family size and higher household incomes due to the greater availability of jobs. Thus, urban areas have greater purchasing power which might be important for marketing a particular product.

Age group segmentation can be simply divided into younger and older generations. The consumption habits and comparisons of these two groups in Myanmar are not well-understood, but in maturer markets the younger generations tend to be very brand conscious and willing to pay more for products that are currently in fashion. They also are very status conscious and more adventurous in trying new quality products. On the other hand, older generations are more down to earth in that they are price conscious and loyal to brands that are reliable. Products that are targeted towards the older generations are more likely to have first mover advantage and to withstand competition from new entrants.

MARKET RESEARCH

Before deciding to promote a product in Myanmar, it is advisable to do a market survey to identify demand. There are very few sources of secondary data that are usable or available. There are local companies in

Myanmar that will carry out market surveys with questionnaires in Burmese. Postal surveys are rarely used because response rates average about 7%. Personal interviews and administered questionnaires are far more effective for acquiring data.

PROVIDING VALUE

Product and Service Availability

Clothing and everyday household necessities are readily available in Myanmar. Larger department stores carry many imported goods and they are equivalent in standard to Singapore's HDB neighbourhood centres. Even a well-stocked pharmacy was encountered.

Consumer goods, such as colour television sets, video cassette recorders, cameras and films, air-conditioning units, imported shirts and jeans, are available in the open market. IBM compatible computers are popular. Apple Computer has moved into the Myanmar market.

Hospital and medical services, however, are very basic. Fully furnished wards in public hospitals are quite rare.

Pricing

Current prices of various products and services given in Table 18–3 can serve as a reasonable guide to some pricing strategies. Average monthly income per worker is US$20–US$30, while average household income is approximately US$100. Many people supplement their income with part-time jobs. Those working in the government sector receive subsidised education for their children and high level staff are provided with cars. Spouses can easily get a licence to operate small family-run businesses like shops. From a marketing perspective, what needs to be considered in pricing a product is total household income plus secondary income, rather than the officially published individual incomes. This is especially true when products are for use by the whole family and not for personal consumption. For example, televisions, which cost about US$200–US$400, are owned by about 50% of the households.

Distribution (Place)

In Myanmar, distribution usually takes place via local wholesalers. The trust and relationship between wholesaler and retailer is very important in ensuring the success of new product promotions. Business deals are often made over the phone and confirmed with a handshake. Written contracts are almost non-existent or secondary. Like elsewhere in Asia, *guanxi* is the key to successfully distributing your products in Myanmar. For that reason, it is advisable to appoint a good successful local wholesaler to distribute your products rather than doing it yourself. In terms of incentives for the retailer, discounts are normally given if certain quotas are exceeded and prizes, such as cars, are given to encourage quick penetration of products into the market.

TABLE 18–3
Prices of Selected Consumer Products

Product	Price (kyats)	Price (US$)
Levi's jeans		50–100
U.S. imported shirts (Authentic)		50
Cheap Chinese prints		3–6
Pirated cassettes		1–1.50
Compact discs		25
PC 486 DX-50 MHz, 250MB HDD	200,000	
HP 4L laser printer	115,000	
Epson LQ1170 printer	89,000	
Colour film (36/100)*	230–255	
Sony Walkman*	10,600	
TV**		200–400
Philips electric fan*	7,500	
Handphone*	300,000	
Nike shoe*		60–80
Reconditioned car**		6,000

Sources: Gluckman (1995) and Myanmar Business (October 1994).
*Source: Yuzana Supermarket, Yangon.
**Source: Interview with Tin Onn Myint & Associates Co., Ltd.

COMMUNICATING THE VALUE

The communications and mass media available for marketing are described in Table 18–4.

Sales Promotion and Advertising

Advertising is carried in the press, in cinemas and on poster sites which are subject to government control. Direct mail advertising is available. Posters are seen everywhere; in beauty shops, by street corners and on huge billboards.

TABLE 18–4
Communications and Mass Media Available in Myanmar

Communications	Telephone (including IDD), telegram, telex, facsimile, direct satellite links to eight countries (including Singapore).
Mass Media	• Radio Myanmar broadcasts in Myanmar and English. • Myanmar Television – one channel NTSC system. • Commercial advertisement services available on both radio and television. • In Yangon, three morning papers of which one is in English (*The New Light of Burma*) and one evening paper. • One morning paper in Mandalay.

Sources: *EIU Country Report*, 1995; *Investing in Myanmar*, 1995; Coopers and Lybrand, 1994.

Promotions include sponsoring events such as marathons, national sports, beauty queen contests and donating branded prizes. Sponsoring national events provides valuable air time over the one channel television network and impact through billboards in urban areas. Billboard advertisements, which require a permit from the Municipal City Council, tend to be used as a continuous reminder of a product rather than to promote a new product. The print media, such as newspapers and magazines, are not very effective because their circulations are still low. Yellow page advertisements are also available.

The cost of various advertising mediums in Myanmar is given in Table 18–5. In terms of reach, TV ranks first as coverage is close to 50% of the population. Televisions, although expensive, are viewed as a necessity in Myanmar. TV is one of the few sources of entertainment, especially in rural areas.

TABLE 18–5
Cost of Advertising in Myanmar

TV	US$300 per 30 second
Magazines	K1,500 per page
Newspapers	K350 per square foot
Billboards	US$6 per square foot per annum

Sources: Interviews with accountants of Halliburton and Finance, and Manager of Myint & Associates.

Timing of promotions is very important since Myanmar is agriculture based and generating income generally coincides with the harvest period during the dry season. Sales and promotion activities normally start in October and end in April with the Water Festival.

CASE STUDIES

The following examples outline the experiences of some foreign companies marketing in Myanmar.

Kodak

After only one year of marketing in Myanmar and using the time tested technique of the Kodak film "lucky draw", Kodak's market share rose from 5 to 50% in 1992. Kodak's marketing efforts included a billboard along Sule Pagoda Bridge and the opening of two Kodak mini photo-processing labs in the latter part of 1992. The Burmese live in one of the most culturally cloistered countries in South-east Asia and are woefully lacking in brand consciousness. As one source puts it, "We need to work hard on promoting our product there" (Janssen, 1992).

Konica

Konica, ranked number three in worldwide film sales, has proven to be the true pioneer in the region. They first looked at Indochina in 1988; starting in Vietnam, then Myanmar and then Cambodia. Today Konica has mini-labs throughout Indochina and Myanmar and has taken the concept a step further by setting up "Konica Centres" in each capital city, the first one opening in Yangon in 1990. These centres display

Konica products and mini-lab equipment, and provide technical training for distributors. They reinforce Konica's strong reputation for technical follow-up.

Daewoo

Daewoo is one of the most aggressive conglomerates in Myanmar. When Daewoo opened its department store in Myanmar, it experienced numerous difficulties. More than 80% of sales were in local currency. This resulted in heavy foreign exchange losses and it closed down after one year. Undeterred by this experience, Daewoo has continued its commitment to Myanmar including investment in an electronics company manufacturing refrigerators and colour television sets.

Toshiba

There are tremendous advantages for first movers in developing countries such as Myanmar. Brand loyalty in Myanmar is very strong because of traditional family and community influences. Brand consciousness, on the other hand, is lacking. Toshiba has such a loyal following for its TVs and VCRs, which are known for their quality and service, that even Sony cannot dethrone it with penetrative pricing.

People not only manifest brand loyalty but they also pay attention to the model. Thus, older models command higher prices because the experience of good quality and reliability is passed on to friends and neighbours. The single broadcasting TV channel has resulted in a high TV to VCR ratio (2:1).

General

In addition to the above cases, interviews with three other firms in Myanmar produced more marketing insights. These are summarised below and are a reflection of the views of all three firms.

Distributors appear to have strong bargaining power over retailers. They can often exert pressure on retailers to carry new products even when retailers have not requested them specifically.

A direct sales staff and a wholly-owned fleet of vans are often used to market consumer products. Remuneration is usually based on a fixed salary plus a sales commission based on volume. There is generally no problem recruiting sales staff.

Although independent marketing firms exist, it is common practice to promote and to market products with in-house resources. Margins given to distributors vary from 0.25 to 300% depending on the product. Inventory stockouts of supplies are common. However, distributors and retailers appear to have good grapevine networks for determining stocks.

At least six months are needed to introduce a new product and to open outlets, and before any conclusions on sales trends can be safely made. Building brand loyalty may take two to three years.

Social services provided by companies (and individuals) are highly regarded. These include donations to support schools, hospitals, pagodas and public events. The image of a caring company is important for both social and business reasons.

CONCLUSION

The marketing function in Myanmar has some unique characteristics. The ones which require special consideration are:

(i) Market research is necessary to identify potential demand.
(ii) Segment the market into two main categories, namely age group and geographical location.
(iii) Find a wholesaler with a good track record to distribute products; it is less costly than doing it yourself.
(iv) TV is the recommended advertising medium for obtaining wide coverage and it provides the most value added per dollar of cost.
(v) The timing of promotions is very important and it should coincide with the harvest period during the dry season.
(vi) A minimum of six months is necessary for the introduction of new products before any conclusions on sales trends can be drawn.

Patience is the key to dealing with the complex business environment in Myanmar. With the country in transition from a socialist to a market-oriented economy, the Ministry of Trade is still issuing new trade rules and regulations. Notifications and orders are frequently amended and lead to confusion and uncertainty in the business community. Good local contacts are essential for keeping up to date with changing conditions.

Social service is an important aspect of business. The Buddhist tradition and culture of Myanmar have evolved a people who are gentle in nature. Marketing practices imported intact from developed economies are unlikely to succeed in Myanmar.

REFERENCES

Chun Sang-Kyun, "Myanmar's Allure and Challenges", *Business Korea*, April 1993.

Myanmar: A Guide for Businessmen and Investors, Coopers and Lybrand, 1994.

Country Profile Series – The Union of Burma, Singapore Trade Development Board, April 1995.

EIU Country Report 1st Quarter 1995 – Myanmar (Burma), The Economic Intelligence Unit, 1995.

Gluckman, "Rock Around Rangoon", *Asian Wall Street Journal*, 17–18 March 1995.

Janssen, Peter, "First Shots in a Photo War", *Asian Business*, October 1992.

Kotler, Philip, *Marketing Management – Analysis, Planning, Implementation, and Control*, Prentice Hall, 8th edition, 1994.

Michael J. Lanning and Edward G. Michaels, "A Business is a Value Delivery System", Mckinsey staff paper, Mckinsey & Co., Inc., No. 41, June 1988.

Myanmar Business, Vol. 1, No. 7, 5 October 1994.

Chapter 19

Transportation in Myanmar

BY
Hugh CATLIN
Kelvin LIM Gim Chong
Andy YEO Wei Lok

INTRODUCTION

THIS CHAPTER FOCUSES on the transportation infrastructure in Myanmar. The scope includes road, rail, shipping and air transportation within the country. Specifically, the current state of these transportation modes and potential constraints on supporting business needs are examined. Future needs and development plans are then explored. Investment opportunities in the transportation infrastructure areas also are identified.

Myanmar, with a total land area of 676,577 square kilometres, is the largest country on mainland South-east Asia. It shares 5,858 kilometres of international borders with Bangladesh and India to the north-west, China and Laos to the north-east, and Thailand to the south-east. The country stretches 2,090 kilometres from north to south and 925 kilometres from east to west at its widest point, and has a sprawling 2,832 kilometres coastline facing the Bay of Bengal and the Andaman Sea.

Three parallel chains of mountain ranges run from north to south: the Western Yoma (or Rakhine Yoma), the Bago Yoma (formerly Pegu) and the Shan Plateau. They separate the country into three major river systems: the Ayeyarwaddy, the Sittoung and the Thanlwin.

The Ayeyarwaddy, which is about 2,170 kilometres long, and its major tributary the Chindwin (it joins the Ayeyarwaddy south of Mandalay in the geographic middle of the country), which is about 960 kilometres long, constitute the greatest riverine system in the country. As it enters the sea, the Ayeyarwaddy forms a vast delta of 240 kilometres by 210 kilometres.

Economic reform since 1988 has resulted in a GDP growth of 6% in 1993–94, with 6.4% growth projected for 1994–95. The promotion of tourism yielded a 230% increase in foreign visitors in 1993–94 to 61,000, and an expected 100,000 visitors in 1994–95. With 1996 earmarked as Visit Myanmar Year, the number of visitors is expected to grow even higher (STDB, 1995, p. 8).

With the enormous growth in the economy, the transportation infrastructure is set to change significantly. Expansion of existing roads and highways, increases in the frequency of international and domestic flights, and building of deep water ports for container vessels, are areas on which the Ministry of Transport is actively working to allow the economy to grow as planned.

ROAD AND RAIL TRANSPORTATION INFRASTRUCTURE

Audit and Assessment of Existing Infrastructure

Growth in trade has spurred much of the recent development of Myanmar's inland transportation system. In 1993, overland freight was 920 million metric tonnes as compared to 63.7 million metric tonnes in 1979 (EIU, 1995). Two ministries oversee road and rail transportation. The Ministry of Transport has a land transport division while the Ministry of Rail Transportation has a Myanmar railways division and a road transport division.

In 1993, the railway system consisted of a track network of 4,689 kilometres. The main railway connects Yangon, Mandalay and Myitkyina, with branches spanning the northern and central Shan Plateau. Mawlamyine in the East and Pyay in the middle West Region are also linked by railway. Myanmar Railways rolling stock consisted of 270 diesel locomotives, some steam locomotives, 1,200 carriages and 8,065 wagons. According to a Belgian consultant, the railways are in poor condition, with obsolete infrastructure and rolling stock, have weak management, and derailments and accidents are frequent (EIU, 1995).

The country is mapped by 24,228 kilometres of main roads. Roads in the major cities of Yangon and Mandalay are in good condition and they are generally capable of handling the present amount of traffic. Union highways and other roads linking the cities and townships are a different matter. They are, in general, single lane roads in moderate to poor condition. Many are not passable in bad weather.

Improvement of the Yangon-Mandalay highway, according to the Director-General of the Planning Department at the Ministry of National Development, is of the highest priority. At present, it is an all-weather road and single lane for much of its length. The highway north from Yangon has been widened to six lanes as far as Bago, the site of the newly planned international airport. This expansion is planned for the rest of the existing road to Mandalay. Completion of this improvement, however, will cut only three hours from the present 12- to 13-hour journey as bottlenecks will still occur at townships and villages that the road passes through.

Legitimate border trade with Yunnan province (in China) is estimated at four million tonnes a year, almost equivalent to the present capacity of Yangon port (TUM, 1990). This trade is conducted by truck convoys mostly through border crossings in the Shan state. In contrast to the generally poor state of interior highways, most of the roads connecting the Chinese and Thai border outposts, such as the newly renovated Burma Road, are relatively modern because they were built with foreign assistance. The impact of Chinese assistance is most conspicuous in northern Myanmar where the city of Mandalay has become the hub of trade with China.

Apart from other limitations and the relatively modest priority assigned to roads and bridges in new construction work, the other major bottleneck concerns fuel supplies. The fuel rationing system makes travel expensive. Private citizens are allocated no more than 8 gallons a month. Government officials are allowed 80 gallons a month. They tend to sell their rations on the black market where petrol costs K200 per gallon as compared to the official price of K16 per gallon (EIU, 1995).

Planned Developments

According to U San Khup, Director-General of the Planning Department in the Ministry of National Development, planned government development of infrastructure is limited to improving existing roads. The rail network, however, is to be extended in frontier regions to exploit natural resources.

An agreement has been signed with the Sukanand Company of Thailand to construct 163 kilometres of road linking Chiang Rai in northern Thailand to the border town of Kung Ton in Myanmar. The Thai company won the contract in competition with several other Thai companies. The estimated cost of the project is around 325 million bahts (S$13 million). It will take at least a year and a half to complete. Toll revenue collected from the drivers will be shared 60:40, between the Myanmar government and the Sukanand Company for 15 years, after which time the road will be transferred to Myanmar (EIU, 1995). In what has been billed as Beijing's "largest ever" foreign aid project, China is building the road network around Mandalay to bind the region closer to Yunnan province (*Asian Wall Street Journal*; 4 November 1994).

Constraints and Opportunities

The major land transportation linkages in Myanmar are from north to south. However, with a trend towards regionalisation, a more extensive land network is required. East to west road networks are required but there is some reluctance by the government to approve these as this may add impetus to the already burgeoning illegal trade (Hill and Jayasuriy, 1986).

Infrastructure development by the government is limited by lack of funds. This makes road, rail and bridge construction by build, operate and transfer (BOT) contracts the preferred means of infrastructure development. Agreements to enhance trade between Myanmar and other countries are bringing new opportunities for infrastructure development. One example is the trade arrangement with Thailand which opened the Three Pagodas Pass road for more trade. New roads to Tavoy and Mergui via Thai-Myanmar roads create opportunities for people in the Tenasserim area. Trade with India in the future could conceivably be on the same scale as that with China. This would provide many opportunities for infrastructure development.

Outside the trade routes, good infrastructure links between the two main urban centres of Yangon and Mandalay is increasingly vital because of Myanmar's increasing industrialisation.

Integration of land and river transportation brings synergistic advantages. Such synergy is applicable in the Kachin region, Arakan, and in the Chin and Naga hills where new roads and the Chindwin-Ayeyarwaddy rivers transport system could complement one another.

WATER TRANSPORTATION INFRASTRUCTURE

Audit and Assessment of Existing Infrastructure

Myanmar has a huge network of inland waterways. The Ayeyarwaddy is navigable for 1,550 kilometres and is the backbone of the country's inland waterway transport system, while 792 kilometres of the Chindwin is navigable from Yesagyo to Hkamti. In the south, the riverine transport in the Ayeyarwaddy delta connects Yangon and Pathein, touching Myaungmya, Maubin, Pyapon and Kyaiklat. The Sittaung river is not navigable but it is useful for rafting logs. Of the Thanlwin, the second largest river in Myanmar, only a stretch of 89 kilometres from Mawlamyine to Shwegun is navigable. On the west coast of Rakhine state, the Kaladan and Saing Tin rivers are useful for riverine transport (*Myanmar Business*, 1994).

Since the early 1970s, development of water transportation infrastructure has been a low priority in the national development of transportation infrastructure. This is mainly due to the limitations of geography and the rundown state of the inland boat fleet. At present, inland waterways remain an important means of transport between Mandalay and Myitkyina in the north, and within the Ayeyarwaddy delta.

Yangon port handles 85 to 90% of overseas trade and the capital has waterway, road and railway links with the rest of Myanmar. The port handles both conventional and container cargo although the bulk of the cargo passing through is conventional break-bulk cargo. The port currently is operating at near capacity which is four to five million tonnes a year (TUM, March 1994).

Aside from Yangon, there are eight other ports known as outports. They are grouped regionally as Sittwe, Kyaukpyu and Thandwe ports in the Rakhine State, Pathein Port in the Ayeyarwaddy Division; Mawlamyine Port in the Mon State; and Dawei, Myeik and Kawthoung ports in the Taninthari Division. The outports mainly serve domestic coastal traffic. Among them, Pathein and Sittwe also are used as international exporting ports (TUM, March 1994).

Operation-Ownership

Myanmar's ports are administered by the Myanmar Port Authority (MPA) which is responsible for providing terminal facilities and services for shipping. Services provided by the MPA include the provision and maintenance of berthing and storage facilities, access channels, navigational aids, pilotage, towage and cargo handling facilities. The MPA also undertakes shipping agency business through its Shipping Agency Department in addition to its normal port functions (TUM, March 1994).

Myanmar Five Star Line (MFSL) is the state-owned shipping line. It operates coastal and overseas services with a fleet of 25 vessels. MFSL operates coastal services to Thandwe, Kyaukpyu and Sittwe along the Rakhine coastline, and services to Mawlamyine, Dawei, Myeik and Kawthaung along the Tanintharyi coastline. It also serves Pathein in the delta.

Internationally, MFSL operates monthly liner services to Britain and the European Continent, and to Hong Kong, South Korea and Japan. There are three sailings a month to Singapore. When cargo is available, the line operates to India, Bangladesh, Malaysia, Thailand and Indonesia. Although most of the cargo carried by MFSL is break-bulk cargo, limited container traffic within Asia is catered for. Twenty-foot and reefer containers are carried on liner services to Korea and Japan. A limited container service is available on the Yangon-Singapore route.

There is no direct service to the United States and Canada, but MFSL does have a transhipment agreement with Japan's Nippon Liner Service (NLS). MFSL serves the Myanmar-Japan sector and NLS serves the Japan-U.S. sector. A similar transhipment arrangement has been made with the Australian National Line (ANL). MFSL serves the Myanmar-Singapore sector and ANL covers the Singapore-Australia sector (*Myanmar Business*, 1994). Foreign shipping lines entering Myanmar's ports include the China Overseas Shipping Co. (COSCO), Mitsui OSK Line and Nippon Yusen Kaisha Line (NYK).

Inland water transport services are provided by Inland Water Transport (IWT), a state-owned enterprise. The fleet of IWT is composed of various types, lines, shapes, and sizes of river navigating vessels. Most of the fleet is overaged. Urgent investment, therefore, is required for the rehabilitation of the fleet. IWT also owns five dockyards and one engine-repair facility, mainly for repairing and maintaining its own fleet. As of 1993, the fleet consisted of 351 powered vessels, 264 cargo barges and 72 station flats, all operating in different regions of Myanmar. Existing shipyards are in a dilapidated condition and cannot cope with the annual docking requirements. In fact, only 50% of the annual docking requirements are being fulfilled currently (TUM, 1994).

Planned Developments

Discussions reportedly have been held with Chinese officials about the joint development of a proposed deepwater port at Kyaukpyu. The Chinese are searching for routes to the Burmese coast to transport goods from Yunnan and other landlocked Chinese provinces. They need a port for the onward sea borne re-export of their products. The export capacity of Yunnan Province has been estimated at around four million tonnes of various cargo. Since Yunnan is only about 60 kilometres away from Bamaw there is interest in using Bamaw as a transit inland port. Export goods from Yunnan may be stored in Bamaw, transported down the Ayeyarwaddy river and exported through Yangon Port (TUM, 1994).

The Yangon Port facilities are not sufficient to cope with anticipated container traffic and, thus, it is necessary to expand the number of berths. With urban growth , the possibilities for expansion are limited on the Yangon site. Thilawa has long been identified as the most convenient location for the expansion of port facilities with deeper water and is regarded as the best and most economical site. The Thilawa site is on the left bank of Yangon river, some 16 kilometres downstream from the present port. The hinterland around this port site is slated to be an industrial area known as the Thanlyin-Kyauktan Area Development Project. The port at Thilawa will be able to handle larger vessels and up to 15,000 DWT laden. Vessels entering or leaving Yangon Port partly loaded will be able to enter and leave fully loaded from Thilawa. This will allow an increase in the size of shipments (TUM, 1994).

The productivity of the Thilawa terminal will be much higher than the present Yangon Port because the terminal will be better equipped. The location will permit the largest category of vessel that can negotiate the outer bar to sail in and out by day and night during 80% of the high tide period, thus reducing waiting time. The width of the river at the

Thilawa site will also allow vessels to manoeuvre in and out more easily than in Yangon.

The contract to develop Thilawa port has been awarded to an international consortium led by the Singapore logistic C&P Group and two companies from China. Total investment is estimated to exceed US$50 million. Construction is scheduled to start in October 1995 and to be completed in June 1997. The contract is on a BOT basis with a 25-year lease, excluding the construction period (*The Straits Times,* 26 June 1995).

Constraints and Opportunities

External transportation is impeded mainly by poor port facilities. A major programme to rehabilitate Yangon's port complex commenced in 1984. The creation of a new set of ports and rail links will streamline Myanmar's transportation system and offer great opportunity for economic growth in the delta, the Tenasserim, lower Arakan, and the arid lands to the west of Prome, Myingyan, and up to Monywa. The existing ports of Yangon, Moulmein and Bassein lack deep water facilities.

The Thilawa site is still not suitable for the largest carriers using the major ports of the world. If economic development necessitates larger vessels, then a new site for a deep sea commercial port can be selected from among alternative sites on the western coastline of Myanmar (TUM, 1994).

Kyaukpyu, which is an important port for the rice exports, has been earmarked as a possible future deep sea port site, based on preliminary surveys. Kyaukpyu is on an island off the Rakhine coast and is not well-connected by road and rail to the rest of the country. Development of a container port at Kyaukpyu would raise the importance of modernising and expanding the coastal fleet.

AIR TRANSPORTATION INFRASTRUCTURE

Audit and Assessment of Existing Infrastructure

(i) ***International Air Routes:*** As of December 1994, there were five airlines flying from six cities, offering 33 flights a week to and from Yangon. There are no scheduled international flights to any other city in Myanmar. This gives a total of just over 300,000 available seats a year. These are supplemented by occasional charter flights for tourists, mostly from Chiangmai in Thailand to Mandalay, Bagan and Tachilek.

The busiest carrier is Myanmar Airways International, a 60-40 joint venture formed in February 1993 between QAF Ltd. of Singapore, better known as the bakers of Gardenia bread, and the state-owned Myanmar Airways. QAF supplied the capital to start up the airline and, in return, was awarded Myanmar Airways' international routes, airport and staff support in Yangon. The airline has a "wet lease" agreement with Malaysia Airlines to operate two Boeing 737s. The lease agreement includes pilots and maintenance of the aircraft by Malaysia Airlines (*Asian Wall Street Journal*, 7 April 1995).

(ii) ***Domestic Air Routes:*** Myanmar's geographic size, terrain and inadequate roads make internal air transport very important. Domestic air routes are operated by Air Mandalay and Myanmar Airways.

Air Mandalay is a 60-40 joint venture between Techmat Holdings Pte. Ltd. of Singapore and Myanmar Airways. Air Mandalay commenced operations in the latter part of 1994 with two ATR-72 turboprop aircraft. There are daily return flights from Yangon to Mandalay and Bagan. These 66-seat aircraft can be chartered and operated from most airports. Flights from the tourism centres of Heho and Thandwe to Yangon are now operational. Fares must be paid in U.S. dollars.

Myanmar Airways was the original national carrier. Relegated to domestic routes by the formation of Myanmar Airways International, it has a reputation for unreliability and a bad safety record. The main reason for this is the equipment; the Fokker F-27s, F-28s, and DHC Twin Otters, range from 15 to 20 years old and have been inadequately maintained. Profits from the joint ventures are helping to correct this situation. Myanmar Airways operates the most comprehensive network in the country and serves 21 destinations. Myanmar kyats may be used to pay for fares.

(iii) ***Airports:*** The Department of Civil Aviation of the Ministry of Transportation administers 66 airports. Seven have been designated as Customs and Excise Airports which means they can accept international traffic. Airports outside Yangon do not have suitable facilities for modern jet airlines, and even Yangon International Airport's runway of 8,100 feet × 200 feet is barely adequate for wide-body jets like the Boeing 757. Most airlines operate the smaller Boeing 737.

The existing international airport at Mandalay is severely limited by runway length. Charter flights from Thailand (Phuket and Chiangmai) use this airport. The only scheduled flights are domestic.

Planned Developments

(i) ***Airlines:*** The Managing Director of Myanmar Airways, U Thura Win, indicated that there are plans for new routes to Madras and Perth via Singapore. Another aircraft will be leased from MAS under the same terms. Air Mandalay does not intend to expand domestic routes but has plans for new scheduled routes from Chiangmai and Phuket to destinations in Myanmar. Also, there are no plans to replace Myanmar Airways' older aircraft although talks with commuter aircraft manufacturers ATR of France and Saab of Sweden are continuing. However, there is a desire for new joint ventures for the domestic airlines. This appears to be one strategy for replacing old aircraft on many existing routes.

(ii) ***Airports:*** The new Hanthawaddy International Airport is being built 50 miles from Yangon in Bago Division. This was a major factor in the improvement of the road from Yangon to Bago which is part of the Yangon-Mandalay highway. Planned facilities for this airport will be able to accommodate all aircraft. The target date for completion of the airport was prior to the start "Visit Myanmar Year" in October 1996. However, with firm contracts secured for the new international airport at Mandalay, this project has been given second priority (TUM, March 1994).

Work on the new Mandalay airport south of the city began in 1994. In May 1995, Singapore Technologies Industrial Corporation was awarded a build, operate and transfer contract to design and construct the new airport. The estimated cost of the project is US$360 million and the completion date is expected to be in mid-1996. The new airport is capable of handling all types of aircraft and the air traffic control equipment meets international standards (*Business Times*, June 1995).

Constraints and Opportunities

The lack of adequate airport facilities and limited seat capacity on international flights does not pose a major constraint to doing business in Myanmar. But with the likelihood of increased tourist flows during "Visit Myanmar Year" in 1996–97, this may change. Domestic air travel suffers from a seasonal shortage of seats and this situation is unlikely to change. Delays and diversions due to bad weather are not uncommon on internal flights because of the lack of modern navigation and flight safety equipment. Only seven airports have limited night landing facilities and none have standards used by international airlines.

Opportunities, therefore, include a joint venture with Myanmar Airways for a third domestic airline. The commuter aircraft market is a competitive one and aircraft manufacturers are willing to offer generous financing. At present, demand is insufficient to make such a venture profitable, but the situation is likely to change. Since there are no domestic or international air cargo services available, a joint venture air-cargo service is another investment opportunity worth investigating once industrial developments are more advanced.

Upgrading projects for domestic airports are another opportunity for foreign investment. These would be on a much smaller scale than in Mandalay and include runway lengthening, terminal building extensions and installation of air navigation and flight safety equipment. Likely areas for development are Heho, Thandwe, Kawthoung, Putao and Kyaukpyu.

CONCLUSION

Rapid economic reform is straining the existing transportation infrastructure. The government realises this and is trying to improve critical areas in order to support economic growth. Attractive foreign investment packages are one of the tools used to facilitate transportation infrastructure improvement. Completion of the Yangon-Mandalay highway expansion will provide opportunities for more road travel and related services. Road transportation services between the new airport at Bago and Yangon is another area for investment. A non-stop expressway, bypassing the towns between Yangon and Mandalay, provides another potential opportunity for highway building projects. The building of deep water container port facilities suggests the need for transportation related services. Overall, investment opportunities and the climate for transportation services are excellent in the short run.

REFERENCES

Country Profile Series – The Union of Myanmar, Singapore Trade Development Board, April 1995, p. 8.

EIU Country Profile 1993–1994, The Economist Intelligence Unit, 1995.

Hill H. and S. Jayasuriy, *Myanmar Dilemmas and Options – The Challenge of Economic Transition in the 1990s*, Institute of Southeast Asian Studies, 1986.

Jordan M., "Entrepreneurs Overhaul Burmese Aviation", *Asian Wall Street Journal*, 7 April 1995.

"Local Group ... Wins Yangon Contract", *The Straits Times*, 26 June 1995.

Loh H. Y., "STIC to Build New Mandalay Airport", *Business Times*, 6 June 1995.

Review of the Financial, Economic and Social Conditions for 1990-91, Ministry of Planning & Finance, The Union of Myanmar, 1990.

"Slumming with SLORC", *Asian Wall Street Journal*, 4 November 1994.

The *Myanmar Business Handbook – A Comprehensive Guide to Trade and Investment in the Emerging Market Economy of Myanmar*, compiled and written by the editors, Myanmar Business, 1994.

Walsh J, "The Lady Emerges", *Time*, 3 October 1984.

Yangon Port, Ministry of Transport, Myanmar Port Authority, Union of Myanmar, March 1994.

LABOUR AND HUMAN RESOURCES MANAGEMENT

Chapter 20

Characteristics of Myanmar's Labour Force

BY
TAN See Chen
T'NG Siew Ang
YAP Say Jou

INTRODUCTION

THIS CHAPTER PROVIDES some insight into the labour situation in Myanmar and its suitability to support foreign investment, especially in the manufacturing and tourism industries. With the opening of Myanmar's economy, foreign investors can tap the large labour force available in Myanmar, especially in major centres such as Yangon and Mandalay. There is also an increase of female participation in the labour force.

Myanmar has an education system in place to provide a pool of highly literate workers. English is now the medium of instruction in high school and university. Also, vocational training, which is emphasised by the government, provides a steady supply of skilled workers. More importantly, the people are perceived to be keen to work in foreign-owned companies and have excellent work attitudes.

A conciliatory approach to disputes and the absence of reported industrial disputes in foreign-owned and local foreign joint venture companies are plus factors for foreign investors. Many of Myanmar's laws are based on English laws and 15 International Labour Organisation (ILO) conventions have been ratified by Myanmar. These laws are more acceptable to foreign investors than unknown local laws. The various labour services provided by the Ministry of Labour can also aid foreign investors. This chapter suggests that the current labour situation is ideal for labour-intensive and low-technology manufacturing firms, and the tourism industry.

This chapter analyses the labour situation and labour potential for foreign investments in Myanmar. In Singapore, information was gathered from seminars conducted at Nanyang Technological University (NTU) as well as from visits to the Trade Development Board (TDB), public libraries and the Myanmar Embassy. Additional information was amassed during the Business Study Mission in Myanmar and all of the information was verified through observation, discussion and data from various sources.

BACKGROUND

Population

Myanmar consists of seven states namely, Kachin, Kayah, Karen, Chin, Shan, Rakhine and Mon. There are also seven divisions which are Sagaing, Mandalay, Magway, Bago, Ayeyarwaddy, Tanintharyi and Yangon. The population in Myanmar is spread over these seven states and seven divisions and, as of 1993, it was estimated to be 43.13 million. Myanmar is inhabited by many ethnic nationalities. There are approximately 135 national groups. The Bamars form the largest group and comprise about 69% of the total population (EIU, 1995).

In 1993, 35% of the population was less than 14 years of age, 59% was between the ages of 15 and 59, and 7% was over the age of 60. The population growth is estimated to be 1.9% per annum. The urban population was 23% of the total population in 1970 and grew to about 33% by 1992 (EIU, 1995).

Yangon's population was estimated at 3.45 million in 1993 and Mandalay's at 0.7 million. The populations of Yangon and Mandalay Divisions were estimated at 4.9 million and 5.7 million in 1993, respectively (Win Myint, 1995; *Statistical Yearbook*, 1993).

Religion

About 85% of the population is Buddhist, 4.5% Christian and 4% Muslim. The Buddhists are comprised of the Bamars, Shans, Mons, Rakhines, and some Kayins, while the Christians are mainly Kayins, Kachins and Chins. The Muslims are mainly people of Indian origin (EIU, 1995).

Education

In 1993–94, there were 37,567 primary schools, 2,062 middle schools and 857 high schools, 151 technical and vocational schools, and 42 universities and colleges. The proportion of the population over the age of 15 years, able to read and write, increased from about 71% in 1970 to 82% in 1992. In 1990, approximately 97% of appropriately aged children were enrolled in primary schools, 24% in secondary schools, and 5% in institutions of higher education (EIU, 1995).

In 1988, the government reintroduced English as the medium of instruction for standard nine and above (equivalent to high school or junior college). The government also sends some students abroad to study in the hope of raising Myanmar's educational levels nearer international standards.

Vocational Skills Training

The Ministry of Labour (MOL) implemented the National Vocational Training Project in 1972 to ensure a steady supply of various levels of skilled workers and to improve the productivity of workers through structured training. The MOL encourages employers to provide in-house training courses by undertaking the education of trainers. It also provides required assistance for outside lecture services to entrepreneurs and private organisations (Htin Aung, 1995).

Wages and Prices

In 1993, the inflation rate was 33% based on the official consumer price index for Yangon. In real terms, however, inflation in Yangon was thought to be increasing at an annual rate of 150 to 200%. Since September 1988, prices have increased rapidly. However, the effect has been somewhat mitigated for workers in the public sector because wages increased for the first time in a decade in April 1989 and by another 25% in March 1993.

The minimum daily wage rate for an unskilled worker in the state sector was also increased in April 1993, from K15 to K20 (*Statistical Yearbook*, 1993). Workers' wages in private enterprises are usually fixed by mutual agreement between the employers and workers. As an example, a low-level factory worker in the manufacturing industry has a monthly wage of approximately K2,000 to K3,000, while for higher level supervisory staff the monthly wage can be as high as K10,000 to K12,000 per month.[1] Table 20–1 shows some examples of typical working hours.

TABLE 20–1
Examples of Working Hours

Activity	Working Hours
In shops, companies, trading centres, services enterprises, entertainment houses.	8 hours a day. 48 hours a week.
In factories, oil fields and mines.	8 hours a day. 44 hours a week.
In factories engaged in continuous production.	8 hours a day.
In underground mines.	8 hours a day. 40 hours a week.

Income distribution is by no means egalitarian. Although the disparities are less marked than in neighbouring Thailand, there are obvious differences, especially between urban and rural areas. The distribution of wealth is probably less varied than that of income (EIU, 1995).

Labour Force

Myanmar's labour force constitutes one of the primary resources of the country. The estimated active labour force was about 16.8 million in 1993. Fairly well-trained manpower and skilled labour are available for most industrial activities. An average of about 30,000 students graduate from universities, institutes and colleges each year; and about 8,000 students are trained at agricultural, technical and vocational training schools. All graduates are bilingual (*Statistical Yearbook*, 1993).

There are no restrictions on foreign investors hiring Myanmar labour according to existing laws. The employment of foreign technical staff is not restricted. Foreign personnel may also be engaged, if neces-

---

1 Visit to Myanmar Daewoo International Ltd., garment factory.

sary, with the approval of the Foreign Investment Commission (Coopers and Lybrand, 1994).

The procedures for the recruitment of workers through township labour offices are relatively straightforward. First, a private or cooperative business employing five workers or more must notify the Township Labour Office of the intention to recruit workers in the prescribed form. Second, the labour office will prepare a list of candidates that meet the requirements mentioned in the form and then send these candidates to the employer. Third, the employer selects the most suitable person(s) from among the candidates submitted by the labour office. It should be emphasised that employers can also hire directly from the labour market through advertisements or local employment agencies (KPMG, 1994).

Labour Laws and Services

Myanmar has a system of labour laws which was initially implemented in the early 1920s based on English common law. The last one to be enacted was the Employment Restriction Act, 1959. In view of the recent economic reforms, the government is in the process of modifying existing labour laws and introducing new ones. One area that the government is considering deals with labour unions. Currently, there are no labour unions in Myanmar.

The labour administration system in Myanmar is handled by the Ministry of Labour which coordinates labour issues among employers, government agencies and workers. The Ministry of Labour consists of the Department of Labour, the Social Security Board (SSB), the Central Inland Freight Handling Committee, the Factories and General Labour Laws Inspection Department (FGLID), and the Central Trade Disputes Committee. One of the primary objectives is to actively promote national development through rendering services to workers and employers. The ministry also enforces labour laws to protect the rights of workers and encourages fair labour practices so that industrial peace can be maintained.

SOME GENERAL FINDINGS

The manufacturing and tourism industries are growing rapidly and they are attracting foreign investments from all over the world, especially from Asian countries. The local people are very keen to join foreign companies. High salaries and good job prospects appear to be the main motivating factors drawing them to these industries.

A visit to Myanmar Daewoo garment factory, which is a government-foreign joint venture enterprise, yielded some interesting information on salaries. A factory operator earns about K2,000 to K3,000 per month. Salaries in private sector joint ventures are higher, and there is a year-end bonus (average is about 2.5 months) and an annual increment of around 10%. Local supervisors earn between K6,000 and K12,000 per month. Senior civil servants, on the other hand, earn less than K2,000 per month, excluding fringe benefits that they are entitled to receive.

Most joint venture factories are located either in new industrial areas or outside the city. Factories in the industrial areas are generally new establishments and, thus, offer a better working environment. Companies normally provide transport and accommodation. Working conditions in these factories are certainly better than in the local cottage industries.

In the government-foreign joint venture companies, such as the Myanmar Daewoo garment factory, management screens out graduates from working as operators in the factory. This is to discourage highly qualified people from working in low level jobs. The screening is possible because high ranking civil servants or military personnel sit on the company's management team.

The Summit Parkview Hotel, built and operated by Singapore investors, employs a large number of local university graduates working as porters, waiters, front desk receptionists, cashiers and various other non-managerial positions. Part of the reason for so many graduates working in lower level positions in this hotel is because university graduates are abundant in the labour market.

The staff in the hotel speak quite acceptable conversational English but most of the managerial positions are still held by foreigners because the Myanmar workers do not have the relevant experience and skills as yet. The pay scheme in this wholly foreign-owned hotel is in line with local foreign joint venture factories. The pay for lower level staff at the hotel is approximately K2,000 per month, excluding the tips that they may receive.

Staff turnover in wholly foreign-owned and joint venture companies is relatively low. Employees in these companies are generally happy with their working environment and compensation. From conversations with some of the staff at the Summit Parkview Hotel, the growth prospects in the hotel industry looks bright and these employees are highly motivated. As noted earlier, women form a substantial part of the labour force. The female workforce enjoys equal employment opportunities and there are no reported cases of discrimination against them.

There appear to be no reported industrial disputes in foreign-owned or local foreign joint venture companies. As a rule, industrial disputes in Myanmar are few. People attribute this outcome to their culture, religion and the existing labour laws. Clearly, the government's strong control over the country may also play a part in mitigating industrial disputes.

There is no indication in official reports on how the population growth is distributed over urban centres. As in other agricultural societies, young people tend to move to the cities seeking job opportunities. This increases the labour supply in major towns and cities. However, as the economy grows, the additional labour supply should be absorbed by the creation of new jobs.

The mortality rate is on the high side. Average life expectancy is only 57 years of age according to 1992 data (Myat Then, 1995). The retirement age in the public sector is 55. This limit is probably based on the system inherited from the British. There is no official retirement age in the private sector. Retirement is subject to agreements between employees and employers. If life expectancy increases with growing affluence, and the retirement age increases, then this can add tremendously to the pool of workers.

Labour offices in townships only serve those aged 18 years and above. The official legal working age in industrial establishments is 16 years of age. However, the legal working age limit is not strictly enforced by the authorities. The analysis of the economically active population, made from the *1993 Statistical Yearbook*, is based on a population aged 10 years and above. This implies that some of the employed population is in the 10 to 17 age group.

There is an abundance of labour in the townships, especially Yangon City. Data shows that from 1993 to 1994, 16,781 submissions for 7,383 vacancies were posted through the labour offices in Yangon City alone. For other townships during the same period, vacancies posted were 51,779 but submissions were only 33,713. This discrepancy may be due to the more rapid development in Yangon City compared to other places.

The official reported inflation rate has been consistently high (about

20%) for the past six years. The 1993–94 inflation rate was over 30%. The unofficial rate may even be higher. This high inflation rate places upward pressure on wages. Any wage increase in the public sector would probably be followed by an increase in the private sector. The last wage increase in the public sector was in March 1993 and that was a hefty 25%.

It is beneficial to employers that the literacy rate and the number of English-speaking people are increasing every year. This gives employers a larger pool of qualified candidates from which to choose. Besides this, the eagerness of workers to stay on in foreign-owned companies also reduces staff turnover.

The government encourages promising students in the outlying regions to study and train as teachers in Yangon. Once their studies are completed, they normally return to their hometown to educate others. This initiative is increasing the literacy rate and English-speaking ability throughout the country. It also facilitates the finding of qualified workers in areas outside the major urban centres.

Although there is no discrimination against women in the workplace, their participation in the labour force still lags behind males. Only 46% of females above ten years of age participated in the labour force in 1990 compared with 76% for males. However, female participation in the labour force increased from 31% in 1973 to 46% in 1990 while male participation increased from 65 to 77% over the same period. The number of female graduates relative to male graduates also is increasing. But despite equal opportunities for employment and respect in society, there are few women currently holding top managerial positions in public or private organisations.

Employers are allowed to dismiss workers who violate their employment agreement. When this happens, employers must make a submission to the labour township office. The various services provided by the Department of Labour are very useful to foreign investors. In the absence of labour unions, the township workers' supervisory committees are responsible for negotiation and conciliation between employers and workers. Due to the culture and religious background of the people, negotiation is the primary means of settling disputes. It is important for foreign investors to note that labour disputes should be settled in a non-confrontational manner whenever possible. Arbitration is the last resort if all other means, and conciliation, are not successful.

CONCLUSION

Myanmar's labour force generally has a basic education and a positive working attitude which makes training easy. There is an abundance of labour, especially in the major cities, following the opening of the economy to foreign investment. Since the manufacturing sector is in its early stages of development, the available labour supply is more than adequate for low technology and labour-intensive operations.

English-speaking labour is readily available for the tourism industry. Firms in this industry should be prepared to train and develop potential managers so that they can begin performing more value added work.

Meanwhile, the government should continue to emphasise the importance of vocational and technical training. This progressive training will provide the foundation for medium to high technology industries which Myanmar will need in the future. Moreover, additional incentives, in the form of a skills development fund or tax rebates to encourage companies to continually train and develop their workers, should be considered by the government.

The Ministry of Labour provides labour placement services and a labour dispute settlement structure which are helpful for foreign investors. But beyond this, the Ministry of Labour should also actively promote the formation of a tripartite labour relationship between employees, employers and government, to minimise any possibility of labour unrest. A more pro-active approach can serve to promote a conducive and stable environment that contributes positively to the suitability of labour.

REFERENCES

Country Profile Series – The Union of Myanmar, Singapore Trade Development Board, April 1995.

EIU Country Profile, The Economist Intelligence Unit Ltd., 1995.

Htin Aung, "Human Resources Management", Seminar Paper, MBA Business Study Mission to Myanmar, 16 June 1995.

Investing in Myanmar, KPMG, 1994.

Khin San May, "Economic Role of Mandalay and The Surrounding Regions", Seminar Paper, MBA Business Study Mission to Myanmar,

19 June 1995.

Myanmar: A Guide for Businessmen and Investors, Coopers & Lybrand, 1994.

Myat Thien, "Socio-economic and Cultural Background of Myanmar", Seminar Paper, MBA Business Study Mission to Myanmar, 15 June 1995.

Review of the Financial, Economic and Social Conditions for 1993–94, Ministry of National Planning and Economic Development, Yangon, 1994.

"Selected Monthly Economic Indicators", Statistical Paper No. 3, Ministry of National Planning and Economic Development, Yangon, January/ February 1995.

Statistical Yearbook 1993, Ministry of National Planning and Economic Development, Myanmar, 1994.

Tun Shin, "Corporate and Commercial Laws of Myanmar", Seminar Paper, MBA Business Study Mission to Myanmar, 16 June 1995.

Win Myint, "Master Plan for Regional Development of Yangon", Seminar Paper, MBA Business Study Mission to Myanmar, 16 June 1995.

Chapter 21

Human Resources Management

BY
HTIN AUNG*

PRINCIPLES OF HUMAN RESOURCES MANAGEMENT

HUMAN RESOURCES MANAGEMENT is the systematic planning and utilisation of human resources for better work performance and economic performance of an organisation with a view to increasing productivity. The success or achievement of an organisation is not the only goal. Workers and employees, who are the main resource, should have the right to enjoy the fruits of their effort. The focal point should be human beings who are responsible for the achievements.

The performance of an organisation, or success of a plan or programme, depends on the following factors: knowledge, skill, environment, attitude, ability, motivation, worker's performance and resources. All of these are necessary. Motivation is the most essential factor. This is governed by environment and attitude. Environment is concerned with the rights and privileges provided for workers/ employers, including wage and salary levels, and social protection, among others. A positive attitude and optimism should be developed among workers/employees through education, along with

* Director-General, Ministry of Labour, Yangon, Myanmar.

improvement of their environment. Only then will they be motivated. Without motivation, performance is unlikely to improve. Ability alone is insufficient.

LABOUR ADMINISTRATION

The Ministry of Labour carries out its functions with the coordination of employers, government agencies and workers' organisations. These comprise the system of labour administration.

In Myanmar, the system of labour administration has undergone change over recent decades. In the early 1940s, its main preoccupation was the protection of workers through the enactment of labour laws. In the early 1950s, industrial relations and the protection of workers' privileges, according to the prevailing labour laws, became important. In the early 1960s, the scope of labour administration became enlarged. It took on a developmental role and was less involved in labour dispute settlements.

Today, labour administration is fully committed to development and is concerned with labour productivity, economic efficiency and the realisation of social objectives and human resource policy objectives. Its aim is full employment, with optimum utilisation of human resources and development of the individual. Human resources are regarded as the most important in every economic endeavour and they are the determining success factor for development objectives.

The Role of the Ministry of Labour

The Ministry of Labour participates in national development through its services to workers and employers. Labour laws protect and ensure worker rights. Their enforcement aims encourage fair labour practices and cordial relations among employers and workers.

Organisation of the Ministry of Labour

There are five different organisations under the ministry and they include the following:

(i) Department of Labour;
(ii) Social Security Board;

(iii) Central Inland Freight Handling Committee;
(iv) Factories and General Labour Laws Inspection Department; and
(v) Central Trade Disputes Committee.

MAJOR FUNCTIONS OF THE MINISTRY OF LABOUR

Industrial Relations Service

There are several services relating to industrial relations. These are undertaken by the Regional Coordination Division of the Department of Labour. Labour Relations are managed by the Township Workers' Supervisory Committees responsible for negotiations and conciliation between employers and workers in the case of disputes. Arbitration is the last resort if, and only if, conciliation is not successful. Also, these committees have been formed to settle workmen's compensation cases according to the Workmen's Compensation Act.

Minimum wage councils fix wage rates for selected industries. At present, there are two minimum wage councils. One is for the rice milling industry and the other is for cheroot- and cigar-rolling industry. The Department of Labour initiates the formation of workers' welfare committees in industries and establishments to look after welfare and grievances of workers. Finally, the Department of Labour's model work rules aim to encourage employers and workers to model their own sets of rules upon these. An advisory service is available.

Employment Service

(i) ***Local Employment Service:*** The Employment and Training Division of the Department of Labour provides manpower supply services to industries and establishments in the public, co-operative and private sectors through its network of 78 township labour offices. Job seekers can register with these offices. Local employment services are provided free of charge. Job seekers are free to choose their employment and employer. This service is backed by the Employment and Training Act and Employment Restriction Act.

(ii) ***Overseas Employment Service:*** Overseas employment is a recent initiative of the Department of Labour. The Overseas Employment Division was set up in 1990 for the recruitment and placement of Myanmar workers abroad. To date, over 2,000 workers have found placement in Asian countries. Recent improvements have resulted in easy access to this service for end-users, and foreign and local recruiting agents.

Vocational Training Service

The Ministry of Labour implemented the National Vocational Training Project in 1972 under the technical assistance programme of the UNDP and ILO. A National Vocational Training Centre (VTC) was established with the following objectives:

(i) To ensure a steady supply of skilled workers to meet the needs of industries.
(ii) To increase the productive capacity of all workers through systematic training. This is undertaken by industrial establishments and enterprises themselves, off or on-the-job, or both. The VTC currently conducts nine regular training courses in skills development for both the public and private sectors. The VTC also provides technical and advisory services to industrial establishments implementing training schemes.

Labour Research, Labour Education and Human Resource Information Service

The Research and Planning Division of the Department of Labour is taking initiatives in matters relating to labour research. A labour library is maintained for general reading and research purposes. Reviewing existing labour laws is one of the main tasks of this division. This requires research into labour laws in different countries and international labour standards adopted by the ILO.

Today, the importance of labour education is widely recognised by employers and workers. Regular in-house training courses enhance labour. A lecture service is available upon request for entrepreneurs and workers.

The Human Resource Information Service manages a manpower database to aid human resource planning. A number of projects have been implemented with the cooperation and assistance of the UNDP, UNFPA and ILO.

The Manpower Statistics Division provides statistical data on the labour force, employment, labour market information and human resource development indicators. The Department of Labour, under the Ministry of Labour, serves as the national focal point for human resource development matters. A National Nucleus Commission for human resource development is being formed with the Director-General of the Department of Labour as Chairman. Officials from relevant ministries are members. A Manpower Planning Coordination Committee is also headed by the Director-General of the Department of Labour, with representatives from various ministries as its members.

Industrial Safety and Health Service

The Factories and General Labour Laws Inspection Department (FGLID) provides safety and health information and consultancy services to industrial establishments. It also monitors, surveys and does research on safety and health issues. The department publicises safety and health measures and conducts related training courses. It helps to form safety and health committees and encourages them to take voluntary safety and health measures. Through the promotion of safety and health awareness, the FGLID aims to create better working environments and conditions.

The FGLID is responsible for the inspection of industrial establishments, work places, shops and establishments with the aim of enforcing labour laws. The FGLID's inspectors are empowered to serve as revenue officers who can collect revenue due for non-compliance with trade disputes committee awards, workmen's compensations committee payments and delayed social security contributions from employers.

Implementation of Social Security Scheme

The Social Security Board (SSB) is one of the important organs of the Ministry of Labour. The Social Security Act established the Social Security Scheme and the SSB in 1956 with the main objective of providing social care for insured workers in the case of incapacity, sickness, maternity, injury or death. Relief to dependants was provided. The Act covers industries and establishments employing a minimum of five workers. Employers are required to insure their workers with the SSB. The Social Security Scheme is financed by contributions from the state, employers and employees.

SETTLEMENT OF TRADE DISPUTES

Any disagreement or conflict between employer and worker is brought to the Township Workers' Supervisory Committee (TWSC) for preliminary negotiation. If mutual agreement cannot be reached after serious negotiations, then the TWSC exercises its power of conciliation to settle the dispute. If conciliation is not successful, then the case is referred to the Township Trade Disputes Committee for arbitration.

Arbitration is the last resort for the settlement of trade disputes. There are three arbitration stages. In the first stage, a Township Trade Dispute Committee (TDC) hears the issues and makes an award. If the award is not accepted by either party, then an appeal can be made to the Trade Disputes Appeal Committee. The latter is formed at the state/division level. An appeal committee reviews the case, comments and make a decision on the award of the TDC. If either party is not satisfied with the decisions of the Appeal Committee, then they may apply for final revision to the Central Trade Disputes Committee. The Central Trade Disputes Committee is the third and final stage for arbitration. The decision here is final.

EXISTING LABOUR LAWS

The following ILO conventions have been ratified by Myanmar:

(a) Hours of Work (Industry), 1919.
(b) Unemployment, 1919.
(c) Night Work (Young Persons), 1919.
(d) Right of Association (Agriculture), 1921.
(e) Weekly Rest (Industry), 1921.
(f) Minimum Age (Trimmers and Stokers), 1921.
(g) Medical Examination of Young Persons (Sea), 1921.
(h) Workmen's Compensation (Accidents), 1925.
(i) Workmen's Compensation (Occupational Diseases), 1925.
(j) Equality of Treatment (Accident Compensation), 1925.
(k) Inspection of Emigrants, 1926.
(l) Seamen's Articles of Agreement, 1926.
(m) Minimum Wage Fixing Machinery, 1928.
(n) Making of Weight (Packages Transported by Vessels), 1929.

(o) Forced Labour, 1930.
(p) Workmen's Compensation (Occupational Diseases) (Revised), 1936.
(q) Holidays with Pay, 1936.
(r) Statistics of Wages and Hours of Work, 1938.
(s) Freedom of Association and Protection of the Right to Organise, 1948.

Also, the following list summarises existing labour laws in Myanmar:

(a) Employment and Training Act, 1950.
(b) Employment Restriction Act, 1959.
(c) Employment Statistics Act, 1948.
(d) Factories Act, 1951.
(e) The Leave and Holidays Act, 1951.
(f) Minimum Wages Act, 1949.
(g) Payment of Wages Acts, 1936.
(h) Social Security Act, 1954.
(i) Shops and Establishments Act, 1951.
(j) Trade Disputes Acts, 1929.
(k) Workmen's Compensation Act, 1923.

TOURISM AND HOSPITALITY

Chapter 22

Tourism Development and Visit Myanmar Year

BY
NAW ANGELENE*

INTRODUCTION

THEN, A GOLDEN mystery upheaved itself on the horizon – a beautiful, winking wonder that blazed in the Sun, of a shape that was neither Muslim dome nor Hindu temple spire. It stood upon a great knoll ... "There's the old Shwedagon," said my companion. The golden dome said, "This is Burma, and it will be quite unlike any land you know about."

These words were written by Ruyard Kipling nearly a century ago in 1898 when the country, under British rule, was named Burma after the main ethnic group, the Bamar. Today, it is again called Myanmar, the original name long used by our people. It is a name that is associated with a nation of many ethnic groups.

If Ruyard Kipling were to return today, then he would hold to his original impression and say, "This is Myanmar, and it is quite unlike any land you know about." Indeed, it is still a land of mystery to many outsiders. Because Myanmar was isolated for many years, it has been left largely untouched by outside and modern influences. Its natural beauty is unspoilt and its peo-

* Director, Department of Planning and Tourism, Ministry of Hotels and Tourism, Yangon, Myanmar.

ple are similarly simple and pure of spirit, rare characteristics in a technologically advanced society.

TOURISM IN MYANMAR

Myanmar, with a total area of 676,577 square kilometres, is the largest country in South-east Asia. Its topography varies from flatlands at sea-level and along river valleys, to snow-capped mountain peaks and deep ravines.

Three parallel mountain ranges, running north-south, extend down from the eastern extremity of the Himalaya mountain range. Snow-capped Hka Kabo Razi at 5,881 metres (19,296 feet), is the highest mountain in South-east Asia. Myanmar's mountainous and hilly regions have enormous potential for mountaineering, trekking, skiing and other kinds of adventure travel.

With the mountain chains come three big rivers, the Ayeyarwaddy, Sittoung and Than-Lwin. The Ayeyarwaddy, which flows 2,170 kilometres from west to south, has great potential for cruising. Myanmar also has a long coastline with many beautiful white sandy beaches.

A cultural heritage based on 2,000 years of civilisation makes it a land rich in ancient archaeological sites and monuments. Buddhism, which flourished in the Bagan period (11th to 13th centuries), has made Myanmar not only the land of pagodas but also has given rise to an ancient architecture which can compete with Angkor Wat and Borobudur.

The 135 ethnic groups, each with their own customs, dress, dialects, music, dances and handicrafts, are an important tourist attraction, and so are the priceless gemstones like jade, ruby and sapphire which are mined in Myanmar. Although blessed with a diversity of tourism products which combine a unique culture, traditional arts and crafts, scenic beauty and the hospitality of its people, Myanmar is still little known. This is because tourism has not been encouraged in the past. It is one of the few countries that still exist as an "unexplored" destination in the modern world.

STRUCTURAL CHANGE

Concerns about cultural preservation inhibited tourism promotion and development for many years. But the change from a centrally planned to a market-oriented economy has prompted a review of the situation. Recognising the potential of tourism, the State Law and Order Restoration Council (SLORC) passed the Myanmar Tourism Law in June 1990. This opened up the hotel and tourism industry, which had previously been a state monopoly for nearly 30 years, to the private sector and foreign investment.

The basic aim of the Tourism Law is to increase the contribution of tourism by generating foreign exchange, aiding regional development and creating employment while ensuring the preservation and protection of Myanmar's cultural heritage and natural environment. Tourism became firmly established and systematically organised with the formation of the Ministry of Hotels and Tourism in September 1992. This ministry is responsible for policy formulation, planning, marketing, facilitation and regulation of the private sector.

To accelerate smooth growth and to give proper policy guidelines, the Tourism Development Management Committee was formed at the national level in April 1994. Secretary One of SLORC is the Chairman and the Minister for Hotels and Tourism is the Vice-Chairman. The committee comprised 12 sub-committees headed by ministers and deputy ministers of various tourism-related ministries. The committee meets monthly and gives guidelines to the 12 sub-committees to ensure an integrated action plan. Since its formation, the Ministry of Hotels and Tourism has made an all out effort to promote Myanmar as an international tourist destination. The designation of 1996 as "Visit Myanmar Year" is one outcome of the second meeting of this committee.

Entry Formalities Eased

Entry formalities have been liberalised and entry visas are easily available for any type of visitor. The tourist visa has been extended from 14 to 28 days. Visas can be issued with prior arrangement to tourists on charter flights, group tours and cruise ships. Customs' procedures have been simplified, and green and red channels at airports aid in fast processing.

To facilitate currency exchange, the foreign exchange certificate (FEC) has been created. FECs can be exchanged for U.S. dollars or pound sterling. The FEC is equivalent to 100 kyats. Payment by FECs is accepted by any person in Myanmar. Visitors are not required to declare foreign currency below US$2,000 brought into Myanmar.

Entry Points

Until 1992, Yangon was the only gateway to Myanmar. Now there are many border checkpoints open along the Myanmar-Yunnan (China) and Myanmar-Thai borders. On the Myanmar-Yunnan border, tourists are allowed to enter through Lwe-Ge, Nam-Kham, Mu-Se, Kyu-koke and Kun-Lone, and they can travel to Yangon via Lashio and Mandalay.

Tourists crossing the Myanmar-Thai border are allowed to travel from Mae-Sai to Kyaing-Tone. Many then proceed to Jing-jong (Sipxhaungbara) in Yunnan through Mai-Lar. In the south, Kawthaung (formerly known as Victoria Point) is open to tourists crossing the straits from Ranong in Thailand. Since opening the border land routes, accessibility and transportation have improved.

Plans are underway to link Myanmar, China, Laos and Thailand in a golden quadrangular tour. These four cultural locations may be visited by road, air or river. The vast Mekong River plays a vital role in linking the four countries.

Air Transport Links

At present, three airlines (MAI, Thai International and Silk Air) operate scheduled services to Yangon with a total capacity of 5,611 seats per week. Two other airlines (CAAC and Biman) also fly once a week to Kunming and Decca with a total capacity of 190 seats. Total international capacity is 5,801 seats per week. Thus, more flights are required to meet the goal of 500,000 visitors for "Visit Myanmar Year".

Mandalay, Bagan, Heho, Tachileik, Kyaing Tong and Mawlamyaing are open to charter flights from Chiangmai and Chiang Rai. These flights are operated by Bangkok Airways and Thai Flying Service.

The Civil Aviation Department has amended the law to give an air operator certificate to Air Mandalay, a joint venture between Myanmar Airways and Techmat Ltd. of Singapore, for operations within Myanmar. Air Mandalay currently operates scheduled flights to the major tourist sites of Bagan, Mandalay, Heho and Ngapali. A scheduled charter service, between Chiangmai, Bagan and Mandalay is planned for the very near future.

At present, major constraints to growth are airport terminals and runways. To solve these problems, two new international airports are under construction: one is near Bago and the other is at Tada-Oo which is 50 kilometres from Mandalay. The two airports are scheduled to be operational in three years' time.

Travel Operator

The Ministry of Hotels and Tourism is encouraging private sector involvement in the tourism industry. As of June 1995, licences have been issued to 285 tour operators/travel agencies, 825 transport businesses and 600 tour guides. One firm from South Korea and two other foreign joint venture companies are among the travel agencies.

Tourist Arrivals

Tourists entering Myanmar are categorised into four main types: package tour, foreign independent traveller, business traveller and visiting friends and relatives. Following the easing of visa regulations, visitor arrivals have increased from 26,000 in 1992–93 to 61,000 in 1993–94. These figures exclude cross-border traffic which totalled over 100,000 visits. In 1994–95, arrivals at Yangon Airport totalled 88,301. Some 3,447 tourists visited Yangon via Muse-Namkham making the cumulative total 91,748 visits, an increase of 147% over 1993–94.

Of the 88,000 air arrivals, 15% were package tours, 39% were independent travellers, 28% were business groups and 18% were visiting friends and relatives. Approximately 85% of foreign visitors entering Yangon went to Bagan, 80% to Mandalay and 50% to the Inle/Taung Gyi area.

Myanmar's main sources of tourists used to be North America and Europe, but recently the trend has changed. Potential markets today are in the Asia Pacific region. In 1994–95, 54% of arrivals were from Asia, 32% from Europe, 9% from North America, 3% from Middle East and 2% from Oceania. Thailand, Singapore, Malaysia and Taiwan are important potential markets because of the growth in trade and investment.

Tourist Earnings

The average spending per day by a visitor is US$100. The average length of stay is seven days for tourists and four days for business travellers. Total tourism receipts in fiscal year 1994–95 were US$34 million, Thai Bhat seven million and Chinese Juan two million.

Border tourism has increased steadily and there is enormous potential for growth. An entry fee of US$18, or conversion of 300 FECs, is required for tourists arriving by the Muse, Namkham, Kun-lone, Mandalay to Yangon route. Tourists entering by the Tachileik-Kyaingtong route have to pay US$18 or convert 100 FECs. In 1994–95, total income was US$942,000 from Muse; US$320,000 from Tachileik, US$9,000 from Paya-Thonezu, US$900 from Myawaddy and US$1,280 from Kawthaung. Total receipts from border sectors amounted to US$1.28 million.

Recently, Myanmar has become a popular port of call for cruise ships. In fiscal year 1994–95, 12 cruise ships called at Yangon port, adding US$1 million to tourism receipts.

THE HOTEL INDUSTRY

Since the liberalisation of tourism, the hotel industry has developed fast along with the growth of foreign investment opportunities. At present, there are 1,900 rooms in Yangon, 1,600 rooms in Mandalay, 343 rooms in Bagan and 360 rooms in the Inle Lake area. If construction schedules are met, then there will be 2,000 rooms of international standard in Yangon by the end of 1996. Currently, there is a shortage of international class hotels in Bagan, Mandalay and the Inle Lake area.

The Ministry of Hotels and Tourism has encouraged private sector development by leasing state-owned hotels to private local management companies and by issuing licences for private construction and operation. As of June 1995, 18 hotels and motels were leased and 195 licences were issued to private hoteliers.

Foreign investors account for 16 hotel projects with four more in the contracting stage. These include one resort hotel in the Golden Triangle area, two island resorts near Kawthaung and one floating hotel. Most of the projects are in the Yangon area. There are two projects in Mandalay. Shangri-La, Sofitel and Novotel (Accor Group), New World, Aman Resorts and Central Plaza are among the major investors.

Foreign projects are generally on the build-operate-transfer (BOT) basis with 100% foreign equity. Leases are for 30 years with an option for an additional three five-year terms for management as an operator. An investor has to pay a land use premium based on the location and size of the project, and a yearly lease of around 5% of gross revenue.

Myanmar Foreign Investment Law incentives permit 100% foreign-owned investment, or a joint venture with a state enterprise or local partner. Construction materials and equipment are exempt from import duty and there is a three-year tax holiday from the date of operation. The law guarantees no nationalisation and allows for repatriation of profits.

INFRASTRUCTURAL DEVELOPMENT

Myanmar's long term objective is to develop tourism as a major foreign exchange earner. In the meantime, infrastructural improvements, international and tourism promotion are priorities.

To complement the building and improving of transport and accommodation, adequate energy, electricity and water supplies provision is essential to speeding up tourism development. To meet the growing demand from hotels and travel agencies for skilled labour, the Ministry of Hotels and Tourism is conducting training courses, workshops and seminars in cooperation with Baiyoke Kandawgyi Hotel and Myanmar Computer Centre. A master plan for tourism development is being drawn up which will identify priorities and prepare feasibility studies for each area.

Tourism Promotion and Visit Myanmar Year

The Ministry of Hotels and Tourism's main promotional task is to enhance international awareness of Myanmar. The ministry is making video tapes of tourist spots and attractions to distribute to embassies and travel agents. A bi-monthly tourism magazine called *Myanmar This Month* is published in cooperation with McComm Advertising Ltd. of Singapore. *Hotel and Travel Magazine*, published by Magic Productions of Thailand, regularly carries one section exclusively devoted to Myanmar tourism. Travel writers invited to Myanmar have reported on the local situation and tourist attractions. Familiarisation trips have been conducted for travel agents.

The year 1996 has been designated "Visit Myanmar Year" (VMY) and the main objectives are making Myanmar better known and attracting more visitors. VMY is regarded as the start-up year for future action plans and development. The official opening of VMY will be in October 1996.

VMY will start in earnest in January 1997 with traditional festivals and fairs featuring special programmes and arrangements. January corresponds to the Myanmar lunar month of Pyatho. In ancient times, Myanmar kings annually held a royal equestrian festival in this month to select heroes for the royal army. This was known as Myin-Khinn Thabin. This festival also demonstrated the prowess of the Myanmar monarch. To revive Myanmar cultural traits that ceased to exist during the colonial period, and to keep patriotism alive, the present government now holds this equestrian festival in January.

Independence was gained on 4 January 1948, and it also is celebrated in January with fireworks, funfairs, open-air shows and musical performances. Kachin people celebrate Kachin State Day on 10 January with traditional costumes, fairs, food and performances. All of these traditional January events will be celebrated in 1997 with greater splendour and grandeur than usual to make VMY a special year.

Throughout the year, traditional boat races, religious and ethnic festivals, trade fairs, travel fairs, fashion shows, co-op bazaars, Miss Tourism contests, flower and fruit shows will take place to create an enjoyable and memorable atmosphere. The following promotional activities are also being undertaken as part of VMY:

(i) The Directorate of Hotels and Tourism, collaborating with local vocalists and composers, has produced seven VMY songs in English and Burmese.
(ii) A series of video tapes on tourist sites and destinations are being made for publicity abroad. These are being distributed through Myanmar embassies.
(iii) Ministry of Hotels and Tourism officials and cultural troupes are participating in overseas travel fairs and conferences (e.g., ITB Berlin, ITS Bangkok and ATM Singapore).
(iv) A handbook on VMY celebrations published in September 1995 highlights special events and illustrates pictures of the sights and attractions of Myanmar.
(v) The Singapore Myanmar Investment and Leisure Enterprise (SMILE), which comprises investors, hoteliers and other businesses in Singapore, is cooperating with the Ministry of Hotels and Tourism to promote VMY in Singapore.

VMY Arrivals

There are 500,000 visitors targeted for VMY which runs from October 1996 to September 1997. This quantity cannot be achieved through Yangon because there are not enough airlines seats into Yangon in a year at the moment. Nor will there be enough rooms of acceptable standard to accommodate 500,000 visitors. If border visits are included, then this number will be exceeded.

But the success of VMY should not be measured only by arrival figures. In addition to numbers, the quality of visitors is important. While welcoming all kinds of visitors, those who contribute substantially to the economy are preferred.

CONCLUSION

Tourism is the fastest growing industry in the world. In this region, there are four countries – Myanmar, Cambodia, Laos and Vietnam – that have recently opened their doors to tourists. Among these, Myanmar has enormous potential. At this point, business development has not grown as fast in Myanmar as in neighbouring countries. A lot more Asian and Western companies have rushed into China, Vietnam and Cambodia, than into Myanmar. This is because people are more familiar with these countries. Very few people have heard about Myanmar because of 26 years of isolation and its recent name change from the more familiar Burma. Also, the Western press is giving Myanmar a difficult time by especially focusing on the human rights issue. However, with political support from ASEAN, businessmen are beginning to take a serious look at Myanmar. Companies with successful operations in Myanmar will encourage others to venture in, especially if projects in China and Vietnam fail to match expectations.

The government is committed to tourism, and the private sector and foreign investors are being encouraged by new incentives. The opening up of the country, together with the adoption of a market economy, are the single most important factors in attracting businessmen to Myanmar. The ministry firmly believes that tourists follow businessmen. For more than a year now, the demand for hotel rooms of international standard has outstripped the supply. Most of those wanting international standards are businessmen who need rooms with a writing desk, adequate lighting, telephone and fax facilities, secretarial support, good food and some form of entertainment. The increasing number of business visitors augurs well for the future of hotel developers.

While rapid growth is encouraged, Myanmar is well aware of the negative impacts that accompany uncontrolled tourism. The government is cautious and is taking measures to safeguard their culture and environment because of the damage that tourism can cause.

Chapter 23

The Tourism Industry in Myanmar

BY
CHONG Wai Hoon
KOH Tse San
SEOW Kok Boon
TIO Guat Kuan

INTRODUCTION

TOURISM CAN PLAY a vital role in Myanmar's development. The government is promoting tourism in order to maximise foreign exchange earnings, increase employment opportunities, distribute economic benefits and narrow the gap between the rich and the poor, and encourage cultural and economic exchange. The importance of tourism for Myanmar is reflected in the relative number of project approvals granted by the government. This sector is second only to manufacturing in terms of number of projects. This chapter takes a brief look at the existing infrastructure of tourism, reviews the present marketing plan of the Ministry of Hotels and Tourism and, finally, discusses several emerging possibilities for investment in this sector.

EXISTING TOURISM INFRASTRUCTURE

Accommodation

There are only a handful of international hotels in Myanmar including the Strand Hotel, The Narawat and the newly opened Summit Parkview. All these hotels are located in Yangon. So far, foreign investors have put more than

US$700 million into 17 hotel projects in Myanmar.[1] Most of these will be completed in 1998 and will boost the number of hotel rooms in the country to 5,672. Some of the major names involved are Shangri-La, Novotel, Sedona and Mandarin-Oriental.

A serious inhibitor to business development is the shortage of IDD facilities in hotels, especially outside Yangon. For instance, at one of the best hotels in Mandalay, the Mandalay Swan Hotel, an IDD call has first to be connected by the reception and then requires a wait of at least four hours before the connection is made. The Thiripyitsaya Hotel in Bagan offers IDD facilities but the call can only be made in a tiny cubicle in the reception area. Power outages are common in Myanmar.

Accessibility

At present, five airlines – Myanmar Airways International, Silk Air, Thai International, CAAC and Biman Airlines – operate scheduled international flights to Yangon. Total seat capacity is 5,801 per week, or 301,652 per year (Naw Angelene, 1995). Many more seats, therefore, are required to meet the goal of 500,000 visitors for "Visit Myanmar Year 1996".

Short and narrow runways, outdated terminals and inadequate navigation aids are among the major constraints on access expansion. To alleviate this situation, two new international airports are under construction. One is located near Bago, 50 kilometres from Yangon, and the other is at Tada-Oo, 48 kilometres away from Mandalay. These airports are scheduled to be operational in 1998.

Attractions

In the inaugural issue of *Myanmar This Month*, published by the Ministry of Hotels and Tourism in October 1994, four tourist attractions are recommended for visitors, namely, Yangon, Mandalay, Bagan and Inle Lake. Some of the highlights of these destinations are as follows:

(i) ***Yangon:*** Yangon's not-to-be-missed attraction is the magnificent Shwedagon Pagoda, considered by many to be the greatest and most impressive Buddhist pagoda in Myanmar. The pagoda, which en-

[1] See Appendix 23–1: "Foreign Hotel Investments in Myanmar", extracted from *Welcome to Myanmar: A Handbook on Tourism & Business*, April 1995.

shrines strands of Buddha's hair and other old relics, is more than 2,500 years old, and stands close to 100 metres high.

Other major attractions are the Museum, colourful Bogyoke Market and The Karaweik where classic handicrafts, exquisite gems, historical exhibits and so forth can be found.

(ii) ***Mandalay:*** Mandalay is well-known for the "world's largest book" – 729 upright stone slabs inscribed with the complete Buddhist scriptures which surround a pagoda built by King Mindon in 1857.

Other attractions in Mandalay include Mandalay Hill, Mandalay Palace and Shwe Nandaw Kyaung, a monastery well-known for its outstanding wooden architecture.

(iii) ***Bagan:*** Founded in A.D. 849, Bagan is a rich archaeological site with 5,000 magnificent stupas and pagodas dating from the 12th century.

(iv) ***Inle Lake:*** Scenic Inle Lake, the fascinating Pindaya Caves, and the cool and colourful hill towns of Taunggyi and Kalaw make up an attractive mountainous region in Shan State.

Affordability

This factor currently weighs strongly against tourism. The authorities make it clear that their intention is to discourage budget travellers, and to encourage those who bring ample foreign exchange with them. High rates for hotel rooms, airline tickets and tours, make Myanmar an expensive tourist destination and uncompetitive relative to its ASEAN neighbours. For example, a return ticket between Singapore and Yangon costs as much as one between Singapore and Perth, despite of being help the distance.

The disparity between the official exchange rate and the unofficial rate (official rate: US$1 for 6 kyats; unofficial rate: US$1 for 110 kyats) creates problems for business travellers and tourists.

GOVERNMENT EFFORTS IN TOURISM

In the last few years, the government has considered tourism as a priority industry which can stimulate the economy. The 1996–97 "Visit Myanmar Year" campaign is forecast to generate US$150 million in tourism receipts from a hoped-for 500,000 visitors.

The following important steps have been taken by the government since 1990:

(i) In June 1990, the *Myanmar Hotel and Tourism Law* was passed. This opened up the hotel and tourism industry to private sector investment and development.
(ii) In September 1992, the Ministry of Hotels and Tourism (MHT) was formed. This is a body responsible for tourism policy formulation, planning, marketing, facilitation and regulation of the private sector.
(iii) In April 1994, the Tourism Development Management Committee (TDMC) was formed. This committee is responsible for accelerating the development of tourism in Myanmar. It is chaired by Secretary 1 of SLORC with the Minister of MHT as Vice-Chairman. This powerful committee includes 12 sub-committees headed by Ministers and Deputy Ministers of various tourism-related ministries.

The Ministry of Hotels and Tourism has implemented several promotional initiatives. First, it is lending support to a monthly publication entitled *Myanmar This Month* published by McComm Advertising Ltd. of Singapore. Second, it is lending support to a publication entitled *Hotel and Travel Magazine* published by Magic Productions of Thailand which carries one section exclusively on Myanmar tourism news. Also, the Ministry hosts familiarisation trips for foreign travel writers and journalists.

TOURISM MARKETING

There are a number of aspects that need attention as Myanmar markets itself.

Product

As a tourist destination, Myanmar needs to emphasise the following features to distinguish itself from neighbouring competing destinations:

(i) Unspoiled natural environment.
(ii) Scenic beauty.
(iii) Diverse cultural differences of ethnic groups.

(iv) The ancient city of Bagan and its archaeological appeal.
(v) Priceless gemstones like jade, sapphires, rubies, and other precious and semi-precious stones.
(vi) Buddhist religion including pagodas, temples and heritage.
(vii) Hospitable people.
(viii) Traditional arts and crafts, like lacquerware and tapestry.

The transportation infrastructure has to be upgraded, built or acquired. Although improvements are not possible in the short term, effort must be made to give priority to the top tourist attractions.

Service is an important aspect of tourism. All staff coming into contact with tourists must be customer-oriented in order to deliver quality service. Failure to do so leaves a negative impression on visitors.

This requires training on a massive scale at a national level. However, the generally mild and hospitable nature of the people makes this task much easier. Personnel to be considered for training should include airport immigration officers, tour guides, taxi drivers, shop attendants, tourist attraction reception staff, hotel staff and, perhaps, even policemen. A special school could be set up to assist the tourism industry to train staff.

Pricing

As mentioned earlier, it is quite expensive to visit Myanmar because there are not many commercial packages available. For example, a ten-day trip may cost S$2,000 to S$3,000. The high cost can be attributed to the lack of competition and economies of scale in areas like accommodation, transportation (especially internal flights) and tour packages.

Since a major objective of the MHT is to increase the awareness of Myanmar, adopting a penetration pricing strategy would be most effective (Agustono *et al.*, 1995). It is recognised that pricing is usually beyond the control of the MHT and lies in the hands of the tour agents, operators, hotels and airlines. Despite this, MHT can arrange for joint promotions with the national airline, major hotels, and tour agencies in other countries, to offer promotional prices and packages.

Since tour packages are usually for holiday-makers, prices should include admission charges, meals, airfares, accommodation and other incidental charges. These people are usually more price sensitive. Hence, competitive pricing or value-for-money packages are important.

Businessmen are usually less price sensitive than holiday-makers because their visits are made out of necessity. They require flights and accommodation. Meals are usually arranged by business contacts in the country. Moreover, they usually demand hotels with international standards. Prices need to match the quality of service provided.

Independent individual travellers are one type of visitor that MHT should not encourage because they are usually budget travellers and, hence, foreign exchange earnings are low.

Advertising and Promotion

Awareness of Myanmar's attractions must be created in order to attract more visitors to the country. Limited funds and resources require that promotion strategies are selected for their cost effectiveness. Mass consumer advertising is probably not feasible. So inviting foreign journalists on familiarisation trips to see Myanmar's attractions firsthand is a more cost effective technique for getting media coverage.

Journalists need carefully planned arrangements since they are well-seasoned travellers and can be quite demanding. All hosts, be they airlines, hotels, travel agents or restaurants, must be ready to provide interesting story lines for the media in order to get coverage.

Distribution

The goal of distribution is to motivate travel intermediaries to distribute to potential visitors tourism brochures, and to use promotional materials like videos and cassette tapes on Myanmar. Private sector enterprises, like hotels and inbound tour operators, need to link with overseas partners to promote travel to Myanmar. A notable example of MHT cooperation with overseas companies is the link with a group of 17 Singapore companies that have strong interest in the growth of tourism to Myanmar. The group, which is called the Singapore-Myanmar International Leisure Enterprise (SMILE), coordinated a high-profile Myanmar Week in Singapore in 1995 (see Appendix 23–2 for a list of SMILE members).

The MHT must consider setting up branch offices overseas to fulfil the multiple roles of disseminating tourist information, coordinating media familiarisation trips and working with tour wholesalers. These offices can also serve as listening posts, which observe market trends and changes in consumer taste and behaviour, and identify market niches. They can monitor competitive activities and indicate to head office any need for strategy shifts or possible collaborations.

INVESTMENT OPPORTUNITIES

Hotels

Since permitting private hotel ownership in 1990, the hotel industry in Myanmar has developed rapidly. As of mid-1995, 18 formerly state-owned hotels have been leased and 195 licences issued to private hoteliers. At present, the hotel room inventory is about 1,900 rooms in Yangon, 1,600 rooms in Mandalay and 343 rooms in Bagan (Naw Angelene, 1995).

However, if "Visit Myanmar Year 1996" achieves its target of 500,000 visitors, then Yangon will need 2,055 rooms, Mandalay 1,644 rooms and Bagan 1,233 rooms (Agustono *et al.*, 1995). It seems, therefore, that Bagan, with the greatest shortfall, promises the most potential for new hotel construction. Two international chains are reportedly evaluating potential sites in Bagan.

Yangon and Mandalay also have potential for international standard hotels, but more detailed studies need to be done, especially into future visitor projections, niche marketing and market segmentation. There would appear to be potential for the mid-market, three- to four-star, hotel category.

Travel Agents and Ground Operators

Although licences have been granted to local travel agents, Myanmar needs more experienced ground operators which are international customer-oriented and which are skilled in recruiting and training professional guides, and organising tours. In addition, more and better coaches are needed for transfers and tours.

Training

There is a general shortage of trained manpower in the tourism industry. MHT presently conducts training courses in co-operation with a hotel and computer centre but the output is insufficient for the expected number of visitors, especially once the new airports at Bago and Tada-Oo are ready. Currently, there are only about 600 trained tourist guides in Myanmar;[2] or one per 833 visitors in 1996. There are opportunities for the private sector to work with MHT in its manpower training effort.

APPENDIX 23–1
Foreign Hotel Investment in Myanmar (approved)

Company	No. of Rooms	US$ (Millions)	Country
Strand Hotel International Ltd.	341	22.0	Hong Kong
Emerald Development	500	25.0	Hong Kong
M.C.G. Ltd.	450	35.0	Japan
Baiyoke Hotel Co. Ltd.	197	26.0	Thailand
Union Farm Ltd. (V.E.S. Group)	200	25.0	Thailand
Vitavas International Ltd. (Golden Triangle)	200	18.0	Thailand
Central Floating Hotel Ltd. (Central Plaza)	132	10.0	Thailand
L.P. Holding Ltd. (Sule Central Plot)	270	46.0	Thailand
Thai Industrial Connection Ltd.	240	25.0	Thailand
System Built Ltd.	50	29.0	Singapore
Straits Green Field Ltd	450	85.0	Singapore
Myanmar Swan Co.	112	3.2	Singapore
Nawarat Land Ltd	80	8.0	Singapore
Shangri-La Group	1,100	180.0	Singapore
New Mandalay Hotel Project	300	50.0	Singapore
Atlantic Outline Myanmar	250	44.0	Malaysia
Idris Hydraulic	600	157.0	Malaysia
TOTAL	**5,472**	**788.2**	

Source: All information extracted from *Welcome to Myanmar: A Handbook on Tourism and Business*, April 1995.

2 Interview with U Myat Wunna, Assistant General Manager, Tour Mandalay, June 1995.

APPENDIX 23–2

Singapore-Myanmar International Leisure Enterprises (SMILE) (As of 27 March 1995)

(1) Amara International Hotels and Resorts Pte Ltd.
(2) Civil Aviation Authority of Singapore
(3) Intraco Ltd.
(4) Ken-Air Leisure Group
(5) Keppel Corporation Ltd.
(6) Natsteel Ltd.
(7) Presidential Pacific Limousine Pte. Ltd.
(8) Representations International Pte. Ltd.
(9) SAFE Enterprise Pte. Ltd.
(10) Shangri-La Hotels Ltd.
(11) Singapore International Airlines Ltd.
(12) Singapore Bus Services Ltd.
(13) Singapore Changi Airport Enterprise Pte. Ltd.
(14) Singapore Explorer Pte. Ltd.
(15) Singapore Tourist Promotion Board
(16) Straits Steamship Land Ltd.

REFERENCES

Ambar Agustono, Ong Joo Hua and Seow Kok Boon, "Marketing Myanmar as a Tourism Destination", Marketing Management Paper, Nanyang Technological University, 1995.

Asian Business, February 1995.

"Changes in Myanmar's Policies Spell New Openings for Investors", *The Straits Times,* 19 September 1994.

"Foreign Hotel Investments in Myanmar", extracted from *Welcome to Myanmar: A Handbook on Tourism and Business*, April 1995.

"Invitations Accepted", *Asian Wall Street Journal*, 2 February 1995.

"Japanese May Return to Burma if Grip on Dissidents is Relaxed", *Asian Wall Street Journal*, 12 July 1995.

Myanmar: A Guide for Businessmen and Investors, Coopers & Lybrand, 1994.

Myanmar Hotel and Tourism Law, The Union of Myanmar, The State

Law and Order Restoration Council, 23 October 1993.

"Myanmar Releases Aung San Suu Kyi", *The Straits Times,* 11 July 1995.

Naw Angelene, "Tourism Development in Myanmar, Visit Myanmar Year, Hotel and Tourism Infrastructure", Seminar Paper, MBA Business Study Mission to Myanmar, 16 June 1995.

Chapter 24

Human Resources Management in Myanmar's Hotel Industry

BY
CHER Choon Teck
CHONG Weng Hoe
TAN Juay Hiang
TAN Hock Chuan
WONG Kum Cheong

INTRODUCTION

HUMAN RESOURCES DEVELOPMENT is a basic strategy for companies in the 1990s. To stay ahead of the competition, managing of human resources is as important as dealing with financial or marketing strategies. Human resources management is also important at the government level. Education and training is now a major part of many political manifestos.

This chapter focuses on the development of human resources in Myanmar in the tourism industry, a sector considered to have great investment potential and which has attracted much attention from both local and foreign interests.

The main objective of this chapter is to provide potential investors in the hotel industry with an appreciation of the human resources problems that they might encounter in Myanmar. More specifically, this chapter addresses the following:

(i) Identification of human resources policies adopted by private and government-owned hotels.
(ii) Differentiation of the policies adopted by

the two sectors.

(iii) Recommendation of human resources management strategies.

(iv) Identification of potential investment opportunities.

Data was collected through interviews with persons related directly or indirectly with human resources management in the tourism industry. Interviews were conducted with staff working in the following hotels:

(i) The Summit Parkview, Nawarat Concorde and The Strand in Yangon; The Mandalay-Swan Hotel in Mandalay; and The Thiripyitsaya Hotel in Bagan. All except the last, which is a 100% government-owned hotel, are either foreign-owned or are joint ventures between foreign organisations and the government.

(ii) Interviews were held with government officials from the Ministry of Hotels and Tourism, the Ministry of Labour, the Ministry of National Planning and Economic Development, the Institute of Economics and the Institute of Technology; and with Myanmar Travels and Tours, a tour agent operating in Myanmar.

HUMAN RESOURCES PLANNING

In the case of foreign-owned and joint venture hotels, planning of human resources is done by a management team in Myanmar, but budgeting is controlled by head offices overseas in Singapore. The planning cycle varies from once to twice a year. Expected staff turnover is 1 to 2% per year. This rate is low because of high unemployment in Myanmar. In addition, most personnel are very inexperienced in this industry and, so, job mobility is minimal (Ghih, 1995; Kumar, 1995; Swe Swe Tan, 1995).

All of the foreign-owned and joint venture hotels have the intention of gradually localising the management, although none have formulated any concrete plans to implement this strategy. At present, there is a lack of experienced staff at the supervisory level and it will take time to train and develop capable local personnel to assume such a role and, ultimately, to lead the management team (Ghih, 1995; Kumar, 1995).

At the Nawarat Hotel, the budget for human resources is about 18% of the total budget (Kumar, 1995). This is high because of the large expenditure required for the benefits and living expenses of the expatriate management staff. Moreover, at this early stage, the hotel needs to incur higher training costs to elevate their staff to acceptable standards of proficiency.

The government has declared 1996 as "Visit Myanmar Year" and an influx of tourists is expected. However, most of the hotels have not planned their human resource needs to cope with this influx.

Human resources planning for government-owned hotels is done centrally by the Ministry of Hotels and Tourism (Ohn Kyaw, 1995). The Ministry not only does the planning for all government hotels in the country, but it also recruits, selects and trains the staff (Naw Angelene, 1995).

In summary, there is a lack of human resources planning in many of the hotels in Myanmar. As the industry matures, human resource planners must not only examine budget and staff replacement planning but also reconsider a range of other issues. For example, career enhancement and career succession will become critical in a more competitive environment. Currently, many hotels adopt the planning system used at the company's head office. However, this may not be compatible with Myanmar's culture, and economic and political system. Individual hotels should begin to benchmark their human resources planning system against industry leaders in Myanmar. This may create new perspectives in managing human resources in a manner that provides a competitive advantage.

RECRUITMENT

There is often a desire by firms to recruit the "best" staff or employees. Likewise, workers often dream of being recruited by the "best" company. Hence, there is a bad fit if a company has good human resources planning but bad recruitment. Doing business in Myanmar requires that firms strive for a good fit.

In Myanmar, there is no problem recruiting unskilled labour for the hotel industry but it is extremely difficult to find individuals with the relevant experience. When the Summit and Nawarat hotels started recruiting, there were hundreds of applicants with qualifications ranging from primary school education to university degrees (Abdul, 1995; Kumar, 1995). The methods of recruitment used by most privately owned hotels are through write-in, walk-in or word-of-mouth recommendation. There are no private employment agencies, executive search firms or professional associations where individuals can apply for jobs (Htin Aung, 1995). These institutions need to be established but there is no appropriate legislation as yet (Tun Shin, 1995).

The only mass media used for recruiting are newspapers, where recruitment advertisements are placed. Television and radio are not used for recruitment. The Nawarat Hotel places advertisements which explain each job and its scope in some detail. In this way, they hope to filter out inappropriate and unqualified candidates from applying, and helps in the shortlisting of those with appropriate credentials (Abdul, 1995; Kumar, 1995; Swe Swe Tan, 1995).

Another recruitment source, that has not been tapped by the privately owned hotels, is the Employment and Training Division of the Department of Labour which provides manpower supply services through its network of Township Labour offices. This local employment service is provided free of charge (Htin Aung, 1995).

It is common practice to have a formal contract between the employer and employee at the time of job acceptance. A probationary period is also applied across all staff levels in privately owned hotels, unlike in government hotels where staff are confirmed upon completion of their training programme (Ghil, 1995; Swe Swe Tan, 1995; Ohn Kyaw, 1995).

The hotel industry does not practise alternative forms of staff recruitment such as temporary employment, part-time employment, daily wage employment, employee leasing or contract employment (Htin Aung, 1995; Kumar, 1995; Naw Angelene, 1995). This can be explained by the large labour supply and the fact that these forms of employment are not really appropriate for the service industry.

Overall, the methods used for recruitment are extremely limited. Although currently satisfying hotel needs, new media are required for the future when labour shortages may occur, or when higher levels of experienced staff need to be recruited locally. Other recruitment techniques might include open houses, career seminars, multimedia shows, billboards, mobil advertisements, broadcasting and canvassing on campuses. When recruitment agencies and executive recruitment companies exist in Myanmar, these will be useful for recruiting expatriates and experienced senior management staff.

SELECTION

After recruitment, the next stage is the selection of candidates for the job. Here, the right match between the candidate and the job is important. If the match is unsuccessful, then both the organisation and the employee will suffer in terms of lost time, economic losses and low morale.

Only government hotels appear to engage in the practice of conducting pre-selection examinations (Ohn Kyaw, 1995). All hotels call shortlisted candidates for interviews with a maximum of two interviews for certain staff positions. It was discovered that the selection criteria used by different hotels are quite similar, namely: command of English, a minimum of ten years of education, previous experience and physical appearance. University graduates are desired for positions of a supervisory nature (Abdul, 1995; Kumar, 1995; Swe Swe Tan, 1995).

Hotels can only recruit candidates who have registered with the Ministry of Labour (Htin Aung, 1995; Kumar, 1995). They are required to inform the Ministry of Labour if they received a job offer. It is mandatory for candidates to undergo a medical examination before commencing work. In the case of kitchen staff, medical reviews are required twice a year.

Hotels in Myanmar need to review selection criteria as the industry matures. They also need to gain a competitive edge through quality service. Therefore, they must be able to recruit high calibre staff to meet higher expectations from the job. This means recruiting workers with better education qualifications and better skills. Finally, aptitude tests should be considered in shortlisting candidates for interviews.

COMPENSATION AND BENEFITS

The largest employer in Myanmar is the government. It manages all kinds of industries including the hotel industry. The minimum monthly pay in the public sector is K600. For an army colonel or a professor in the university, the pay is about K2,500 to K3,500. However, besides take-home pay, senior public servants are given other benefits such as a car with chauffeur, subsidised prices for housing and daily necessities. Converting kyats into U.S. dollars at US$1 to 100 kyats (which is more commonly used than the official exchange rate), means that salaries are extremely low as compared to other countries such as Singapore. Foreign investors in the hotel industry are attracted by low labour costs despite the lack of skilled labour in the hospitality field (Htin Aung, 1995; Kan Zaw, 1995; Khin Maung Nyunt, 1995).

Basic wages for general staff, such as waiters and front desk receptionists in hotels (fully-owned by foreigners or joint ventures with a Myanmar national or the Myanmar government), range from K1,500 to K4,000 depending on the location of the hotels and their ownership. For example, the foreign-owned Summit Hotel in Yangon pays restaurant staff an average of US$35 per month excluding profit sharing, service allowance and bonus (Swe Swe Tan, 1995). Another foreign-owned hotel in Yangon pays its general staff up to US$60 gross per month (Kumar, 1995). But for the Mandalay Hotel, which is jointly owned by the Myanmar government and a foreign firm, the basic salary was maintained at US$40 per month after the foreign investor took over the management from the government in August 1995 (Ghil, 1995). The economic development in the area and the competition for labour from other hotels are the main factors contributing to these differences in basic wages.

The government discourages private companies from offering high pay with annual increments. This is to prevent the difference in pay between private and public sectors from being too large, which already seems to be the case. Legislation requires a social security contribution at a rate of 4% of an employee's pay; 1% is from the employer and 3% is from the employee. The contribution is capped at a maximum of K60 per month up to a monthly salary of K1,500 (Htin Aung, 1995; Kumar, 1995; Swe Swe Tan, 1995).

Singapore-owned hotels in Myanmar are very competitive in terms of attracting staff. A high basic salary is the most important reason. In fact, during recruitment interviews, foreign-owned hotels were never asked any questions by applicants about compensation and benefits schemes. Other factors such as a conducive working environment and performance-based promotion, become important in attracting skilled and trained workers from other hotels.

Compensation and benefits schemes are based on the particular policy of each hotel, with adaptations for the local environment. Most of the Singaporean hotels in Myanmar are relatively new and they are still in the process of fine tuning their schemes. Basic schemes such as annual leave, overtime pay, medical benefits and bonuses are commonly practised. The various compensation and benefit schemes practised by foreign-owned hotels in Myanmar are summarised in Table 24–1 below.

In addition to the above schemes, individual hotels provide various non-monetary rewards to staff. For example, one hotel gives US$150 to outstanding staff to enrol in self-improvement courses as a reward (Kumar, 1995), while others send their staff overseas for training (Reitz, 1995; Swe Swe Tan, 1995).

TABLE 24–1
Compensation and Benefits Provided by Foreign-owned Hotels

Type of Compensation and Benefits Scheme	High End	Low End
Basic monthly salary for local unskilled workers such as waiters	US$50	US$10
Basic monthly salary for local supervisory staff such as captains and managers	US$250	US$12
Overtime pay rate	Double	None
Daily working hours	8 hours	8 hours
Weekly working hours	Maximum 48 hours	Maximum 48 hours
Bonus	US$120 biannually	1 month pay annually
Profit sharing	Based on hotel performance	None
Pay increment	Depends on level of seniority	None
Transport allowance	Provide transport for night shift	Provide transport for night shift
Tips and service charges	Shared by all employees based on seniority	30% retained by hotel to provide employee welfare
Paid annual vacation leave	Minimum 14 days	Minimum 6 days
Medical benefits	For staff only	For staff only
Dental benefits	None	None

Most hotels indicate that they have other schemes in the pipeline depending on the needs and practice of the industry as a whole. Social functions, such as a dinner and dance, and company outings are not common, but this may change. Managements may also set up employee welfare committees and provide financial assistance for education assistance and grant staff loans. However, other areas, such as staff insurance, retirement plans and retrenchment plans, have not been considered.

It may appear to potential foreign investors that operating expenditures in terms of staff compensation and benefits are low and, therefore, very attractive. One literally can exploit the labour market especially in areas outside of the major cities. However, the foreign hotels in Yangon generally offer relatively higher wages and better benefits. Since trained and experienced staff are still scarce in the hotel industry, anyone with some experience is very marketable. As the industry matures, a higher turnover of staff should be expected.

One major problem in the current situation is the large wage discrepancy between the private and public sectors. It appears that the government is not planning any policy changes to reduce this gap. As the largest employer in the country, the government controls the largest proportion of human resources. It is not easy for a public sector employee to resign and join the private sector because replacement has to be found before the resignation is accepted (Ohn Kyaw, 1995).

Discontentment felt by public sector employees, as a result of the wage difference, may give rise to unforeseen social or political problems. In a bid to further discourage the private sector from paying high wages, the government might even impose wage ceilings, which may affect the attractiveness of investing in Myanmar.

PERFORMANCE APPRAISAL

In general, the appraisal system is mainly used by hotels in Myanmar to evaluate the performance of hotel staff. However, some hotels highlighted secondary objectives, such as career planning and development (Kumar, 1995), identification of training and development needs (Htin Aung, 1995a), and internal employee relations (Swe Swe Tan, 1995), as other uses of the appraisal system.

Most of the private hotels have adopted formal, but open, appraisal systems. Some of the performance criteria highlighted are punctuality and quality of service. The normal appraisal frequency ranges from semi-annual to annual although hotel staff are also appraised after their probation period. When there is a need to monitor the progress of hotel staff during a transition from state to private ownership, assessment can be more frequent. For the Mandalay Hotel, a weekly assessment was conducted for staff under training and the appraisal cycle was six weeks (Ghil, 1995).

All staff in private hotels are normally appraised by their immediate supervisor and the assessments are subsequently endorsed by department managers. However, in the case of the Nawarat Hotel where supervisors are lacking, department managers are responsible for appraising all their staff. To cope with the large number of appraisals, only the top 5% and the bottom 5% of staff receive formal appraisals. All appraisals are eventually reviewed by the human resources manager. When an adverse appraisal is given to a staff member which may result in termination, the human resources manager confirms it with the department manager and the staff member concerned (Kumar, 1995).

In government-owned hotels, the appraisal system is usually confidential and closed. This is similar to other government offices such as the Education Ministry (Khin Maung Nyunt, 1995; Ohn Kyaw, 1995). Staff appraisal is conducted semi-annually by the supervisor and endorsed by the department manager. However, a difference from private hotels is that government-owned hotels need to submit their staff appraisals to the Ministry of Hotels and Tourism for the final review. Resignations must also be submitted to the Ministry and approval is granted only if a replacement is available (Ohn Kyaw, 1995).

One interesting fact about the appraisal system is that, at the end of the process, some hotels may not give any salary increments. Instead, increments are reserved for promotions.

In summary, the hotel industry pays high salaries as compared to the public sector and the disparity within the industry is increasing as more new hotels compete for the small pool of trained staff. The challenge for hotels is to correctly identify the needs of employees and to offer sufficient incentives to retain their services. To achieve this end, hotels must implement a comprehensive appraisal system to communicate more effectively with their employees. This will allow management to assess the needs of employees more effectively. Also, employees need to receive feedback on performance including future expectations. The open communication established through an effective appraisal system will allow management to understand their staff better and it will facilitate the development of appropriate strategies to retain staff.

TRAINING AND DEVELOPMENT

It is apparent that there is a lack of skilled workers for the hotel industry. Though experienced hotel staff are available from government-owned hotels, they are insufficient in number to meet the growing demand in the hotel industry. To acquire skilled labour, hotels usually have to employ unskilled labour and then provide basic training. Hence, training and development is one of the main human resources management activities for this industry in Myanmar.

There are limited training institutions for the hotel industry in Myanmar. The Ministry of Hotel and Tourism operates a training course in cooperation with the Baiyoke Kandawgyi Hotel and Myanmar Computer Centre (Htin Aung, 1995b). Courses are offered in the following areas:

(a) Reception.
(b) Housekeeping.
(c) Food and Beverages.
(d) Kitchen.

These courses are open to the public but applicants must meet the minimum qualification of tenth Standard. The course ranges from two to six months and cost between K2,000 and K5,000. Class size is limited to about 30 trainees. Upon completion of the course, trainees are awarded certificates endorsed by International Labour Organisation (ILO), World Tourism Organisation (WTO) and the United Nations Development Program (UNDP) (Swe Swe Tan, 1995).

However, due to insufficient training facilities, private hotels usually conduct their own in-house training for their entry level staff, as mentioned previously. In-house courses are usually conducted by expatriate department heads who are responsible for providing basic training in their area of expertise. For example, the food and beverage manager is responsible for training the waiters and bar tenders for the cafe, bar and restaurant in the hotel. After basic training, staff members are given practical training in technical skills. Such training methods are common for new hotels, such as the Summit Parkview and the Nawarat Hotel, which recruit large numbers of unskilled staff and wish to start operations quickly.

In addition to technical training, it is common for hotels to engage either expatriate staff or external teachers to conduct English courses for all staff members. If requested, the Ministry of Labour will provide assistance to the hotels with outside lecture services (Naw Angelene, 1995b). There is also a growing trend among the hotels to sponsor staff on overseas training/attachment or part-time upgrading courses. Those who qualify for these training schemes are usually staff at the supervisory or management level. Hotels differ in their policies of bonding staff after they finish their training or courses (Kumar, 1995; Reitz, 1995; Swe Swe Tan, 1995).

At the moment, there is no plan by the Ministry of Hotels and Tourism to set up more institutions specialising in hotel training nor any plan to expand the current curriculum to offer refresher and advanced courses. Also, there is no government subsidy or tax relief to offset training costs incurred by the hotels (Naw Angelene, 1995; Swe Swe Tan, 1995). However, as more state-run hotels are privatised and new hotels are built, there will be a serious shortage of skilled labour in the hotel industry if the current practices are not revised.

Eighteen government hotels/motels have already been leased to private management and 195 licences have been issued to private hotels (Naw Angelene, 1995b). There will be a large and growing demand for skilled labour in the industry. Current training capacity offered by the Ministry of Hotels and Tourism, is unlikely to result in sufficient skilled staff. As a result, hotels can expect some pirating of their experienced staff. Although hotels can continue to train unskilled staff for replacement, this is not sustainable in the long run because of escalating training costs.

CAREER PLANNING AND DEVELOPMENT

Faced with a shortage of skilled labour and increasing competition, many hotels are beginning to respond to these problems by developing plans to retain their experienced staff. Besides monetary incentives, hotels are providing career planning for their staff. Particularly in the private hotels in Myanmar, career paths for each position are now clearly defined (Kumar, 1995; Win Kyi, 1995). For example, a typical entry level staff member, such as a waiter, will be promoted to the supervisory position of a chief waiter, followed by captain, assistant food and beverage manager and eventually food and beverage manager. Thus, each staff member knows the next position and the time it takes to achieve that position.

Entry level employees who perform exceptionally well can expect to be promoted within six months while higher level positions require a minimum of eight to twelve months. Career planning is also practised in the government-owned hotels but it is done centrally by the Ministry of Hotels and Tourism (Abdul, 1995; Ohn Kyaw, 1995).

With the growth in hotels, there is also a shortage of supervisory staff. It may take as long as three years to train an entry level employee to assume a supervisory position. Hence, hotels are using career planning to identify individuals with good potential from among their staff and to develop them to fill supervisory positions. Those staff members selected will either be subsidised by the hotel for part-time upgrading courses, or be sponsored for overseas training, or attachment to other hotels (Kumar, 1995).

In the long run, some hotels also intend to transfer management responsibilities to the local staff. Therefore, hotels are actively identifying and grooming local staff for management positions. Some of the current management development programmes include local and overseas full-time management courses and attachment to other overseas hotels.

INDUSTRIAL RELATIONS

Labour unions were disbanded when the State Law and Order Restoration Council took over control of the country in September 1988. Presently, there are no formal labour unions in Myanmar even though a Trade Unions Act (1926) exists. In its place, another system has been set up and administered by the Ministry of Labour with responsibility to coordinate employers, other government agencies, workers' organisations and to settle disputes. Other functions of the Ministry of Labour include enhancing labour productivity, promoting economic efficiency and working towards the attainment of full employment with the optimum utilisation of human resources.

The Ministry of Labour has several measures at its disposal to enforce labour laws which protect and ensure the rights of workers. However, caution is exercised in enforcement to ensure that it does not hinder and impede the momentum of business or encourage unfair labour practices.

In place of trade unions, the Ministry of Labour requires a company with more than ten workers to set up a worker's compensation committee, comprised of management and non-management staff. The main responsibility of the committee is to settle any industrial disputes that arise within the company through negotiation and reconciliation. No size restriction has been imposed on this workers' compensation committee (Htin Aung, 1995b).

Upon establishing a workers' compensation committee, the Township Workers' Supervisory Committee (under the umbrella of the Ministry of Labour) must be informed and ensure that the committee has been properly set up within the company.

Any disputes that cannot be settled within the company are brought to the Township Workers' Supervisory Committee (TWSC) for preliminary negotiation. If mutual agreement cannot be reached, then the TWSC tries to settle the dispute. If this is not successful, then the case is referred to the Township Trade Dispute Committee for arbitration. However, it should be noted that arbitration is the last resort for settlement of trade disputes and that negotiation and reconciliation are always the preferred means of settlement.

There are three stages in the arbitration process. At the first stage, a Township Trade Dispute Committee (TDC) hears the issues of the dispute and gives a decision or award regarding the case. If the award made by the TDC is not acceptable to one or both of the parties, an appeal can be made to the Trade Disputes Appeal Committee which is formed at the State level. This committee reviews the case and gives comments, and decides on the award of the TDC. Again, if one, or both, parties are not satisfied with the decision, an application for final revision to the Central Trade Dispute Committee can be made. In the third and final stage, the Central Trade Dispute Committee reviews the case again and makes a final decision (Htin Aung, 1995b).

The industrial relations arrangements and infrastructure currently set up by the Ministry of Labour appear to be rather simple and unsophisticated. It is understandable that this area has not been accorded priority by the government given the fact that labour supply far exceeds demand. Also, the working premise is that the culture of Myanmar steers people towards an atmosphere of cordial relations and industrial peace, and avoids confrontation.

It is quite evident that, at Myanmar's present stage of development, there is no great need for a sophisticated structure to settle trade disputes. The fact that some hotel personnel managers are not even aware of the presence of such an avenue with the Ministry of Labour seems to support this belief. However, as Myanmar develops and the workforce gains sophistication, some revamping may be necessary to enable the system to keep pace with the needs of the future workforce.

RECOMMENDATIONS

Due to the government's lack of resources and experience in running hotel training and management courses, hotels are currently conducting their own training for unskilled staff. This requires additional resources and distracts management from the daily operations of the hotel. The establishment of a commercial institute would enable a larger pool of skilled labour to be readily available. Thus, there is an investment opportunity for experienced hoteliers to establish a hotel training school.

The private hotels have indicated that communication between management and local employees is a major problem in their daily operations. Burmese is a tonal language like Thai. The English used by local staff is not sufficiently good and causes communication problems. There is an opportunity for an English language school to train employees in general and "hotel" English. Although the state has introduced English into schools, there are good opportunities for commercial institutes to conduct more specialised courses such as business communication, presentation skills, public speaking and so forth.

Since declaring 1996 "Visit Myanmar Year", the government has recognised the importance of tourism to the economy. It should provide assistance by providing scholarships or training grants, and subsidies, to attract the talent into careers in the hospitality industry. Also, the government has to gradually reduce the disparity in salaries between state-run hotels and private hotels. However, as the state intends to privatise all hotels, this disparity might dissolve. With the impending privatisation of more government-owned hotels, the state needs expertise in organising the privatisation process, such as looking for suitable buyers to enter into joint ventures. There are tremendous opportunities for venture capitalists and management consultants to assist the Myanmar government in the privatisation process.

If legislation permits, then there may be investment opportunities for establishing employment agencies and executive search firms. Currently, hotels have to conduct their own recruitment. Employment agencies can make available a larger pool of relevant skilled human resources and greatly reduce the selection process time and subsequent training. These agencies could also provide temporary or part-time workers to meet peak season demand.

CONCLUSION

This chapter has provided potential investors with some appreciation of the issues in human resources management that they may face in the hotel industry in Myanmar. Potential investors should consider the human resource element in their business plan when evaluating investment opportunities. The issues raised may also provide a human resources manager with some basis for planning future needs. The major difference in human resources management policies between the government-owned and privately owned hotels have also been highlighted.

In particular, the issues discussed in this chapter should be useful to expatriate managers in the industry who are considering a posting to Myanmar. There are some recommendations that the government of Myanmar might wish to consider in its bid to accelerate the growth of the economy. Also highlighted are some areas of investment opportunities that entrepreneurs might wish to evaluate further.

The hotel industry in Myanmar is relatively new and it is growing rapidly. Since the essence of a good hotel is quality of service, and since this is dependent on the quality of staff, human resources management is certainly an area which should receive close attention from hoteliers.

REFERENCES

Abdul Karim Noor, Assistant Front Office Manager, Summit Parkview, 350 Ahlone Road, Dagon Township Yangon, Myanmar, tel: 95-1-27966, fax: 95-1-27995 (interviewed 14 June 1995).

Ghil Levi, Mandalay Hotel, Belmont International Hotels, Director of Operations, 161-B Thomson Road, Goldhill Centre, Singapore

307614, tel: 2530212, fax: 3521962 (interviewed 19 June 1995).

Htin Aung, Director (Research and Planning), Directorate of Labour, Ministry of Labour, 52 Strand Road, Yangon, Myanmar, tel: 82169 (interviewed 16 June 1995a).

Htin Aung, "Human Resource Management", Seminar Paper, MBA Business Study Mission to Myanmar, 16 June 1995b.

Kan Zaw, Lecturer, Institute of Economics, Regional and Environmental Studies, Department of Economics, Yangon 11041, Myanmar, tel: 951-433/9 (interviewed 15 June 1995).

Khin Maung Nyunt, Professor (interviewed 22 June 1995).

Kumar Chakrabarty, Hotel Manager, Nawarat Concorde Hotel, 257 Insein Rd, Yangon, Myanmar, tel: 951-67888 (interviewed 22 June 1995).

Kyin Soe, Director, Yangon Institute of Technology, 14 Y.I.T Compound, Insein P.O. 11011, Yangon, Myanmar, tel: 65678 (interviewed 15 June 1995).

Maw Than, Head, Department of Commerce, Institute of Economics, University Estate, Yangon, Myanmar, tel: 32433 (interviewed 15 June 1995).

Myanmar: A Guide for Businessmen and Investors, Coopers & Lybrand, 1994.

Naw Angelene, "Tourism Development in Myanmar, Visit Myanmar Year, Hotel and Tourism Infrastructure", Seminar Paper, MBA Business Study Mission to Myanmar, 16 June 1995.

Naw Angelene, Director (Hotels and Tours), Ministry of Hotels and Tourism, No 77/91, Sule Pagoda Road, Yangon, tel: 951-40089 (interviewed 22 June 1995).

Ohn Kyaw, Thiripyitsaya Hotel, Archaeological Zone, Hotel Manager, tel: 951-89000 (interviewed 21 June 1995).

Reitz Sue, Manager, The Strand, 92 Strand Rd, Yangon, Myanmar, tel: 951-81532 (interviewed 22 June 1995).

Swe Swe Tan, HR Executive, Summit Parkview Hotel, 350 Ahlone Road, Dagon Township Yangon, Myanmar, tel: 95-1-27966, fax: 951-27995 (interviewed 16 June 1995).

Tun Shin, Legal Advisor, Ministry of National Planning and Economic Development, Yangon, Myanmar (interviewed 16 June 1995).

Win Kyi, General Manager, Myanmar Travels and Tours, 77/91, Sule Pagoda Road, Yangon, Myanmar, tel: 80317, fax: 095-01-82535 (interviewed 15 June 1995).

Chapter 25

Development of the Summit Parkview Hotel, Myanmar

BY
Daisy LOO
TAN Tee Meng
Nellie YEO Sok Leng
Lester YEO Gim Seng

INTRODUCTION

MYANMAR, UNDER THE State Law and Order Restoration Committee, opened its doors to foreign investments in late 1988. The establishment of a liberal foreign investment law ensued. By February 1995, the *Asian Wall Street Journal* reported that 112 projects worth US$1,295.2 million had been committed by foreign investors. Of these, the hotel and tourism sector comprises 26 projects totalling US$529.9 million (see Table 25–1).

One of the earliest foreign investment hotel projects was the Summit Parkview Hotel in Yangon, a joint venture between Liang Court Holdings, Unicorn International, Timas Pte. Ltd. and the Singapore Technologies Industrial Corporation. It was the first, purpose-built business hotel of international standard built in Yangon. Its nearest competitor, the Nawarat Hotel, which opened a year or so earlier, was developed from a non-hotel building.

This chapter looks at the development of the Summit Parkview Hotel in terms of tourism, financial analysis, design and construction as well as the operation, recruitment, training and transfer of management expertise.

BACKGROUND

While "Visit Myanmar Year" 1996 is the first priority in Myanmar's short-term vision for tourism, there is a long-term master plan for tourism development with a five-year review cycle.[1] This plan addresses infrastructure, cultural tourism (which promotes aspect of Myanmar's culture and Buddhist heritage) and tourist attractions development. More specifically it highlights, among other things, a new international airport at Mandalay; hotels for Yangon, Mandalay and Bagan; and historical sites, beach and hill resorts earmarked for development.

TABLE 25–1
Foreign Investments in Burma by Sector

Sector	Number of Projects	Amount US$ Million
Agriculture	1	2.7
Manufacturing	42	125.3
Fisheries	10	90.8
Oil and Gas	20	381.1
Mining	11	163.4
Hotels and Tourism	**26**	**529.9**
Transport	2	2.0
Total	112	1,295.2

Note: Figures do not include Burmese partners' contributions to joint ventures.
Source: *Asian Wall Street Journal*, 2 February 1995.

Currently, there are more than 150 hotels (local and overseas ownership) in operation along with 134 private hotels and 16 joint venture hotels.[2] Singapore is among the top ten foreign investors with 23 projects worth US$293.35 million. Most of these are in the hotel, fishery and manufacturing sectors.[3] Another source[4] reported that, "Hotel construction is booming, with 17 new hotels coming up in Yangon alone, which will add 5,240 rooms by 1998."

To date, two Singapore-owned hotels are open in Yangon: Hotel

[1] Dr. Naw Angelene, Ministry of Hotels and Tourism. Facsimile interview, 1995.
[2] *Handbook on Tourism and Business*, Ministry of Hotels and Tourism, 1995.
[3] *The Straits Times*, 21 April 1995.
[4] *The Business Times*, 21 November 1994.

Properties Limited's Nawarat Hotel and the Summit Parkview Hotel. Two more, owned by Straits Steamship Land (Sedona Hotel) and Shangri-La (Traders' Hotel), are under construction.

SUMMIT PARKVIEW HOTEL

General

The grand opening of the Summit Parkview Hotel took place on 3 June 1995. The joint venture company formed for the project is Regional Hotel Pte. Ltd.[5] The investment cost was approximately US$28.6 million. A breakdown of this total appears in Appendix 25–1.

Construction

Construction was scheduled to start in May 1993, with completion targeted for 31 October 1994. Actual work began on 18 November 1993 and was completed by 1 December 1994.[6] A concurrent design approach was adopted to include architectural, civil, structural, mechanical and electrical features. The in-house design team consisted of two architects and two engineers from each discipline, and eight full-time designers.

A team was established and sent to Yangon to gather information on government submission requirements. A site visit and an analysis of Yangon's biggest "modern" hotel at that time, the Inya Lake Hotel, were undertaken to enhance construction and design knowledge. The ensuing report consisted of information on procedure, control, contract arrangement and administration, as well as a design action plan.

The construction method favoured pre-fabrication, which included the integration of planning, design, manufacturing of structural elements and site operations. This resulted in a substantial reduction in construction time relative to more traditional methods of construction. It took 11 months to complete the hotel which was two months less than target.

The pre-fabrication method of construction facilitated the planning, organisation and control of construction activities since they were repetitive in nature and not subject to the uncertainties of weather. Other

---

5 *STIC News*, November 1994 to January 1995.

6 Press release, Summit Park View, 3 June 1995.

benefits included better quality control and cost effectiveness because of less waste.

The Chairman of Summit Parkview, Mr. Stewart Yen, attributed the record construction time to an additional factor; the owner, designer, builder and operator of the hotel are the same entity. "Our people worked closely as a team with a common objective, and that was to complete the project on time and within budget," he stated in the grand opening press release.

This accomplishment notwithstanding, the initial outlay was substantial in producing the pre-fabricated components and in acquiring specially designed transport vehicles and other expensive equipment. However, through a feasibility study done earlier, the construction team found that the pre-fabricated components could be transported at a cost which, together with the cost of manufacturing these components, was lower than the cost of construction on site. A major drawback with this alternative was the lack of suitable roads between the port and the hotel site. In the final analysis, however, the total construction cost was well within budget.

Operations

The Summit Parkview has 265 rooms and prides itself on being the first international-class business hotel in Yangon. The rates (from 1 December 1994) are US$140 for single rooms, US$150 for double rooms and from US$250 for suites. The hotel's occupancy rate in mid-1995 was 55% and was projected to increase to 65% by November/December 1995.

The composition of guests is 80% businessmen and 20% holidaymakers. Singaporeans make up the largest share by nationality, followed by Japanese and other Asian nationalities. The Summit targets a business clientele who do not demand service frills but prefer value for money. The cost of "dressing up" the guest rooms is kept to a minimum but without sacrificing comfort and satisfaction. This keeps room rates competitive and yields a solid profit margin.

According to Ms. Linie Cortez, Sales and Marketing Manager, during the construction phase the hotel management team was run by a general manager who played a key role. He provided input with respect to furniture and fittings, mechanical and electrical requirements, as well as designs and other requirements for the hotel's facilities.

Marketing is done by both the Myanmar and Singapore offices with the added advantage of reaching a bigger market. The Singapore office liaises with travellers in the Asia-Pacific region while the Myanmar office concentrates on local marketing, with follow-up by the Singapore office. The Summit made a mistake in delaying the setting up of its marketing team, which was non-existent before June 1995. This resulted in a lower occupancy rate than expected despite it being one of the best business hotels in Myanmar.

Human Resources Management and Cultural Issues

The Summit has 300 staff, including 28 expatriates. The hotel's basic organisation structure is shown in Figure 25–1. Recruiting staff is not a problem because of the labour surplus in Yangon. However, most of those employed lack appropriate skills and speak very little English.

FIGURE 25–1
Summit Parkview Hotel Organisation Structure

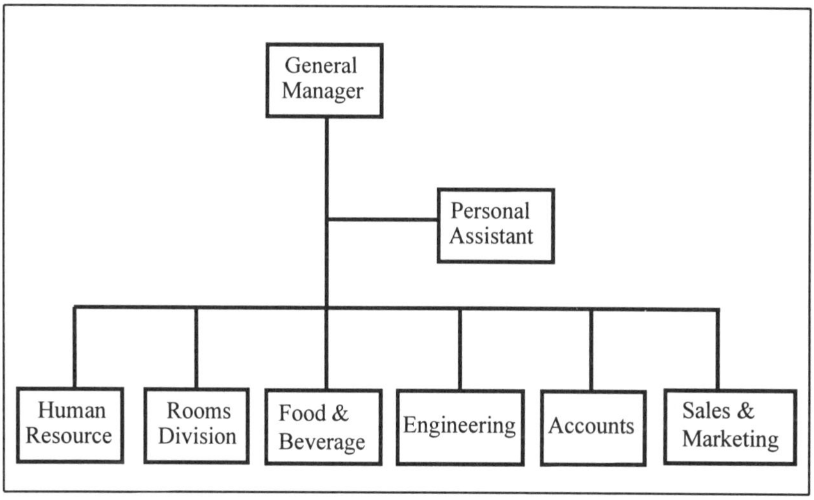

There are no formal institutions for training staff in the hotel industry. As noted by Ms. Cortez, responsibility for training is delegated to individual expatriate managers or supervisors with expertise in specialised areas. These department managers generally furnish their own policies and procedures. According to her, the lack of formal training can result in a "fragmented vision of the hotel's corporate culture".

One manager said that most of his male employees, aged between 30 to 35, have never worked before in their life. They have depended in the past on the support of their parents or sisters. It is not unusual for Myanmar men to stay at home and be pampered while the women work to support the family. He added that the number of staff employed at the Summit is more than would be required for a similar hotel of equivalent size in Singapore. This is not because the cost of labour is much lower but because of the low productivity of staff. For example, it takes two housekeepers to clear a room instead of one. Currently, the turnover of staff is low. However, poaching of trained staff can be expected as more hotels open.

A senior expatriate manager made several telling comments concerning resource allocation. He revealed that some expatriate management staff assigned to the Summit were inexperienced in working with people of a different culture. Any deviation from their own cultural norms are perceived by them as unsocial, backward, or stubborn behaviour. Training in cross-cultural management appears to be vital in preparing foreign managers to work with people of a different cultural orientation in an under-developed country like Myanmar.

This same manager also noted that the transfer of knowledge and training to host country nationals was hindered by language limitations; expatriates do not speak Burmese and local staff know little English. The language barrier also impeded manager/staff working relationships.

Relationships in the hotel are somewhat hierarchical, with respect stemming from age, authority and position. In the Summit, the "power oriented" corporate culture is viewed not as a threat but rather as a nurturing authority, much like a caring leader who knows what is best and good for his subordinates.

Teamwork and cooperation have developed well in a relatively short space of time. This is partly attributable to the Burmese "collectivist" orientation which emphasises an *esprit de corps*, group morale and cohesiveness. In addition, they are generally conscientious, eager to please, and constantly seeking to learn new skills. The most important issue that the manager stressed was the need to establish a distinct corporate culture as soon as possible.

The impending resignation of the general manager, who took the team from day one to the soft opening of the hotel, seems to have aroused apprehension among management and supervisors about his expatriate successor. The transfer to local management is expected to take place three years after opening.

Myanmar needs to commence appropriate training courses and academic programmes to build up the necessary knowledge base. To attain the required level of professional knowledge within three years seems too ambitious based on the current state of progress. It appears that little emphasis and support has been given to the training and development of professionals in the tourism industry. Instead, the government has rushed into opening up the country for tourism with great plans, but lacks a strong supporting base of people and procedures.

Marketing Strategies

The Summit has budgeted 2% of its annual gross revenue for marketing and promotional strategies (interview with Ms. Cortez). Since its soft opening on 2 December 1994, the Summit has worked closely with the Ministry of Hotels and Tourism to publicise Myanmar as a destination rather than the Summit Parkview Hotel itself. It maintains close collaboration with various airlines and travel agencies to promote Myanmar. The Summit's strategy is based on the premise that the country remains unknown to the outside world, due to 50 years of isolation. Making the country known precedes advertising the hotel's facilities or other attractions.

The Summit's corporate office is in Singapore, from where most marketing activity is initiated. Travel shows, advertisements and press releases form the major part of the Summit's marketing activities. Locally, the hotel advertises its function rooms, food and beverage outlets, shops, night club and sports facilities widely in the Myanmar press.

The souvenir shop, restaurant, business centre, banquet and meeting rooms are owned and operated by the Summit. Other units, like the hair and beauty salon, Overseas Union Bank and a 24-hour clinic, are tenants of the hotel's commercial operations.

The Summit does not have any direct competitor in Yangon. The exclusive, expensive and historic Strand Hotel targets individual wealthy tourists. It is too elaborate, formal and costly for many pioneering businessmen. The similarly priced and business traveller oriented Nawarat Hotel is considerably smaller and lacks the full range of facilities required by businessmen which the Summit provides. Furthermore, it is located outside the centre of the city, unlike the Summit which overlooks the Shwedagon Pagoda. However, the Summit is likely to face strong competition once some of the hotels under construction open, like the Sedona Hotel and Traders Hotel.

CONCLUSION

The hotel and tourism industry in Myanmar has tremendous potential, especially with the boost given by the government-backed "Visit Myanmar Year" in 1996. Despite the less than perfect market conditions and lack of supporting infrastructure, many new businesses are moving rapidly into Yangon. Many are adopting a "first-mover advantage" strategy (Porter, 1985). This seems apparent in the development of the Summit Parkview Hotel. As stated by Mr. Derrick Lam, Financial Controller of the Summit (facsimile interview, 27 July 1995), "We are practically the first to open an international business hotel in Yangon. So we take all the risk of being the first ... and enjoy some degree of monopoly before the competition comes in at a later stage." Obviously, the challenge for the Summit is to keep ahead of the impending competition, as Yangon admits more investors into the hotel and tourism industry.

APPENDIX 25–1
Summary of Financial Analysis
(Proposed Parkview Hotel, Yangon)

1.	**Development Costs**	**US$,000**
	Land Lease	2,743
	Building Construction Costs	17,046
	Furniture/Fitting & Equipment	2,163
	Contingency	960
	Construction Management Fee	1,412
	Professional Fee	1,727
	Operating Inventory & Equipment	1,284
	Pre-Opening Expenses	500
	Interest Cost	765
	Total	28,600

APPENDIX 25–1 (cont'd)

2. **Financing for the Project:**

Share Capital	3,125
Loan Capital	4,375
External Loan	21,100
Total	28,600

3. For cashflow purposes, the construction period of the hotel is 13 months from the date of the ground breaking ceremony on 18 November 1993. The project is targeted to be fully completed in December 1994. Soft opening for at least 50 rooms is targeted for November 1994. Hotel revenue is expected from 1995 (Year 2) onwards.

4. The NPV at 10% is US$16.246 million.

5. The IRR for the project is 15.34%.

6. Upon expiration of the lease contract, if the government of the Union of Myanmar desires to operate the proposed Parkview Hotel as a national hotel owned by the government, then the transfer of all assets including the hotel building will be made at book value. The company then can repatriate all the proceeds to Singapore.

7. According to cashflow projections, it is estimated that the external loan of 21 million can be fully repaid by January 1999 (Year 7), while the share and loan capital payback is likely to be in January 2001 (Year 9).

REFERENCES

A Handbook on Tourism and Business, Tourism Development Management Committee, Union of Myanmar, 1995.

"CDC's Yangon Hotel Opens", *The Singapore Technologies Industrial Corporation News*, The Singapore Technologies Industrial Corporation, 1995.

Country Profile Series – The Union of Myanmar, Singapore Trade Development Board, 1993.

Lane Henry W. and Joseph J. DiStefano, *International Management Behavior* (2nd ed.), PWS-Kent Publishing Co., Boston, 1992.

Loh Hui Yin, "The Trials and Tribulations of Investing in Myanmar", *The Business Times*, 21 November 1994.

Porter Michael, *Competitive Advantage*, The Free Press, 1985.

Than Mya, "Myanmar Places Its Bet on Free Market Economy", *The Business Times*, August 1993.

Trade and Development Digest, "Follow the Lion King", *Myanmar Business*, Vol. 1-1, 1994, pp. 1–2.

Wain Barry, "Hotels are Hot", *Asian Wall Street Journal,* 2 February 1995.

Wong Douglas, "Singapore Among Active Investors in Myanmar", *The Straits Times*, 21 April 1995.

FEEDBACK FORM

Thank you for purchasing the Nanyang Business Report series. In order to aid us with the development of other similar books in the future, please give us your opinion in this form and fax or mail it to us at the address given on the back. We would also like to include your name in our mailing list to keep you informed of book promotions which we may have in the future.

Name: ______________________ Occupation: ______________________

Company: ______________________ Type of business: ______________________

Address: ______________________

____

Do you normally purchase this kind of book? ❑ Yes ❑ No

Which title did you buy? ______________________

Why? ______________________

How did you learn about this book? ❑ courses/seminars ❑ recommended text

❑ bookshop ❑ advertisements ❑ Others(please specify) ______________________

What business magazines are you subscribing to? ______________________

____

What seminars do you normally attend? ______________________

What suggestions for improvement would you recommend to the book you bought?

____

____

What kind of areas do you think we should focus on in business publishing?

____

Why? ______________________

____

Would you like to be part of our direct mail/mailing list? ❑ Yes ❑ No

Please list out subject areas ______________________

Would you like to aid us in our publishing decision by being a reviewer of unpublished works? ❑ Yes ❑ No

Please list out subject areas if different from above ______________________

____

Please fax to:

The Managing Editor, Simon & Schuster (Asia) Pte Ltd, fax: 3780 371 or email your response to prenhall@singnet.com.sg

FOLD HERE

FOLD HERE

AFFIX
STAMP

The Managing Editor
Simon & Schuster (Asia) Pte Ltd
317 Alexandra Road
#04-01 IKEA Building
Singapore 159965